Realm Divided

Dan Jones is a bestselling historian, award-winning journalist and a broadcaster. He is the author of *Summer of Blood*, *The Plantagenets*, *The Hollow Crown* and *Magna Carta*. He lives in London.

REVIEWS FOR DAN JONES

REALM DIVIDED

DIVIDED

A Year in the Life of Plantagenet England

DAN JONES

First published in the UK in 2015 by Head of Zeus Ltd

This paperback edition first published in the UK in 2016
by Head of Zeus Ltd

1 3 5 7 9 10 8 6 4 2

A catalogue record for this book is available
from the British Library.

ISBN (PB) 9781781858837
(E) 9781781858813

Printed in the UK by Clays Ltd, St Ives Plc

Designed by Lindsay Nash
Typeset by Ed Pickford

Head of Zeus Ltd
Clerkenwell House
45–47 Clerkenwell Green
London EC1R 0HT

WWW.HEADOFZEUS.COM

In memoriam
H.E.

Contents

'... que sunt, sicut sunt ...'

Frederick II Hohenstaufen (1194–1250)

Introduction

There were many dramatic years in the long history of Plantagenet England. Years of war, years of revolution. Years of popular uprising and devastating plague. Years of triumph, years of humiliation. But few, perhaps none, of these years were as dramatic or as significant as 1215. It was a year of enormous political upheaval and constitutional invention; of rebellion, civil war, siegecraft, religious contention. It was the year that blackened forever the name of the ruling King John, and very nearly swept his royal dynasty out of the pages of British history. It produced the first, short-lived grant of Magna Carta. If we are to think of milestones beside the long road of the middle ages then 1215 is easily as important a year as 1066, which saw the Norman invasion, or 1485, when the battle of Bosworth brought the Tudor dynasty into power.

For some, it was all rather painful. When the biographer of William Marshal, the greatest knight to have lived during the Plantagenet age, came to this particular year in his vibrant nineteen-thousand-word verse story (committed to parchment between 1219 and around 1226), he glossed over the events of 1215 with a wince. 'There were many incidents,' the biographer wrote, 'which it would not be profitable to relate.'[1]

In truth, he couldn't help himself. As is so often the way with William Marshal's biography, the desire of the writer to be modest on his subject's behalf seldom outweighed his wish to show off how much he knew about great events. So, having written that he had nothing to say about 1215, he immediately went on to provide a succinct and perspicacious summary of the political dispute that boiled up and produced a great charter, a massive civil war and a full foreign invasion:

> Suffice it to say that what happened was
> that the barons came to the King
> and asked him to grant them their privileges.
> He refused them, and
> most of them present said
> that, if they did not have their privileges,
> then he could rest assured
> that they would leave his service;
> he might also rest assured that
> he could not place his trust
> in them, and that they would do him harm
> in every way possible.[2]

Looked at one way, this is indeed the essence of what happened in 1215, in high politics at least. There was a serious collapse in relations between the third Plantagenet king of England, John, and his barons, which tore the country down the middle. At Runnymede, near Windsor, in June 1215 a large party of John's barons, allied with churchmen including the impressive and scholarly archbishop of Canterbury, Stephen Langton, demanded that the king confirm in writing (and certify with his Great Seal) a long list of rights and royal obligations that they felt he and his predecessors had neglected, ignored and abused for too long. These rights and obligations were conceived partly as constitutional innovation and partly as a return to a semi-imaginary 'ancient' law-code that had governed a better, older England, which lay in the historical memory somewhere between the days of the last Saxon king, Edward the Confessor, and the more recent times of John's Norman great-grandfather, Henry I. They touched on matters of religion, tax, justice, military service, feudal payments, weights and measures, trading privileges and urban government. Occasionally they reached for grand principle: famously, John was forced to promise that 'no free man is to be arrested, or imprisoned, or disseized, or outlawed, or exiled, or in any other way ruined, nor will we go or send against him, except by the legal judgment of his peers or by the law of the land', and that 'to no one will we sell, to no one will we deny or delay, right or justice'. Otherwise, what was at issue in 1215 was a tight-knit and technical shopping list of feudal demands that was mainly of interest to (and in the interests of) a tiny handful of England's richest and most powerful men, and which applied only to 'free men': at best twenty percent of England's adult population.

It has been our tendency to see the granting of Magna Carta, and its supposed 'invention' of the principles of personal liberty, limited monarchy and restrained government, as the whole story of 1215. This is a big mistake. In fact, the key clause of Magna Carta, often overlooked but absolutely essential to the run of events in the year that produced it and to the life of everyone in England at the time, was that which proposed a conceptually neat but disastrously flawed method for compelling the king to stick to what he had promised. If John reneged on the charter, ran the clause, his barons would renounce their personal loyalty to him, thus invalidating the central relationship on which the whole structure of thirteenth-century society depended. To use Marshal's biographer's phrase, they would 'do him harm in every way possible'. To put it even more simply, they would start a war. This grave threat was reflected in the words of the charter itself, in which John acknowledged that if he failed to keep the promises he had made then his barons could 'distrain and distress us ... by taking castles, lands, possessions ... saving our person and the persons of our queen and children'.[3]

And that is precisely what happened. When we run the tape of 1215 on from the month of June and the glorious moment of baronial victory at Runnymede, we see a rather different picture of the year beginning to emerge. Yes, John's barons had compelled him to grant them a charter of rights and privileges, but they had done so on terms that effectively guaranteed a fight to the death. The king began to wriggle out from beneath the charter's strictures almost as soon as the seal-wax was dry. In 1215 Magna Carta was only legally valid for a little over two months, whereupon it was declared 'shameful and demeaning ... illegal and unjust' by the Pope, who pronounced that any man who observed the charter would 'incur the anger of Almighty God and of St Peter and St Paul His apostles': a polite way of saying that they would burn in the fires of Hell for all eternity.[4] During the full-blown civil war that followed, towns and castles were besieged, men were slaughtered, the royal treasure was (infamously) lost in boggy ground near the Wash and the French king's heir was invited to England to replace John. Once the war was ended by John's death from dysentery during the night of 18–19 October 1216, almost no one would have believed that the charter agreed the previous year was anything more than a brave but flawed attempt to restrain a king, which had failed in the most emphatic circumstances imaginable.

Of course, in the eight hundred years that have passed since Magna Carta was granted by John on 15 June 1215 *in prato quod vocatur Ronimed* – 'in the meadow that is called Runnymede' – it has become perhaps the most iconic document in the western liberal tradition.[5] For that reason (rightly or wrongly) the year 1215 has become in a sense a 'year zero' in the story of the struggle for freedom from tyranny, while the surviving copies of the 1215 Magna Carta, held by the British Library, Lincoln Cathedral and Salisbury Cathedral, are treated with much of the reverence normally accorded ancient religious texts. A 1297 edition of Magna Carta is displayed with pride at Parliament House in Canberra, Australia.* A visitor to the US National Archives in Washington DC will find that Magna Carta is the first thing they see when they pass through the

---

* Magna Carta was reconfirmed and reissued numerous times following the first grant in 1215. These occasions included 1216, 1217, 1225, 1237, 1253, 1265, 1276, 1297 and 1300. More than a hundred official and unofficial thirteenth-century copies of the charter – some combined with the Charter of the Forest – survive today, and they are still being discovered by researchers combing through local archives.

security zone: another 1297 edition, which was bought for more than $20 million at auction in 2007, sits, dimly lit, as the physical and metaphorical starting point for the history of American freedom. It is captioned with a quotation from the great thirty-second president, Franklin D. Roosevelt, who claimed that 'the democratic aspiration is no mere recent phase in human history ... it is written in Magna Carta.' That democracy was possibly the last thing on the minds of the men who made Magna Carta in 1215 is seldom mentioned. To all intents and purposes, the popular narrative holds that 1215 *was* Magna Carta, and Magna Carta *was* 1215.

I beg to differ. I have already written a short book about Magna Carta itself, studying its long-term origins in early Plantagenet history and analysing its clauses. This present book – on which I worked at the same time, but with rather different intentions – aims to do something else. At its heart still lies a narrative of defiance and dispute between John and a group of his barons, who went about for a time under the name 'The Army of God and the Holy Church'. There is, in that sense, the whiff of political and constitutional history to it, and it sits as a companion volume to my previous works on the Plantagenet dynasty, *The Plantagenets* and *The Hollow Crown*. But there is more to this book than that.

1215 was a year of changes and upheavals on an even larger scale than those occasioned by the events in June, and the matters I wish to explore extend well beyond the storm of recrimination between a handful of great men. In France, a long tussle for dominance between Plantagenet kings and their Capetian rivals was moving decisively in favour of the latter, and the people of England were coming to terms with the consequences of the loss of Normandy, which was an event that held just as much significance as had the Norman Conquest of 1066. Meanwhile, the crusading movement had been given real teeth by the belligerent Pope Innocent III; we cannot consider English politics and English society in this period without examining religious life during this extraordinarily muscular era in the history of Christianity. Neither, on that note, should we ignore the fact that 1215 was the year that Innocent's Fourth Lateran Council met in Rome. The Fourth Lateran made substantial alterations to the life of millions of people, issuing new commands on everything from the sacrament of confession to the identifying clothing that was to be worn by Jews and Muslims, to the number of times that parish churches were to be cleaned. Many educated people in 1215 would have considered it a much more important congress than the provincial gathering that took place at Runnymede. That, then, must also have a place in this book.

All this still only takes us some of the way towards a book that properly charts the story of this milestone of a year in the history of Plantagenet England. I have tried here to write about 1215 in the fullest sense, creating a fusion between narrative history and what is often called 'social' history but which is, rather, the history of people: their minds, their worlds, their lives. So as well as describing the high politics of the year, I have built up a picture of what 1215 was really like for people at every level of society: king and barons, knights and merchants, priests and peasants. Wound around the 'high' narrative of the year is a simpler story of how people ate, slept, worked, spoke, thought, fought, worshipped and traded in 1215; what they were called and what they wore, how they lived and how they died. This account of 1215 is equally concerned with stories about the people whom history has tended to ignore as it is with the deeds of kings, popes and barons. To that end I have punctuated the chapters with short essays about some individual aspects of life with which I am particularly fascinated. This book is thus designed as a history 'from the bottom up' as well as 'from the top down'; a book of themes and digressions, but also a story that has forward momentum. By the end, I hope that readers will have a sense both of 1215 as a year of world-changing importance and also of what it was for most people: just another year in the life of medieval England.

I should also say, as I always do, that this is a history designed to inform and to entertain in equal measure. I hope it succeeds in both respects.

Dan Jones
Battersea, London
Summer 2015

A Note on Dates

Today in the west we calculate years from 1 January. In the early thirteenth century, there were more systems at work. The historical year, accounted then as now in years *anno domini*, increasing consecutively from the birth of Christ, had been in use since the time of Bede in the early eighth century. But the moment on which the year changed varied according to circumstances. The administrative and ecclesiastical year began on the Feast of the Annunciation (otherwise known as Lady Day), 25 March. However, many documents, including royal records, were dated using the regnal year, which began at this time on the day of the reigning king's coronation.

King John was crowned on 27 May 1199. Unfortunately this was also Ascension Day, a moveable feast in the church calendar. The years of John's reign therefore varied in length. In 1214 Ascension Day fell on 8 May, marking the beginning of the sixteenth year of John's reign, which was written as 16 John. In 1215 Ascension Day was again on 27 May. This is therefore the start of 17 John.

All this gets rather confusing. I have reckoned 1215 to begin on 1 January, and told my story accordingly.

1

'Christus vincit'

On Christmas Day 1214, John, king of England, listened as the clergymen of his private chapel sang *'Christus vincit'*. He paid them a handsome fee to do so. When the king came to settle his bills the following month the men who led the plainsong chant, Robert of Saintonge and James the Templar, would receive twenty-five shillings – about a week's wages – for their performance.[6] But the music was worth the expense. The Latin words of the multi-voiced chant swirled together, alternating between the two accomplished soloists and the collective chorus of the congregation, gathering toward a triumphant refrain: *'Christus vincit! Christus regnat! Christus imperat!'* ('Christ conquers! Christ reigns! Christ commands!') Yet the theme of this particular chant was more than simply one of Yuletide celebration. Its associations lay much closer to King John's heart, for when sung before a king, *'Christus vincit'* (a song of the type known as *laudes regiae*) was nothing short of a hymn to lordly – and kingly – magnificence. It had been chanted at royal coronations across Europe since the time of Charlemagne, possibly the greatest ruler of the whole middle ages, who had been crowned as

11

Holy Roman Emperor by the Pope on another Christmas Day, in the year 800.* The practice had come to England with the Norman invasion, so John had heard '*Christus vincit*' at his own coronation as king of England in May 1199, and at the coronation of his wife, Queen Isabella, in October the following year. Throughout his reign he had paid for it to be sung at Christmas and Easter; now he listened again as monastic singers opened their lungs and called for the blessing of a long list of holy men and women: from St Peter and the Virgin Mary to St Thomas Becket and St Etheldreda, a seventh-century East Anglian nun who had successfully escaped ravishing by a lascivious king and had grown an ash tree from her walking stick. The well-trained male voices prayed together that their king should enjoy prosperous times. They called for piety and joy. They asked for the peace of Christ to descend on the realm. 'To the king of the English, crowned by God, salvation and victory,' they sang.[7] For a king like John, whose life and reign had been anything but peaceful, there could have been no more fitting Christmas wish.

John was celebrating Christmas in Worcester.[8] The walled city in England's western borderlands had been a favoured stopping point for kings since the days of the Norman Conquest. John was no stranger to its gates. Worcester was, like Gloucester to the south of it and Hereford to the west, a marcher city, rising out of the fertile lands between England and Wales, where lush green countryside was watered by the rivers Wye and Severn as they ran down from the Cambrian

* '*Christus vincit*' remains popular today: it was sung at the inauguration mass of Pope Benedict XVI in 2005.

mountains. This was the westernmost point of civilization, for beyond the marches roamed the Welsh, a strange, wild, quarrelsome people, by turns generous and musical, bold and barbarous, witty in their speech but fierce when they were met riding into battle, the men fighting barefoot, with their moustaches grown long and their faces painted brightly.[9] The Welsh were half-respected and half-feared by their English neighbours. John's father, Henry II, who had reigned between 1154 and 1189 and had fought a number of times both against and alongside Welshmen, once said that they were 'so brave and untamed that, though unarmed themselves, they do not hesitate to do battle with fully armed opponents'.[10] Visitors to Wales reported on a place of freaks and monstrosities, such as killer stags, ape-dog half-breeds and pigs that could hunt for game.[11] Worcester had been fortified against these strange and ancient Britons since the time of William the Conqueror – John's great-great-grandfather – and it remained a royal stronghold after two generations of Plantagenet rule.

Besides being a safe haven, one of Worcester's main attractions as a venue for a royal Christmas was simply that it was big enough to cope. Buildings within the grounds of the town's castle, described as the 'king's houses' in official documents, could cater for the small army of cooks, servants, clerks, scribes and workmen who formed the core of the royal retinue. The monks of the nearby priory could be counted on to provide lavish living quarters for the most prestigious guests, including the king, any of his noble companions and the knights of his household. The monks could also be tasked with hosting a party fit for the royal presence, which was itself no small undertaking: on any given day, let alone a feast day, the king was surrounded by scores and even hundreds of hangers-on whom convention and honour required him to treat generously. It should be said that the forty-seven-year-old King John was not universally celebrated among his subjects for being a man of honour and generosity. (Indeed, there were many who thought him a greedy scoundrel whose name was synonymous with perfidy.) Even John, however, was expected to make an effort at Christmas.

A Christmas court in this age needed considerable planning. The chief midwinter festival was usually celebrated for the full twelve days, from the Nativity on 25 December to Epiphany on 6 January. Along the way it took in the traditionally raucous feast of the Circumcision on 1 January, which according to a hymn by the twelfth-century poet and theologian Walter of Châtillon was both a festival of 'disorder' organized 'to promote fun' and at the same time one in which 'vice' should be 'cut off' (*amputetur vitium*), since 'this is the mystery signified by Christ's circumcision, when his foreskin was removed following Jewish custom.'[12] Whatever the case, Christmas – in the king's presence at least – was expensive and conspicuously indulgent. The daily costs of the court might rocket to seven or eight times their normal levels. During December 1206 John had stopped in Winchester, near the south coast of England; on that occasion the royal kitchens had taken delivery of fifteen hundred chickens, five thousand eggs, twenty oxen, one hundred pigs and one hundred sheep.[13] In 1213, an even grander Christmas had been held at Windsor: the court had then gone through four hundred pigs' heads, a dizzying sixteen thousand hens, ten thousand salted eels and fifteen thousand herrings.[14] Recipe books from later in the middle ages record traditional Christmas dishes such as broiled venison basted in wine and ginger, served in a pepper sauce thick with breadcrumbs and animal fat, and huge pies stuffed with six or seven different types of fowl.[15] This year, too, the revellers would expect to be well fed. Seven weeks earlier, the king had ordered his servants in Yorkshire to go into the forest at Pickering and start catching pigs to slaughter. One hundred were to be taken, the carcasses salted and the heads preserved in wine or beer.[16] Meanwhile, John's longstanding counsellor, administrator and gambling partner Hugh de Neville had brought fifty goats and forty pigs to Worcester from the royal hunting lodge of St Briavels in the Forest of Dean. Twenty silver bowls had been seconded from the recently refurbished kitchens at Marlborough Castle.[17] Along with this would have come supplies ordered in from the rest of the realm, including huge quantities of wine imported from royal lands in southern France, stored in vast barrels in the cellars of castles all over England, and moved around by horse and cart in accordance with the royal itinerary.[18] A large and frequently visited royal castle like Corfe in Dorset would take deliveries of thirty barrels of wine at a time – a consignment of several thousand litres.

The presence of the royal household would have been both a curse and a boon for the people of Worcester. Hosting the king in person could be burdensome on a number of levels. The prior might be ejected from his own living quarters to make way for the king, while the dense flow of human traffic from the royal court would leave the town's streets piled even higher than usual with the dung, animal bones and rotting waste that were a feature of life in any busy medieval town.[19] True, the chance for local merchants to profit from the presence of the court would have been gladly received, and there were times when the king would give something back to the fabric of the town, such as in 1204 when he had ordered the rebuilding of the gatehouse in stone, rather than timber, following a devastating fire.[20] However, in 1214 the sight of the king in Worcester was most likely to have reminded the citizens that John had recently levied several harsh taxes on them, and that other arbitrary taxes on the town, known as tallages, had risen by five hundred percent in the last decade.

Nevertheless, a guest at this Christmas court, wandering the corridors of Worcester Castle for the first time, peering behind curtains and staring out of the windows, would have realized that this was a place imbued with a sense of royal prestige and history. The nearby cathedral, a part of the priory, was in the long process of being rebuilt, since the original Norman building had burned down in a calamitous fire that had swept through Worcester during the high summer of 1113 – the first of four major fires that had reduced the town to ashes in the previous hundred years. Now the cathedral was being raised again, and despite its half-finished appearance it contained the tombs of two esteemed saints. It was the burial-place of St Oswald, the archbishop of York who had died washing the feet of Worcester's poor in AD 992. And close by that tomb lay the remains of St Wulfstan, one of the few English-born bishops who had survived the Norman Conquest and a man who had spent his career sponsoring church-building and book production. The cult of Wulfstan was one of the most popular of the early thirteenth century. He had been canonized in 1203 and a hagiography written in Anglo-Saxon had been translated into Latin by the famous chronicler William of Malmesbury. This book contained accounts of Wulfstan's many miracles and great deeds. These included curing the arthritis of a woman called Segild by writing her a letter, cursing a nut tree whose shade was favoured by gamblers and ne'er-do-wells so that it withered and died, and preaching to slave-traders in Bristol until he had persuaded them to abandon their inhumane business.[21]

Lastly, Worcester had a special place in John's own family history. At Easter in 1159 John's father and mother, Henry II and Eleanor of Aquitaine, had visited Worcester during a tour of their realm and treated a congregation in the cathedral to a ceremonial display of crown-wearing.[22] Although this was some years before John was born he would hold Worcester and St Wulfstan in special reverence until the very last days of his life.

✛

The England in which John had been born and over which he ruled was a unified and sophisticated realm. It occupied the largest part of the British Isles, sharing fluctuating borders in the north with the kingdom of the Scots and in the west with the territories of the Welsh princes. The English also had close links with the Irish, over whom they claimed lordship, with varying degrees of success. Even closer ties lay across the Channel, where – until the early period of John's reign at least – English kings had controlled large swathes of France. Beyond this the Plantagenet family was connected by blood to the ruling houses of Castile, Sicily, the Holy Roman Empire and the kingdom of Jerusalem.

England was mild and wet and fertile and industrious, a land of varying terrain, from the moors and mountains of the north-west to the fertile lowlands that stretched from the midlands to the south coast. The Domesday Book had counted a population of 268,863 in 1086, but this number ignored many more souls than it included. By the time of John's reign, England's population was at the very least two million, and may well have been as high as four million.[23] Most of these lived in small, scattered villages of a few hundred people, and sustained themselves on meagre rations by farming the land and rearing animals.* The most heavily populated counties were those in the east of England – Kent and Essex, East Anglia and the northern sprawl of counties collectively known as Yorkshire – and a belt of counties in the south-west, including Gloucestershire, Wiltshire, Somerset and Devon. England also boasted plenty of thriving towns. London was the largest, a burgeoning hub of commerce and government 'whose peer no one knows', according to the twelfth-century poet Jordan Fantosme.[24] The second tier of cities included Norwich, Bristol,

* The average diet of an ordinary person in thirteenth-century England has been estimated at about 1,500–1,650 calories, of which more than ninety percent came from plants. (S. Broadberry, B. M. S. Campbell and B. van Leeuwen, 'English Medieval Population: Reconciling Time Series and Cross Sectional Evidence', qub.ac.uk (2010), 23.) Today that sort of nutritional intake is only recommended for people attempting rapid weight loss.

Winchester, Lincoln, Carlisle and York, and these were home to a few thousand people each.

The rural villages where most Englishmen and their families lived were grouped into clusters known as manors, ruled over by a lord, who would often hold several manors at one time. The villagers who were categorized as villeins or serfs were 'unfree' and owed their lord several days' labour a week in return for their right to live on a patch of his land. Those who were freemen worked for a wage, paid their rents in cash and – crucially – had access to the royal courts to pursue legal disputes, a privilege denied to the unfree, who were bound only to plead and be judged in the private courts of their lords. The pattern and proportion of landholding varied markedly across the country, with the east being generally 'freer' than the west.

Over these ordinary people ruled a class of rich, powerful and educated men of two distinct sorts. First were the men of God. The English Church was vastly wealthy and endowed with much land through the seventeen bishoprics of England and Wales, and the numerous monastic houses that were homes to monks of various rules. England's abbots, bishops and archbishops were generally of aristocratic and even royal stock, politically active and vital advisers to the king. For much of his reign, indeed, John had fought a furious battle with the Pope for the right to dictate appointments to English bishoprics, a matter that was technically the privilege of Rome.

Then there were the great secular lords. Out of the population of several million, there were about ten thousand lords of a minor sort, who might own a manor or two, be active in local politics and perhaps hold public office in the shires. Above them were around a thousand knights – an office that still implied a military outlook and training, but which also had a political role by virtue of the large amount of land that was required to sustain a man in knightly status. Above these men were England's elite: the barons, of whom there were about one hundred. These were lords of massive wealth, military power and prestige who largely descended from families – including the royal family – that had come to England with or since the Norman Conquest. Elite barons held the title of 'earl' and ruled over huge tracts of the countryside, with estates that covered scores of manors, political interests that might stretch across hundreds of miles, and a direct personal relationship with the king. It was with these men that the king was informally expected to consort, collaborate and consult as he went about the business of ruling England. It was also with these men that a king who ruled a kingdom incompetently or unjustly could expect to clash. For the last two years of his reign John had been clashing with his barons in spectacular fashion.

✝

John was the youngest son of a famous family which today we call the Plantagenets. His father, Henry II, had taken the crown in 1154 following a devastating civil war known as the Anarchy, in which royal authority had reached a nadir. Henry had spent his thirty-five-year reign restoring that authority. He had created a strong, stable and centralized system of government based around the pervasive Common Law. Henry developed new legal processes and took uncompromising action against barons who defied him. By the end of Henry's reign, when he was succeeded by his second adult son, Richard I 'the Lionheart', England was heavily but efficiently administered, with the authority of the crown at an unprecedented high.

John had inherited his kingdom in 1199 after his brother Richard died while besieging a castle at Châlus-Chabrol in the Limousin. Richard had been shot through the shoulder with a crossbow bolt, developed gangrene at an inoperable point in his body and died an excruciating and lingering death – although perhaps not as excruciating as that suffered by his killer, Bertram de Gurdun, who was subsequently captured and flayed alive.[25] Since the Lionheart had never had children, there were two plausible heirs: one was John; the other was Arthur of Brittany, the twelve-year-old son of John's dead elder brother Geoffrey. John had won the day, but there had been murmurings even at that early stage that he was not a universally popular choice as king.

The lands that John inherited in 1199 were vast. During the reign of his father, Henry II, the English crown had been yoked through conquest, inheritance and marriage to a series of continental lordships that comprised around a third of the landmass of modern France and virtually her entire western seaboard.* John's full set of titles, as stated in official royal documents, was 'king of England, duke of Normandy, duke

* Henry II inherited the crown and the duchy of Normandy from his mother, and the counties of Anjou, Maine and Touraine from his father. His marriage in 1152 to Eleanor, duchess of Aquitaine, brought him that sprawling southern French lordship. Conquest gave him effective command of Brittany.

of Aquitaine, count of Anjou and lord of Ireland'. This was, to put it mildly, a challenging set of territories for anyone to hold together, particularly since the French kings, including the present king Philip II 'Augustus', took very unkindly to the existence of a single lord, let a rival king, ruling so much of 'their' territory. Richard the Lionheart had managed, by bearing down on his enemies with every ounce of his formidable military talent, to keep this enormous and unlikely patchwork empire together.

What John had inherited, however, he set about losing with almost bewildering speed. In the years between his accession and the winter of 1203–4, John was driven out of Anjou, Maine, Touraine, much of Aquitaine (save for a small area around Bordeaux in the region known as Gascony) and, most seriously of all, Normandy. His reputation for cruelty and changeability preceded him, as did the general suspicion that he lacked his brother's stomach for a fight, and a trickle of dissent in the early years soon became a torrent of defectors, who streamed away from John's side and swore loyalty instead to Philip Augustus. It was variously the honour and the fate of medieval rulers to be assigned blunt nicknames, and John's at the time of the loss of Normandy was brutal. The chronicler Gervase of Canterbury reported that almost as soon as he had been crowned, the new king was being called *molle gladium*: John Softsword.[26]

The loss of this empire – and particularly of Normandy – had created for John a number of awkward problems. Firstly, he had presided over a political rupture that affected the English barons more powerfully than any event since the

22

Conquest of 1066. This was embarrassing. In fact, it was seismic. Before 1204 many aristocratic English families held land on both sides of the Channel. When Normandy was taken by the French, many of these families' lands were split in two. All land in either realm was held on the basis of feudal tenure: the landholder was obliged to pay homage – pledging personal allegiance and promising military support – to the king who was the ultimate lord. It was practically impossible to pay homage to two different kings, particularly two such as John and Philip who were regularly at war with one another. Thus, in 1204, many of England's barons had suffered materially as a result of John's military failure.

The second consequence of the loss of Normandy was that John was determined to get it back. This was a mission that had defined a decade of his life and dictated the whole political thrust of his reign. It had informed his financial policies: John had exploited every source of royal revenue he could find in order to fund the armies he needed to launch a series of invasions across the Channel. It had affected his relations with the Church: he had almost gleefully accepted a five-year Interdict – the suspension by the Pope of all church services in his realm – because it allowed him to extort vast sums of money from the English clergy. But more than anything else, perhaps, the loss of Normandy had moulded John's personal relations with the English barons. For years they had been accustomed to absentee kings, whose demands for money had been tempered by their physical distance. Under John, England had come to know a king who was more or less ever-present, greedy for money on a scale never before known, and determined that he was going to use every bit of his considerable personal energy and cunning to wring it out of the men at the top of the social structure. The personalities of all John's family were connected by a common ruthlessness and abrasive ambition. This was so well known as to be a standing joke: John's brother Richard had boasted that the family was descended from the devil and would return to the devil; their father Henry II had commissioned in his castle at Winchester a large mural portraying himself as an eagle being torn to pieces by its four chicks, each of which represented one of his feckless sons. In the mural, the smallest eaglet – John – sat on the parent's neck, waiting to peck his eyes out. Henry II had been an astute judge of character, and although extremely fond of John he had also correctly surmised that his youngest son was the most treacherous of the lot. John's barons, once the young man had grown up to be king, had found much cause to agree.

Thirdly, the loss of John's family inheritance had, in the eyes of a group of his leading subjects, made this king answerable for all the sins that had been committed in putting the Plantagenet empire together. This, as much as anything else, lay behind a political crisis that had been building for many months, and which at Christmas 1214 appeared ready to explode. As a consequence, although John was in Worcester to hold his Christmas court, and although he had paid rather a lot of money to lay on feasting and to hear his favourite Christmas music, in truth he had no wish to linger over the celebrations, nor any intention of staying in the city a moment longer than was necessary. A couple of days of devouring wine-pickled swine-heads was more than enough distraction from the pressing business of saving what remained of his shattered inheritance. The Twelve Days of Christmas in 1214 were to be spent on the move. On the feast of St Stephen, 26 December, John ordered his possessions to be packed away onto the horse-drawn carts that formed his royal caravan train and set out in the direction of London.[7]

Crowns, gowns . . .
and slippers

In the spring of 1890 the coffin of Hubert Walter, King John's first archbishop of Canterbury, was opened at Canterbury Cathedral. Hubert had been interred on 14 July 1205 and during the intervening centuries he had lain peacefully and unmolested beneath the cool stone of his large, oblong tomb in the Trinity Chapel, dressed in death as he would have been on the greatest days of his life: as a man of rank and splendour.

The treasures found in Hubert's tomb are today preserved in Canterbury Cathedral archives and they give us an immediate sense of how the most powerful people in England dressed during the age of Magna Carta. As primate of the English Church, Hubert had access to rich, luxurious fabrics and gems and finely crafted garments, and he clearly made full use of it. His mitre was made of gold-coloured silk, which still shimmers impressively today. A pair of buskins – decorative cloth boots – are covered in embroidered stars and hung with tassels; they would have reached to just below Hubert's knees. The tomb also contained a pair of soft and comfortable-looking ceremonial slippers, with precious stones attached and dragons or griffins stitched just below the ankle. Large fragments of the archbishop's stole match the golden silk of his mitre, but are covered in bold geometric patterns in what would once have been bright colours.

The intricate needlework on Hubert Walter's vestments is a very good example of English embroidery, known as *opus anglicanum*. (During the course of the thirteenth century England would develop a reputation as the best place in the world to have both vestments and secular clothing decorated; this reputation was just beginning to take off during the years following Hubert's death.) The silk was probably imported from Spain or the Middle East. Some of it may even have been brought in by Hubert himself, for he had been to the Holy Land alongside Richard the Lionheart and would certainly have had the opportunity to trade with cloth merchants of that region. Certainly, other men of similar status are known to have brought back lengths of the beautiful fabrics that could be obtained from the lands around Jerusalem: William Marshal was buried in funeral clothes made from fabric that he bought during the Third Crusade in the 1190s and kept safe for more than two decades. It is not inconceivable that Hubert did something similar. In any case, we know that the quality of the clothing found in Hubert's tomb is a fair reflection of the triumphant finery of the age. For these vestments were not even the best that he owned: Hubert left a yet more exquisite set of religious garments in his will to the canons of Canterbury Cathedral. Typically, these were seized by John, who decided to award them instead to his loyal servant and henchman Peter des Roches, on the occasion of des Roches's enthronement as bishop of Winchester in 1206.

The general impression we should draw from the example of Hubert Walter's graveclothes is that England in 1215 was a place where people – or, at least, the richest and most powerful people – cared deeply about what they wore and were prepared to spend a great deal of money on making sure that their status was reflected accordingly. Although it was not until the fourteenth century that sumptuary laws laid out precise rules for dress according to social station, standards of dress were still highly scrutinized and men and women were identifiable immediately by the clothes on their backs.

Thus, for kings and popes, barons, knights and bishops, dress was dazzlingly ornate, assembled from expensive cloth, imported furs and silks decorated with precious stones and embroidered with gold thread in intricate patterns. Matthew Paris's famous ink portrait of John shows this perfectly well: the king sits wrapped in yards of loose-hanging, multicoloured fabric, gathered about his waist with a thin belt and adorned all over with blazing suns and little dots – jewels, perhaps? – arranged in the shape of triangles. Naturally, he wears a golden crown. It is common to locate the start of a really spectacular age of royal dress rather later in the

Middle Ages, at the chivalrous and magnificent courts of kings like Edward III and, later, Edward IV. In fact, by 1215, kings were already well advanced in their sense of high fashion. So too, indeed, were those who kept royal company. We see in the records of John's government from 1215 regular examples of the king awarding loyal men and women of his court furs or lengths of coloured cloth as payment for good service. These rewards were made to everyone from the king's half-brother to his wife's washerwoman. In the presence of royalty, everyone was expected to make an effort.

Clothing was not, however, merely a matter of personal vanity or frivolous court culture. It was political, too. A generation before 1215 John's mother, Eleanor of Aquitaine, had been the subject of some scorn for disguising herself as a man in an attempt to evade her husband's troops during the Great Rebellion of 1173–4. 'Having changed from her woman's clothes, she was apprehended and detained in strict custody,' wrote the chronicler Gervase of Canterbury, who added that Eleanor was 'of noble descent, but flighty'. It is possible that in this passage Gervase was using Eleanor's cross-dressing as a metaphor for her assuming a male political role. But whether he is writing literally or figuratively, the story illustrates the same point: women were not supposed to wear men's clothes. This was spelled out quite uncompromisingly in the Old Testament: Deuteronomy 22:5 dictated that 'the woman shall not wear that which pertaineth unto a man, neither shall a man put on a woman's garment: for all that do so are abomination unto the Lord thy God.' (It should be noted that this, along with many other Biblical prohibitions, was little regarded by John himself, who appeared publicly at times throughout his reign wearing the coronation regalia of his grandmother, the empress Matilda.)

So what were the common forms of dress in 1215? Basic clothing for laymen and women included stockings, a long-sleeved shirt, a tunic or gown that reached to the knees or below, and during winter months a cloak wrapped around the shoulders for warmth. Women's dresses would be cinched at the waist, from where their skirts would flow outwards, while fashionable women wore their sleeves trailing long below the wrists. Thin leather shoes protected the feet and a purse was hooked at the belt, since clothing was made without pockets.

The fashion for excessively long skirts, sleeves and cloaks points us towards an age-old desire among the rich to show off their wealth with unnecessary and conspicuous consumption. However, fashions moved over time, and the acceptable length of clothing on the lower body was changeable. John's father had been known by some as Henry Curtmantle on account of his penchant for a more neatly cut cloak than was traditional; John's great-great-uncle Robert Curthose, duke of Normandy from 1087 until 1106, had also been nicknamed for preferring the feel of the air on his legs.

For the lower orders and (theoretically) for lower members of the clergy, dress was necessarily simpler, rougher and less regularly changed. Peasants wore their skirts shorter than the upper classes, for reasons of cost, and practicality when working. Clearly it was unlikely that a peasant would be able to afford the latest embroidered patterns or foreign silks, and even if he or she had been able to, they would be of little use to anyone working a plough, tending a vegetable patch, or herding sheep. So for peasants, too, clothing was a marker of status, and in a sense a badge advertising their political capital and potency, which is to say that in general they had none.

Yet for some in society, the very rejection of pomp, finery and expensive clothing could in itself be a sign of status, political power or faith. In the same Church that approved of and celebrated the material splendour of a man like Hubert Walter there was, simultaneously, a pronounced strain of reactionary, conservative thought which revered poverty, austerity and chastity. This found its most obvious manifestation in the monasteries and among the orders of holy knights such as the Templars and Hospitallers, who were sworn to defend the Holy Land, and in doing so to forsake the frivolities of secular life.

By 1215 this mindset had been codified in several places. For example, the provisions of the rule of the Templars and the Fourth Lateran Council both took issue with churchmen who adorned themselves too ostentatiously and indulged in gaudy dress. The rule of the Templars ordained that brothers could only wear white, black or brown habits, which were to be 'without finery and without any show of pride'. Fur was banned, and clothes were to be designed not for elegance or show but 'so that each can dress and undress, and put on and take off his boots easily'. Any Templar who complained would swiftly learn his lesson, for in the words of the rule, 'if any brother out of a feeling of pride or arrogance wishes to have as his due a better and finer habit, let him be given the worst.' Elsewhere the rule stated that pointed or laced shoes were an abomination against 'the promise of God himself, who said . . . "Be born as I am born".'

Clearly, this sense of wool-clad piety was admired outside the orders where such rules were maintained. In late 1215 the canons of Pope Innocent III's Fourth Lateran Council sought to spread the doctrine of clerical simplicity to the wider church. Canon 16 stated that clerics were to:

> wear outer garments that are closed, not noticeable by being too short or too long, they are not to indulge in red or green clothes, long sleeves or shoes with embroidery or with curved toes, bridles, saddles, pectorals and spurs that are gilded or have other unnecessary ornamentation. Priests and those in minor dignities are not to wear cloaks with sleeves at divine service . . . and not even elsewhere . . . They are not to wear buckles or belts ornamented with gold or silver, or even rings except those whose dignity it befits to have them.

Papal concern even extended to the hairstyles of the clergy. The tonsure – hair clipped short on the crown of the head – was an important outward marker of clerical status, and its importance was explicitly stated in the canons of Fourth Lateran. Outside the Church, of course, it was a different matter. Hair in this age was grown long for both sexes – men's hair to the shoulders and women's to their backs, where it was worn plaited if they were married and loose if not. Beards were a sign of mature masculinity, and had indeed been the subject of a (humorous) treatise, the *Apologia de barbis*, written by the Cistercian abbot Burchard of Bellevaux, who held forth in some detail on the length, cleanliness and nature of beards and their moral and mystical significance.[28] Most churchmen, however, were clean-shaven.

In contrast to the canons of the Fourth Lateran Council, Magna Carta had precious little to say about clothing, fabrics or outward display, which is just as well, for as splendid a king as John would not have enjoyed strictures being placed on his own dress. Magna Carta did, however, consider clothing indirectly, by mentioning three types of cloth: dyed cloth, russet and 'haberget'. The latter is obscure: the best guess of historians and archaeologists is that it was a cloth whose weave gave it a vague likeness to a hauberk, or chain-mail shirt.

2

Trouble at the Temple

The road that led John out of the marches was one of the kingdom's great highways. It passed through the green, gently rolling landscape of the Thames valley, connecting London – the capital and largest city – with the important marcher town of Gloucester. Other major medieval roads ran from London to Dover and Colchester in the south-east, York and Chester in the north. In places these followed the course of the great Roman roads such as the Fosse Way, Watling Street and Ermine Street, which had been dug out and paved in stone during the occupation of the first four centuries after Christ's birth. Mostly, though, medieval roads were wide, unengineered tracks laid by the footfall of generations. The biggest highways had originated during Saxon times to join up the ports and settlements with places of worship and trade. Smaller highways were slowly carved into the landscape by the wanderings of merchants and drovers, soldiers and messengers, pilgrims and funeral processions.[29] Whatever the road, though, the sight of a Plantagenet king's court travelling along it – 'with carts and sumpter horses, pack-saddles and panniers, hawks and hounds, and a concourse of men and women,' in the words of the twelfth-century courtier and writer Walter Map – was extremely impressive.[30]

The king himself was a striking man. He stood slightly below average height at about five foot six and a half inches. Middle age had begun to grey his hair, although his teeth remained in good condition.[31] He wore expensive cloaks lined with miniver fur,* and he loved jewels: when he lost a necklace in 1202 John rewarded a man called Berchal, who happened to find it, with an annual income of twenty shillings.[32] He was known for the changeability of his moods: in good humour he could be generous and openhanded, although it was hard to know what to expect from him. He was regularly seen sniggering with his closest companions, with whom he shared a sense of humour that delighted in others' misfortunes. When angered John would dissolve into the paroxysms of fury that were characteristic of his family. The chronicler Richard of Devizes sketched John losing his temper: 'wrath cut furrows across his forehead; his burning eyes shot sparks; rage darkened the ruddy colour of his face.' (The same chronicler said of John's elder brother Richard that 'his raving fury terrified his dearest friends'.)[33] His favourite curses also echoed those of his family. Henry II had been fond of exclaiming 'God's eyes!' and Richard I shouted 'God's legs!'[34] John was heard by one writer to curse 'by the Lord's feet!'[35]

Our most famous image of John shows him hunting, colourfully dressed in a red tunic covered by a bright blue cloak, which billows around him as he charges aboard a great

---

* Miniver is pure and unspotted white fur, which is made from the white winter coat of the stoat, or ermine.

white horse tacked with gold stirrups and bit.[36] This ink drawing was produced many years after the king's death and is certainly idealized; John is wearing his crown while chasing a stag, after all. But it still hints at the awesome spectacle of the monarch and his entourage. Certainly the king's servants' outfits were bright and regularly replaced: his greyhound keepers wore blue, his messengers green. John paid attention to the appearance of even his lowliest servants. His wife's washerwoman wore rabbit fur, paid for from the royal Exchequer.[37]

Besides the large numbers of men, women and hunting dogs who travelled with the king, the royal baggage train also included weapons, money, treasure, precious cups and plate, food, wine, tents and even a pop-up chapel containing saints' relics.[38] This was all dragged around by strong horses, some lugging packs and others pulling hide-covered carts, which doubled the beasts' drawing power.[39] A relatively recent innovation saw cartwheels rimmed with iron, which made them more durable when bumping along rutted roads in an English midwinter.[40] This enabled John to keep constantly on the move. On average, the king moved his court about England's roads thirteen times every month, winter or summer, seldom staying anywhere for more than a few days. Although his main business was done in a roughly diamond-shaped patch of central England with its corners at Dover, York, Worcester and Exeter, John also visited corners of his kingdom that had not seen a king for centuries: in 1201 he had been the first king since William Rufus in 1062 to visit the remote north-western town of Carlisle. This restlessness was one of the traits he had either inherited or learned from his father, Henry II. Walter

Map had written of Henry that 'he was ever on his travels, covering distances like a courier and showing no mercy to his household'. The chronicler remembered vividly seeing Henry riding at the head of his band of knights and clerks, deep in conversation with a trusted counsellor, the two of them stifling their laughter when a monk tripped over in the road before them, his habit blowing up to display his bare buttocks.[41] Exactly the same description could have applied to John, with one small but important difference: when the monk fell, John would have ignored princely decorum and laughed uproariously.

Following his abrupt departure from Worcester after Christmas Day, John moved south to Tewkesbury, where he kept a house that had once belonged to his first wife, Isabel of Gloucester. Then the royal train swung west towards Temple Guiting in Gloucestershire.[42] The distance between each of these stages was about fifteen miles – for the court, loaded onto between ten and twenty carts and wagons, this probably represented a full day's travel.

As John travelled he kept up a heavy stream of business. His orders were sent out on small chits of parchment, whose contents were copied for reference by the king's clerks in his office of chancery onto long membranes of vellum (stretched, bleached and treated parchment made of calfskin), which were stitched together and rolled up for easy storage and transport. These survive today as the close rolls and patent rolls: close rolls contained private orders and were sent sealed, while patent rolls were delivered open. John was a keen-eyed and capable administrator and the breadth of government business that he could deal with, quickly and personally, was astonishing. It ranged from deciding the disposal of property that had come into royal hands and granting letters of safe-conduct for merchants, soldiers and envoys to gifting trinkets and animals to those who had found royal favour. At Tewkesbury on 28 December he had sent orders permitting the marcher lord and sometime outlaw Fulk Fitzwarin to capture five deer from the royal forests in Leicestershire.* He also sent a blizzard of commands to men including the mayor of London, the barons of his Exchequer and the sheriffs of Essex, Gloucester, Bedford and York, ordering everything from the payment of bills and the transfer of servants to the regifting of two 'hawks of good breeding' that had been sent to him from the king of Norway.[43] His scribes worked furiously, copying out a vast array of names and orders and sending them to the most far-flung places in the kingdom. John's bureaucratic machine working at speed and on the hoof must have been an awe-inspiring thing to behold.

---

* It is usually but wrongly assumed that the mythical English outlaw Robin Hood was active in John's reign. In fact, the earliest known ballads of Robin Hood are set in the reign of John's grandson, Edward I. Fulk III Fitzwarin, however, was very much an outlaw of the early thirteenth century, a real-life dispossessed nobleman – albeit from Shropshire and not Yorkshire or the midlands – who fell into dispute with John in 1200 when he was denied his rightful inheritance. Fulk and a number of his relatives rebelled and he spent nearly three years as an outlaw, before being received back into royal favour in November 1203. His story was romanticized in the poem 'Fouke le Fitzwarin', which was probably written in the second half of the thirteenth century, and included fanciful episodes such as the young John and Fulk falling out over a game of chess. Fulk's legend may be read in modern translation in T. Ohlgren (ed.), *Medieval Outlaws: Ten Tales in Modern English* (Stroud, 1998).

John arrived in London on 7 January and he lodged, as he often did when he visited the capital, in the New Temple. This was the London headquarters of the Knights Templar, the vastly rich crusading order established in Jerusalem in around 1119, whose power and interests reached across Europe to the Holy Land. Their distinctive, modern Temple church with its round nave of Caen stone, Purbeck marble pillars and elegant Gothic arches was at the heart of a much larger complex of riverside buildings in which John evidently felt at home. His Templar friends – men like Alan Martel, a future Master of the order – walked the grounds dressed in white robes decorated with a bright red cross, which was supposed to symbolize their willingness to shed blood and die in defence of a Christian Holy Land. They slept four hours a night, attended up to seven masses a day and fasted three times a week. Templar knights vowed to remain chaste, to refrain from anger and cursing, to refuse gifts and never to indulge in luxury, a commitment that specifically included rejecting gaudy horse-bridles and shoes with laces, which the original rule of the order considered to be 'abominable things [that] belong to pagans'.[44] It was muttered that the diligence of the order had slackened during the decades in which their wealth had accrued; all the same, it remained a basic fact that the duty of a Templar knight was to concentrate on religious observances and hard military training. These men were not raucous company, but they did make for highly effective bodyguards.

The New Temple was also a convenient spot for a king to stay, standing as it did outside London's thick Roman walls on

Fleet Street, the road that connected the Ludgate on the west side of the city with Westminster, the administrative village that was a mile or so up the Thames. It was a very pretty set of lodgings. An orchard and gardens surrounded the halls, kitchens and cloisters in which the Templar knights lived and worked, and the whole plot abutted the waterfront of the Thames, which thronged with river traffic. An earth-and-stone wall ran around the main precinct, while on the other side of Fleet Street was the Templars' jousting ground known as Fittes Field.[45] John was fond of both the Temple and the Templars, who loaned him money and provided the crown with semi-formal banking services, as they did for princes across Europe. In return, the knight-monks thought unusually highly of the king. During his stay at the Temple in January 1215 John awarded the brothers land worth £10 a year at Radnage – a manor nestled at the edge of the low Chiltern hills in south Buckinghamshire. And he made a personal gift to Brother Aymeric, Grand Master of the Templars in England, of all the houses and palaces in Northampton that were seized by the crown from the wealthy Jewish financier Aaron of Lincoln. Years after John's death the Templars would maintain priests specifically to sing masses in the Temple church for his soul as it passed through Purgatory.[46]

As John set up court at the New Temple between 7 and 15 January, however, there was little time to admire the beautiful surroundings and the wealthy austerity of his companions. He had to attend to difficult business with a group of his nobles. A dozen bishops and at least as many barons of the highest rank had come to town to meet John at the Temple.[47] Some were friendly or neutral – these included Stephen Langton, archbishop of Canterbury, and William Marshal, the loyalist earl of Pembroke – but there were far more barons in London whose fidelity John had cause to suspect. They, too, had spent Christmas trudging along England's highways, descending on London from all over the realm – and particularly from the north. They had come for a pre-arranged meeting, set to begin on Thursday 8 January. And they had come armed.

The purpose of this meeting between king and country was to thrash out business that had been hanging around since the previous autumn, when John had returned from his French lands in disgrace. The issues at stake were many and varied, and ranged from matters entirely of John's making to bones of contention that had been gnawed over for more than fifty years. What brought all of the problems together, however, were the catastrophic events that had taken place the previous summer, on Sunday 27 July 1214 in a field in Flanders near the village of Bouvines. There, in a single clash between two armies, all of John's aims and ambitions in foreign policy had been ground into the dust.

✝

Many flags flew over the two large armies that met on that warm Sunday afternoon in Bouvines, but the two that most impressed men on the battlefield belonged to John's nephew Otto of Saxony, Holy Roman Emperor, and Philip Augustus, king of France. A chronicler called William the Breton, who was present, described Otto's banner: it was pushed about on a cart and consisted of a long pole around which twined a dragon, 'its tail and wings bloated by the winds, showing its terrifying teeth and opening its enormous mouth. Above the dragon hovers Jupiter's bird with golden wings while the whole of the surface of the chariot, resplendent with gold, rivals the sun and even boasts of shining with a brighter light.' Philip's banner was simpler. It was the Oriflamme: the sacred banner of France, 'a simple silken cloth of bright red', which 'has the right to be carried in all battles, ahead of every other banner.'[48] But John's flag, bearing the Plantagenet leopards – or lions passant gardant, to use their alternative heraldic name – was nowhere to be seen. This was because John was not present at the battle of Bouvines. Instead, on 27 July 1214 he was waiting four hundred miles away near La Rochelle, oblivious to the action taking place in the north, despite the fact that he had paid for a significant part of Otto's army himself.

The strategy that led to the battle of Bouvines was on the face of it straightforward. John had paid a fortune to maintain a coalition of Philip Augustus's common enemies, including Otto and the counts of Flanders and Boulogne. He had developed this coalition over the course of several years, and by 1214 was ready to strike at France, with the ultimate aim of clawing back as much as he could of what had been lost in 1204. In the summer of 1214 John had intended to land in Poitou, gather up his southern allies and raid north through French territory; meanwhile the rest of his allies, accompanied by his half-brother William Longuespée, would punch down from the north, pincering Philip between them and – ideally – laying siege to Paris. Sadly for John, all this had started to unravel from an early stage. He managed to land in Poitou and enjoyed some early success, but Philip declined to meet him head on. Instead, the French king went north, leaving his son Prince Louis to face down John. This was enough to cause John's allies from Poitou to lose their nerve. They abandoned him and John was forced into a red-faced retreat from Louis's forces during the early days of July. Placed under the slightest pressure, one half of the pincer had simply snapped. John camped at La Rochelle and planned his next move.

In the north, meanwhile, Philip and Otto's armies shadowed each other for some time until battle could be avoided no longer. That time was Sunday 27 July. It was thought very low to contemplate fighting on Sunday, the holiest day of the week, but this did not seem to trouble Otto and his allies. Otto had been excommunicated from the Church as the result of a long-running dispute with Pope Innocent III, and though some companies of his men decorated their armour with small crosses made from strips of fabric, it was the view of at least one chronicler that these were the cynical badges of a bad bunch, worn 'much less for the glory and honour of Christ's cross than for the growth of their wickedness'.[49]

For his part, the forty-nine-year-old Philip was sitting under an ash tree enjoying some respite from the midsummer's blaze when his messengers informed him of his enemies' wish to sully the Sabbath by spilling Christian blood. This presented him with a dilemma: to disgrace the conventions of holy warfare, or to stain his own honour by retreating and being thought of as a coward. The decision did not take long.

Although no French king had fought a pitched battle for more than a century, Philip buckled on his armour, made a quick trip to a church to pray and prepared to fight.

The battle site chosen, just outside Bouvines, was close to a marshland that spread out from the banks of the river Marque, and large enough for the two armies to be arrayed in long lines facing one another. On both sides stamped heavily armoured horses, ridden by similarly well-protected men: 'each knight covered his members with several layers of iron and enclosed his chest with armour, pieces of leather and other types of breastplate,' wrote William the Breton. Emperors, kings, dukes, earls and counts commanded the various divisions of cavalry and foot-soldiers. It was highly unusual for these men to be preparing to do battle in an open field, for the preferred mode of warfare in this period was the siege: a slower but far more predictable means of conflict. Nevertheless, this was also a golden age for tournaments, and the best men in both armies would have experienced fighting in the melée: a codified form of sparring between armed knights which mimicked most of the aspects of real fighting, and which was designed, in theory at least, to prepare a man for a day like Bouvines. Despite the inherent novelty of a battle, then, men on both sides stood ready and willing to fight. Trumpets blared. The fighting began.

The sun beat down on pure carnage. Whereas knights and commanders were considered too valuable to kill – the ransoms that could be earned from capturing noblemen were dizzying – there was still a savage range of weapons brought to bear. 'Lances are shattering, swords and daggers hit each other, combatants split each other's heads with their two-sided axes, and their lowered swords plunge in the bowels of the horses,' wrote William the Breton. A number of bishops rode into battle, wielding maces and clubs instead of swords, taking a strictly literal view of the Church's ruling that men of God ought not to spill blood; in practice this meant that churchmen could not wield bladed weapons, but a bishop could still crack a skull with a blunt instrument. Some of the worst violence at Bouvines was committed against horses, since attacking a man's beast was a sure way of sending him tumbling, vulnerable, to the floor. (At one point Philip Augustus himself was knocked from his mount, but rose to continue fighting.) William the Breton saw terrible things that day:

> You could see horses here and there lying in the meadow and letting out their last breath; others, wounded in the stomach, were vomiting their entrails while others were lying down with their hocks severed; still others wandered here and there without their masters and freely offered themselves to whomever wanted to be transported by them: there was scarcely a spot where one did not find corpses or dying horses stretched out.

Amid all this, some men stood bewildered, shocked by the brute chaos of war. 'Here a cavalryman, there a foot-soldier voluntarily surrender, fearing more to be killed than to live vanquished.'

After hours of this melée, the orderly lines in which the

armies had begun had splintered. John's brother William Longuespée and the counts of Flanders and Boulogne were taken prisoner, while the emperor Otto fled the battlefield. A final stand of coalition cavalry, in which knights made sorties against the French from within a circle of pikemen, was eventually overwhelmed for lack of numbers. The day thus ended with a resounding victory for Philip Augustus. It was, recorded William Marshal's biographer, 'a large-scale rout'.[50] It took a number of days for the news to make its way south to Poitou. When it did, John realized the game was up. He had to make expensive arrangements for the release of his half-brother, agree an eighteen-month truce with Philip Augustus and return home to face the music. 'And thereafter began the war, the strife and criminal conflict between the king and the barons,' continued Marshal's biographer, with disdain.[51]

✝

Losing a battle on the scale of Bouvines would have been humiliating for any king, for the judgment of the Lord was always implicit in a crushing military defeat. Yet for John, defeat presented an even more severe problem. Although he had not been personally present on the battlefield, he had nevertheless gambled around ten years of controversial and increasingly divisive royal policy on the outcome of the battle. He had lost. When he faced his barons in a series of meetings in London on his return, he was under enormous pressure to provide assurances that things were going to be different from now on.

There had been a shared truculence – part reformist, part rebellious – among a group of England's barons for at least two years before Bouvines, fed by a whole range of grievances against John's kingship in particular and Plantagenet kingship in general. This combination – of long-term problems exacerbated by John's short-term failings – would be the essence of what was expressed in Magna Carta.

There was no doubt that John himself had done much to earn the enmity of his barons. He had treated a number of them extremely badly. Outwardly John projected the grandeur of a king, but this was tempered by a tendency to fall out very acrimoniously with his leading barons and churchmen. In his day John was described as mean-spirited and unchivalrous: traits quite unbecoming to a prince. He was suspicious, paranoid and absurdly secretive: he would establish elaborate codes and passwords by which to differentiate his real orders from fake instructions sent to mask his true purpose, then would forget the passwords.[52] His treatment of prisoners was infamously cruel: those who fell foul of him could expect to be fettered or chained in dungeons, where they would be starved or worse. It was most notoriously said that John had murdered his nephew and rival Arthur of Brittany at Rouen Castle in 1203. All of this combined to leave a lasting but not always a happy impression on many of his most prominent subjects.[53]

These personal quirks did not, however, significantly mark John out from his predecessors. Kings were not supposed or expected to be nice. (Those who were too holy, such as Louis VII 'the Pious' of France, were mocked behind

their backs.) John's great-grandfather Henry I was said personally to have pushed one of his own brother's servants to his death from the top of the tower in Rouen Castle. His father, Henry II, once ordered a group of wandering Cathar heretics arrested in Oxfordshire to be scourged and branded, before sending them out into the freezing winter to die. Henry II subsequently gained Europe-wide notoriety for ordering – albeit unwittingly – the murder of Archbishop Thomas Becket in Canterbury Cathedral. John's brother Richard the Lionheart ordered the murder of hundreds of prisoners of war during the Third Crusade, while making so many enemies among the European aristocracy that he was imprisoned for eighteen months on his return from Europe, an incarceration which cost him 150,000 marks in ransom.*
Nor was it just violence in which previous English kings had excelled. John was thought to be a lecher who preyed on the wives and daughters of his courtiers, but this was not wildly unusual either. All self-respecting monarchs tended to dally with ladies of the court, many of whom might be inconveniently married to other men.†

So the grievances between John and his barons were more than just a matter of personal animus. What concerned

---

* Richard's ransom is hard to convert into a modern sum, but its value was around four times his royal revenue. A reasonable and probably conservative estimate via measuringworth.com is that the value of the ransom today would be £25 billion ($40 billion). This represents the *economic power* of the ransom.

† Henry I fathered more than twenty bastards during his thirty-five-year reign. Henry II's most famous mistress was Rosamund Clifford, with whom he lived quite openly after imprisoning his wife, Queen Eleanor, in 1174.

England's nobles far more, as they gathered at the Temple and clamoured for reform in January 1215, was the idea that John and his predecessors had been systematically abusing their royal power for two generations. Abuses had to be reined in, by whatever means possible.

Government since the time of Henry II had seen two parallel developments. On the one hand royal authority had penetrated deeper than ever before into the localities of England, with the power of royal officers and the royal courts increasing relative to the power of barons over their own territories. Henry II had passed numerous 'assizes' establishing new legal processes by which litigants could contest land disputes before the royal law. Writs with names such as mort d'ancestor and novel disseisin could be obtained at a relatively affordable price from the royal chancery, and royal justices began to tour England on a circuit known as the general eyre, in which offences would be swept up and dealt with under the supreme jurisdiction of the crown.* Royal justice in this sense had become more routine, bureaucratic, available and efficient.

As government had become more professional, however, it had also become more profitable. Administrative fees charged by government departments for access to the royal law were supplemented with fines levied against those who lost their cases, and against those who fell foul of the criminal

---

* Mort d'ancestor was a process that sought to establish the right of inheritance; novel disseisin was an action that established that land had been taken and restored it to the original holder. These and several other legal processes were established by Henry II as part of the Assizes of Clarendon (1166) and Northampton (1176).

or forest laws. Government offices were frequently auctioned off for profit, not least by Richard I, who conducted a fire-sale of official posts after he was crowned in 1189, as he sought to raise money for the army he eventually took east to the Third Crusade. The Plantagenets, with their territorial and military interests stretching from Northumbria to Jerusalem, needed money constantly and often chronically. A system of law and government that could be run by bureaucrats but which generated a healthy profit for the crown was manifestly beneficial to them.

And if there was one group which Plantagenet government tended to weigh heavily upon it was the baronial class: the men known as 'tenants-in-chief' whose principal dealings with law involved not the decisions of mid-ranking bureaucrats but direct contact with the king himself. For just as the day-to-day operation of many parts of English government was becoming more mechanical, so the experience of royal rule at the top of society had come to seem more arbitrary than ever before. Under Henry II and his sons there was a concerted effort to squeeze as much advantage as possible from their feudal streams of revenue: the profits that accrued from the prerogative powers allotted to the king by virtue of being king. When his eldest son was knighted or his daughter married, the king could levy a charge on his greatest subjects. When the same great men wanted to claim inheritances or to marry, they had to offer the king a fine for the privilege of doing so. Holding great titles and estates came at a cost. It also obliged great men to provide knights for royal armies when required; this could be avoided on the payment of a scutage or 'shield-tax', which was also a healthy source of royal income during wartime.

Feudal payments were generally supposed to be laid down by custom. In theory they were ancient and traditional offerings that did not change much down the years. Under the early Plantagenets in general – but under John in particular – they had been ratcheted up to exorbitant levels. John's chancery records are full of orders to his representatives in far-off parts of the realm, demanding that pressure be put on noblemen to pay large amounts of money, almost always with instructions to 'obtain this sum and a larger one if you can'.[54] In part, this served John's need to raise money to fight in France. More objectionable than that, though, was John's use of financial means to bully, threaten and in some cases ruin those barons who were unlucky enough to displease him. The Exchequer – the government body responsible for collecting royal revenue – had become under John an office not merely of accountancy but of harassment and extortion. Inevitably, by virtue of their position, many of England's barons would find themselves accumulating large debts to the crown. Traditionally, many of these were left either partially paid or unpaid – relief of debt could be a tool of political patronage for those close to the king. Under John, however, enforcement of debt became a primary means of political menace.

There was a long list of men who had found themselves crushed in the jaws of John's financial vice. They included William de Briouze, a one-time servant and close companion of the king who had fallen out with him in

1208, after William's wife Matilda reportedly accused John of having murdered his nephew Arthur of Brittany five years previously. William had incurred huge debts to the crown as a result of being awarded lands and titles; in 1208 John decided to break William by calling those debts in. Citing default, he sent men to confiscate William's estates and arrest him. William fled to Ireland and was sheltered for a time by sympathetic acquaintances. John went after him with an army. William escaped and made his way to France, but his wife and son were thrown into a dungeon and starved to death. This was clearly a despicable act of vendetta on the king's part, but what is most instructive is an open letter that John circulated justifying his conduct in tight, legalistic 'Exchequerese', citing shirked debts, missed deadlines and fishy accounting on the part of Briouze and his wife as reason for hounding the family to its destruction. Read today it has all the matter-of-fact menace of a bailiff's notice, and gives us a chilling vision of John's merciless bureaucratic efficiency.[55]

Briouze died in French exile in 1211, but by 1215 there were plenty of others who nursed deep grudges about John's heavyhanded methods. They included Geoffrey de Mandeville, who in 1214 had been encouraged to marry John's first wife, Isabel of Gloucester, whom the king had divorced shortly after his accession in 1199. Mandeville was charged an exorbitant fine of twenty thousand marks for the privilege of marrying a woman in her early forties, who was past childbearing age and whose landed inheritance had been strictly limited in order to reserve the most lucrative parts for the king. Mandeville was ordered to pay his fine in four instalments of five thousand marks each.* It was no coincidence that he was prominent among the men who lined up to oppose the king from the autumn of 1214 until the meeting in London in January 1215.

✝

All those who came in their armour to the New Temple in January 1215, then, were conscious of a history of resistance to the king that reached back at least three years. Prior to his failed invasion of France in 1214, John had also experienced truculence and in some cases downright refusal when he had demanded that his barons fulfil their feudal obligation to send him troops for his army or pay the scutage that was assessed according to the number of knights that each baron was liable to raise. But in early 1215 the resistance was beginning to take shape in a more organized fashion than ever before.

According to the chronicler Roger of Wendover, a baronial meeting had been held at Bury St Edmunds around the time of John's return from Bouvines. The disgruntled noblemen met there, said Wendover, under the cover of a pilgrimage to the gold-encrusted shrine to the sainted ninth-century Saxon king Edmund; there may have been something doubly suggestive about the fact that they were meeting around the shrine of a famously perfect king whose reign ended when

---

* Twenty thousand marks for a marriage in 1214 equates to something like £500 million today. This is the *economic status* value of income or wealth, calculated at measuringworth.com.

he was assassinated in a hail of arrows.* At Bury, according to Wendover, the assembled barons 'discoursed secretly ... for some time'.[56] The same account went on to claim that Stephen Langton, archbishop of Canterbury, advised them that the best way of restraining the king would be to demand that John confirm the coronation charter of Henry I, whereupon 'they all swore on the great altar that, if the king refused to grant these liberties and laws, they themselves would withdraw from their allegiance to him, and make war on him, till he should, by a charter under his own seal, confirm to them every thing they required; and finally it was unanimously agreed that, after Christmas, they should all go together to the king and demand the confirmation of the aforesaid liberties to them.' The coronation charter of Henry I in 1100 had offered the abolition of 'evil customs by which the kingdom of England has been unjustly oppressed'. It included vows to avoid unjustly battering barons with demands for unreasonable feudal payments, to guarantee the financial rights of widows, to write off old debts to the crown, to avoid taking a range of newfangled and unpopular taxes and to keep the peace.[57]

* St Edmund ruled the kingdom of East Anglia from around AD 855 to 869, when he was killed by a band of Vikings known as the Great Heathen Army. The story of his martyrdom held that he was shot to death with arrows and then beheaded, his head only being recovered after a talking wolf summoned faithful Christians to the woodland spot where it had been discarded. His shrine was one of the greatest in England, richly decorated in precious stones and metals. John himself had promised the monks a large ruby set in gold for the shrine, to be handed over on his death. (R. Yates, *History and Antiquities of the Abbey of St Edmund's Bury*, (London 1843), part II, 40.) The shrine was destroyed during the Reformation.

Whether or not this meeting happened quite like that is a matter of some uncertainty, but what is clear is that there had been tense political discussions among the barons before Christmas 1214, that the realm was in generally mutinous spirit, that a charter similar to that granted by Henry I on his coronation was being demanded, and that if John did not accede to the reformers' demands then he could expect serious and potentially violent consequences.[58] But if there was ever a king to wriggle when he was pinned, it was John. For the best part of a week at the Temple, John listened to the angry complaints of his subjects as they implored him to reconfirm Henry I's charter. Deftly, he sidestepped and stalled. He declared himself unprepared to agree to the barons' demands, which he condemned as a 'novelty', and countered by saying that he would only come to terms on condition that the barons swore a general oath of obedience 'to stand with the king against all men' and promised never to make similar demands of him again.[59] And crucially, just as he had done in the autumn, John played for time. He proposed to give his barons a final answer to their demands at Easter, banking on the fact that they were angry, but not yet so angry as to make war.

John gambled correctly. By Thursday 15 January the meeting at the Temple had broken up, in bad spirits but without a binding resolution or a full descent into violence. John was obviously aware that England was teetering on the brink of outright mutiny, because on the previous day he had prepared orders asking major landowners between London and the north to provide safe-conduct for those 'who came to London at Epiphany ... to appeal to us over their grievances'.[60] Still, he was not ready to concede. Bidding farewell to the Knights Templar and their fine hospitality, the king and his court rolled out once more onto his country's ancient high roads. This time he was heading west, and he had a plan.

Eating, drinking . . . and making merry

When we glance through the records of King John's reign it is impossible not to be struck by the importance of food and drink in the life of a great medieval lord. The king is frequently to be found sending gallons of wine to his hunting lodges and castles. He dispenses patronage by awarding certain favourites the right to capture (and, we presume, to eat) deer and boar from the royal forests. He gifts fish. He orders dozens of beasts to be slaughtered to feed the royal court on feast days. King John was less notable for gluttony than he was for other sins, but it is clear all the same that food was regularly on his mind. When he commissioned work on his castles at Marlborough and Ludgershall in Wiltshire, he specified that their new kitchens should contain ovens that were each big enough to roast two or three oxen at a time.[61] Even when he sent for the fat of forty pigs, to be used to set fire to a mine dug beneath Rochester Castle late in the autumn of 1215, John gave explicit command that the pigs who gave up their lives for this task should be 'of the sort least good for eating'. John was not especially greedy.

He was simply the product of an aristocratic culture that prized largesse and displays of mass public consumption.

The king and his associates were of course extremely fortunate in being rich enough to gorge on feasts such as the week of royal partying that took place in Winchester over Christmas in 1206.[62] At that gathering, five hundred ells of cloth (more than six hundred yards) was used to make the tablecloths alone. This sort of event represented the height of culinary indulgence – and it was noted of John that whatever his other failings, he could always be relied upon to stand a good banquet. The author of the *Histoire des ducs de Normandie et des rois d'Angleterre* wrote that the king 'gave plenty to eat, and did so generously and willingly. People never found the gate or the doors of John's hall barred against them, so that all who wanted to eat at his court could do so.'[63]

Outside the doors of John's hall, things were less extravagant. Yet in good times, people in England still had access to a fairly broad and varied diet. The bulk of calories consumed came ultimately from cereals such as wheat, oats and barley (in that order of commonness). A great deal of this was made into bread and ale, which were the staples of an English family's daily consumption, along with potage – a soup made on a base of grains or pulses, livened up with whatever vegetables were available. Yet evidence from archaeological digs shows that the thirteenth-century diet was by no means wholly bland or repetitious. People ate root vegetables and garden herbs, peas and beans, fresh and dried fruit.

Cows, sheep and pigs were all slaughtered for their meat, providing beef, veal, mutton, lamb, pork, ham and bacon. (Whether one ate pork or bacon was a marker of social status: pork was the preserve of the wealthy, while bacon and ham were foods for the poor – although in any case far more meat was eaten by England's rich than by the lower classes.[64]) Cows and goats produced milk, which could be made into butter and cheese. Chickens could be eaten or kept for their eggs. Animal bones excavated from city rubbish dumps are regularly found hacked open: the marrow inside them was a valuable ingredient for enriching stews and soups.

There were, however, strict rules laid down by the Church about what foodstuffs could be eaten on which days. For those who followed a monastic rule there were great strictures placed on dining. The rule of St Benedict commanded that monks be fed two main meals a day, 'at the sixth and ninth hour' – canonical hours corresponding to midday and mid-afternoon – with each meal consisting of two types of cooked food and fruit or fresh vegetables, if available. A pound of bread was to be allowed for each brother unless the day's work was especially hard, in which case 'it is left to the discretion and power of the Abbot to add something, if he think fit, barring above all things every excess, that a monk be not overtaken by indigestion'. The rule also forbade 'eating the flesh of four-footed animals', except for very sick or weak brethren, although this instruction was not always observed.

It was not only monks whose diets were restricted by doctrine. Nearly half of the days in the medieval calendar were designated for lay fasting, including every Friday and Saturday as well as each Wednesday during Lent and Advent. On these days, and on the numerous other religious feast days, no meat was supposed to be eaten by anyone. The observant would get their protein from dairy or fish. Fishing was therefore big business in thirteenth-century England – one reason why so many fish-traps had been constructed along major rivers such as the Thames and Medway, a source of grievance addressed by Magna Carta. From the sea came piles of herring (often preserved by salting), cod, conger eel, hake, flatfish, mackerel and shellfish.

One of the greatest delicacies in this age was the lamprey: a small, eel-like, jawless fish that sucks up its food through a round mouth encircled by tiny teeth the shape of rose thorns, or occasionally bores into the flesh of other fish to drink their blood. Devoured since Roman times, the lamprey caused the great and good of England to salivate in much the same way that beluga caviar today delights London's oligarchs. Lampreys had been implicated in the demise of John's great-grandfather, Henry I, who was said to have fallen into his final sickness after gorging on them in 1135. This was not enough to warn John off involving himself in business concerning the rubbery but delicious fish. Early in his reign, the king sent a servant called Samson under letters of safe-conduct all the way from Baugé, in

Anjou, to Nantes, eighty miles away in Brittany, in order to fetch back lampreys for the countess of Blois. By the middle of his reign, the fish were still on his mind. Letters patent sent to the sheriff of Gloucester instructed him to ensure that no one was selling lampreys for more than two shillings each (an exorbitant price in an age where it was possible to buy the finest river salmon for the same amount). The punishment for anyone who transgressed these orders was a fine and the loss of property.[65]

Clearly, the availability of foods like the lamprey varied enormously between the ranks of thirteenth-century society, and for every great lord feasting on beasts of the air, sea and ground, there were probably a dozen hungry serfs scrabbling to get by on whatever they could eke out from their smallholding. The rule of St Benedict reminded readers that 'nothing is so contrary to Christians as excess', but not all Christians took this to heart. An indication of the casual gluttony enjoyed by the upper classes is suggested by a dining invitation that survives from the very end of the thirteenth century, addressed from the bishop of Worcester to the prior of the city. 'Next Sunday ... come to us ... at one o'clock to dine with us on good, fat and fresh venison, and an equally fat crane, which chance to have been sent to us, and which we do not like to eat without you ... Farewell in the Lord.'[66]

For those who were invited to eat at great tables, chivalric culture implied and demanded an elaborate set of manners which governed how England's great and good treated one another while dining. The earliest book of English courtesies was the three-thousand-line *Liber urbanus*, drawn up by Daniel of Beccles, most likely a courtier of Henry II. It reminded readers not to ride their horses in the halls of great houses, and to refrain from putting their elbows on the dining table or speaking with their mouths full. Guests at a lord's hall were not to scratch their armpits in public and were to feign illness if the wife of a host should make a pass at them.

'Beware of draining cups greedily like Bacchus,' counselled Beccles, although in an Englishman's court that was easier said than done. Alcohol was a major ingredient in the daily diet at every level of society. Wealthy men and women drank wine. When apples were ripe, cider was available. The most common drink for ordinary people was ale, made from barley malt, herbs, spices and yeast, and drunk fresh, when it was still cloudy and rather bitter.

The result was general drunkenness. Accordingly, for all the chivalric protocol that obsessed medieval courtiers and writers, England in 1215 was an earthy, bawdy place, and in some senses quite unrestrained. The business of toasting drinks sums up the paradox between society's strict protocol and apparent loutish-ness. At table, a cry of 'Wesheil!' was a polite command to reply 'Drincheil!' and drain one's drink. This could be carried on long into the night, until (or beyond) the point where decorum gave way to ribaldry. The waspish chronicler and travel writer Gerald of Wales records a story of Henry II enthusiastically joining in with a toasting contest against a Cistercian abbot, who found himself out of his depth when faced with the practised inebriation of the king. In this sort of company many of the genteel manners of the table were frequently ignored. (John's father once rode a horse into his own hall to dine with a rather affronted Thomas Becket.)

Another (much-flouted) injunction of thirteenth-century chivalry forbade cursing in company. Swearing was less scatological or gynaecological in 1215 than it is today and instead concentrated on blasphemous oaths. 'Do not swear by Christ's advent, birth, passion, body, brain, bowels, heart, tomb, ears, feet, arms [or] legs,' Beccles warned, but we know that he was frequently ignored. King John habitually swore 'by God's teeth', just as his father had been wont to curse by God's eyes.[67] Other oaths invoked God's bones or His nails. All of these were literally profanities: they profaned the sacred and were therefore, in a highly religious and far less squeamish society than our own, much more shocking than any reference to sexual organs or shit.

Although not demonstrably more foul-mouthed when drunk than other peoples of the world, the English were nevertheless famously heroic drinkers, a character trait which seeped into the language used to describe them even in contexts that had little to do with the ale-house. Describing an episode in the crusades, the writer Richard of Devizes knowingly describes Englishmen as being 'drunk with fear'.[68]

In polite circles, this drunkenness was regarded as a vice and a sin to be equated with gluttony. William of Malmesbury considered the Norman Conquest in part a punishment for the English practice of drinking all day 'until they spewed'.[69] Drunkenness among the clergy was regarded as especially abominable. Gerald of Wales and Gervase of Chichester railed against priests who went to feasts or undertook their duties while drunk. The author of the Book of Ely recorded the story of a priest who was so drunk that he could scarcely walk, but attempted nevertheless to perform the mass, only to vomit and defecate on his vestments in front of the congregation.[70]

Alcohol was, therefore, an unsurprisingly common factor in criminal court cases, as one thirteenth-century example from Scott's Acton in Shropshire attests. After sunset on Christmas Day, heard the judges, 'some men [were] singing outside a tavern ... Hugh de Weston, a chaplain, came by the door immensely drunk, and quarrelled with the singers.' The quarrel became a fight in which Hugh charged one singer, John Oaks, with a sword, battering him about the head and 'nearly cutting off two fingers of his left hand'. After further scuffling, John himself drew a knife and stabbed Hugh through the chest, 'killing him instantly'.[71] Little wonder that men like the tenth-century homiletic composer Aelfric considered drunkenness 'a vice of such magnitude that [St] Paul bears witness that drunkards are not able to obtain the kingdom of God.'

3

Taking the Cross

Walter Mauclerk arrived in Rome in the middle of February 1215, feeling rather unwell. His journey from England to the papal court had involved a winter crossing of the Channel and a long ride south through France. A thirteenth-century map made by the St Albans chronicler Matthew Paris shows the several routes from London to Rome: sailing from Dover to Calais or Boulogne, riding on via Paris or Reims to Lyon and then traversing the Alps through the Mont Cenis pass, a route trodden by generations of pilgrims. Travellers then descended through northern Italy via Lucca and Siena to approach Rome from the north.[72] All this seldom took less than three weeks. It had taken Walter even longer than usual to make the trip since, as he wrote in a letter home to King John, 'I was detained by serious illness.'[73] In an age where travel was hard, slow and physical, crossing the continent in faltering health was no light undertaking. Yet this trusted royal confidant and servant, who described himself to the king as a 'faithful and devoted clerk always and everywhere', had done his duty and eventually arrived in the Holy City on Tuesday 17 February. He presented himself at the

Lateran Palace armed with a package of letters from his king asking for papal support in the tussle against England's barons, and he was granted an audience with one of the most formidable men in the recent history of Christendom: Pope Innocent III.

Born Lotario de' Conti, Innocent had worn the papal tiara since he was elected in January 1198 at the unprecedentedly young age of thirty-seven. A fresco painting of him at the Monastery of St Benedict in Subiaco, idealized but unquestionably striking, shows a youthful man with an almond-shaped face and thin features, his brown hair cropped above his ears and his papal splendour expressed in rich ecclesiastical vestments: a bright red cope adorned with a butter-yellow pallium embroidered with blue crosses, which drapes tidily across his shoulders. The magnificence of the image is fitting. During his seventeen years as Pope, Innocent had done everything in his power to raise up the prestige of the papacy and the authority of Rome.

Innocent was well suited to high office. He came from a distinguished family – an uncle had previously served as Pope Clement III – and he was an exceptional scholar, whose training at the universities of Bologna and Paris had left him equally gifted in the fields of canon law and theology. He had written several important theological works, including one called *De contemptu mundi* ('On the Contempt of the World'), which, despite its gloomy title, would be wildly popular for centuries to come. Few previous Popes had ruled with as much self-confidence, political acuity and success. He was by turns ruthless and sensitive, personally domineering yet able to unite and command great swathes of Christendom by reconciling princes who were more naturally eager to tear one another's throats out. He was as exacting and precise when dealing with the political disputes of rival claimants to the title of Holy Roman Emperor as he was when examining petty legal cases concerning the humblest men and women of Europe.*

Innocent had extended or re-extended the power of Rome over the states that surrounded it, as well as over the Norman kingdom of Sicily and the principalities of Germany. The greatest kings in Christendom had felt the sting of his displeasure: the Pope had intervened in the affairs of Philip Augustus, king of France, the Holy Roman Emperor Otto IV and his rival Philip duke of Swabia, the kings of León, Portugal and Aragon and even the kings of Norway. A brutal campaign against Cathars in southern France had resulted in seven years of slaughter, mainly around Toulouse, stories of which might have been related to the sickly Walter Mauclerk as he passed near that terrorized region on his way to Innocent's court.†

---

* He did so quite memorably in 1204, when making a judgment in the case of an Italian woman who had found her husband to be impotent and left him to marry a lover who was better made to satisfy her urges. The woman's bishop had forced her to return to the first husband, but he had been unable to stand the humiliation, so entered a monastery and promptly died of shame. Innocent not only troubled himself with the details of the case but made a ruling redefining the Church's entire position with regard to impotence and marriage. (C. M. Rosseau, 'Neither Bewitched nor Beguiled: Philip Augustus's Alleged Impotence and Innocent III's Response' in *Speculum* 89 (2014).)

† Catharism was a dualistic Christian heresy that spread to southern France and northern Italy from the eastern Roman (Byzantine) empire around the middle of the twelfth century. Believers identified two gods

These were merely the political deeds of the man. Innocent had also made an artistic improvement in the state of his office. To reflect the rising might of the papacy the Lateran, which was the main residence of popes, had been dazzlingly restored under his supervision, so that the poet Dante Alighieri would write around a hundred years later that it 'outsoared all mortal art'.[74] To be granted an audience with Innocent III in the halls of this palace was to stand before a true colossus of his age – perhaps the greatest of all the medieval Popes. Yet as Mauclerk was aware, this was a man with whom King John of England had a rather tarnished history. More concerning still, baronial ambassadors were also circling the papal court, attempting to put forward their own version of recent events in the Plantagenet realm. For the sake of peace in England – and perhaps even his master's crown – it was vital that Mauclerk made a good impression.

✝

It is fair to say that John and his immediate predecessors did not enjoy an unsullied reputation for holy kingship. John's father,

---

(or principles) – one good and one evil – and thought that the material world was the creation of the evil. Medieval Catholicism held that God alone had created the world, so Catharism was a direct assault on the Church's basic monotheistic principle. Innocent III had initially attempted to deal with Catharism with missionaries. But in 1208 a papal legate was murdered after excommunicating Count Raymond VI of Toulouse for his failure to deal sufficiently harshly with the Cathar heresy. Innocent declared the dead man a martyr and launched a full military assault, led by one Simon de Montfort (father of the later English earl and rebel) and known now as the Albigensian Crusade. For good general introductions to the subject see J. Sumption, *The Albigensian Crusade* (London, 1973) and more recently R. I. Moore, *The War on Heresy: Faith and Power in Medieval Europe* (London, 2012).

Henry II, had inadvertently caused the murder of Archbishop Thomas Becket before the altar of Canterbury cathedral. Richard the Lionheart – for all his crusading heroism – was fond of joking that the family was descended from the devil. Others shared a similar view. Gerald of Wales included in his book *De instructione principis* ('On the Instruction of a Prince') an account of a vision received by a northern hermit, songwriter and popular saint called Godric of Finchale, which seemed to sum up that perception. In his vision, Godric had entered a church to see Henry II and his four adult sons prostrating themselves in front of the altar before rising to their feet to dust it with linen cloths. Gradually they began to clamber up the altar, cleaning the legs of the crucifix that hung above. But when they reached the top of the crucifix, 'horrible to relate, they began to defile the altar on every side with their urine and excrement.'[75] Gerald of Wales was an enthusiastic critic of the Plantagenet dynasty whose appetite for tall tales was rivalled only by his pursed-lipped delight in scatology and sex. Yet in the Plantagenets in general, and in John in particular, he had a worthy subject. For John's relations with Innocent III were in themselves an astonishing story, for which Godric of Finchale's vision provided an apt metaphor.

The quarrel between John and Innocent had begun with a death. In the summer of 1205 Hubert Walter, the highly capable but essentially pliant archbishop of Canterbury, suffered a high fever brought on by an infected carbuncle and breathed his last. This was a loss to the crown, but it was also an important opportunity for John to appoint a new man who would, like Hubert (and unlike his father's nemesis Becket) serve the needs of the king as readily as he served his flock. John's choice for the new position was his former chancery clerk and close ally John de Gray, bishop of Norwich. Since the monks of the cathedral chapter in Canterbury claimed the privilege of electing the new archbishop, John leaned on them to choose his man. The monks had other ideas. Instead of electing de Gray they picked Reginald, sub-prior of their chapter, and packed him off to Rome to seek papal confirmation for his new post.

John was livid, and lobbied the Pope to respect his choice. In 1206 Innocent made up his mind. He rejected both claimants and imposed his own candidate, Cardinal Stephen Langton. An Englishman by birth and a brilliant continental scholar by training, Langton was supposed to be a compromise appointment. He would turn out to be anything but.

Langton's appointment enraged John even further. Not only had he been thwarted over de Gray, he was now being asked to accept as primate a man who had spent twenty years living and lecturing at the university of Paris – the capital city of John's most hated rival, Philip Augustus. Worse still, Langton was a scholar in the tradition of Becket and the theologian John of Salisbury, both of whom were severe critics of English kings and defenders of the principle that ecclesiastical authority outranked the power of mere princes. Accordingly, when Innocent consecrated Langton at Viterbo in 1207, John refused to allow him to travel to the realm. A year later, in retaliation, Innocent placed England under papal Interdict, and in 1209 he had levied a personal sentence of excommunication against John himself. A stand-off between two of the most hard-nosed rulers in Europe thus began, and every person living in England had felt its consequences.

The presence and power of the Church pervaded almost every area of medieval life. The English Church had been established in the late seventh century, and by John's time, nearly five hundred years later, it was rich, institutionally self-confident and knitted into politics, law, government, culture, the economy, education, art and architecture at every level of society. The Church baptized and buried virtually every single person born in England. Most people who married did so in accordance with its rites and laws. Thousands of parish churches, scattered the length and breadth of the land and overseen by seventeen English (and four Welsh) bishops, were hubs for both villagers and townsmen. The bells that rang in their square stone towers kept the hours of the day and their services, whether attended or not, were a reassurance to the general population that God was being honoured and his favour sought in the earthly realm. This was more than a matter of theology. People believed that there was a real life after death and that the nature and location of this afterlife – be it in Heaven, Purgatory or Hell – could be affected by deeds done on earth. The Church therefore bore an enormous responsibility for the spiritual wellbeing of every man and woman in the country.

A large section of English society was bound to the Church by employment, training or consecration. Indeed, by John's time as many as one in six of all Englishmen were clerks of some description: entitled among other things to tax relief and the right to be punished for crimes by lenient, non-corporal church courts rather than the king's law, which sentenced many miscreants to mutilation or death. The main institutional hierarchy of the Church consisted of bishops, priests, deacons and sub-deacons, known collectively as the major orders. There were also large numbers of other sorts of cleric who had received some form of church training and wore the tonsure to mark them out from the rest of the population. The minor orders included porters, who looked after church doors; lectors, who read from the New Testament at mass; exorcists, responsible for holy water and therefore involved in baptisms and blessings; and acolytes, who provided assistance to the priest during the Eucharist. Beyond these were secular clerics, ranging from priests employed in the private chapels of lords and kings to educated administrators who had been schooled by the Church in reading and writing and could therefore work as secretaries, scribes or teachers. All were expected to wear the tonsure, to avoid trouble and taverns, to dress plainly and to refrain from bearing arms. Many did so, although not all. Violent crimes committed by clerics had been a major factor in the dispute that erupted in the 1160s between Henry II and Becket, while the stereotype of the randy or roguish priest was a staple throughout the middle ages, summed up nowhere better than in the genre of bawdy French poems known as *fabliaux*, which were popular from the twelfth to the fourteenth centuries. Surviving *fabliaux* include the tale of a sly priest who tricks a guileless peasant into giving him a cow but loses two cows to the peasant as his punishment, and another of a pompous bishop who finds a sparkling, jewelled ring on the path and takes it for himself, then finds to his horror that this is a magic ring which bestows uncontrollable virility on the wearer, giving the bishop a mighty erection that bursts through his breeches and drags along the ground.[76]

There also existed in England large numbers of monks, canons and nuns living under various rules, from the Templars to ordinary brethren who lived simply together in monastic houses under the obedience of an austere rule that celebrated chastity and poverty and rejected individual indulgence of any sort.* Benedictine monks lived by the rule of St Benedict, and were known as 'black monks' thanks to their dark attire, which symbolized their commitment to penance. But by 1215 there were plenty of others, most notably the orders of 'white monks' which had emerged in the late eleventh century. These included the Cistercians (named for their origin in Cîteaux, in Burgundy), whose pale habits represented purity and who deliberately tried to pursue an even more austere and physically grinding lifestyle than the black monks, living in monasteries located in remote areas. England's few Carthusians (named for the Chartreuse mountains in the French Alps, where their founder St Bruno built his first hermitage) were more self-denying still, living in tiny communities and spending most of their time alone in contemplation and suffering. Canons, meanwhile, also obeyed a rule (usually that of St Augustine) and lived in communities, but were often associated with cathedrals or

* It should be said, however, that despite the austerity of their rule, monks also employed large numbers of servants to farm, cook and clean. Some monastic orders included lay brothers: unordained, usually poor and illiterate men who lived separately and performed the more onerous menial tasks in the monastery.

other public places of worship and performed more priestly functions than monks did. Nunneries were less numerous than monasteries: there were around five hundred male religious houses in England in 1215 and only around 150 female ones.[77] There were basic practical difficulties in establishing female religious houses when women were not able to become priests, meaning that they could not celebrate the mass. For this reason nunneries were attached to – and very often built near – monasteries.

Despite differences in dress and outlook between the various orders, a commitment to the monastic life for both men and women meant rejecting property, possessions, violence and sex and embracing a repetitive daily routine that consisted mainly of prayer, religious chanting, physical work, Biblical study and silence. To negotiate the latter elaborate sign languages were developed, one of which was recorded for St Thomas's Abbey in Dublin, a house of Augustinian canons. A hand signal to request a text of the Gospels was performed by extending the hand and moving it like the leaf of a book while making the sign of the Cross on one's forehead with the other hand; to ask a fellow diner to pass a dish of radishes, one would 'extend the finger across the mouth a little opened, on account of the savour which is perceived from them'.[78]

Finally, there were those holy men and women who sat outside the formal structures of the Church. Hermits and anchorites (both male and female) lived in a form of retirement from the world, dwelling in cold stone cells or caves, in conditions of utter scarcity and solitary devotion, seeking through their indigence to transcend the earthly realm and understand the mystery of the sacred kingdom. In the case of anchorites and anchoresses, their enclosure was complete and final – they lived in walled-up cells attached to churches, their only point of contact with the world being a small window through which food could be brought and waste removed. It was popularly thought that religious solitaries could bend the fabric of the world to their will, and miracles or visions were frequently associated with them. Their power could be humble or it could be great. St Wulfric, a Somerset-based hermit who had died a decade or so before John's birth, once cursed a mouse that gnawed his cape so that the mouse dropped dead. By contrast, an illiterate Yorkshireman called Peter of Wakefield, who survived alone on a diet of bread, water and prayer, became famous for his visions of the Christ child, who would appear to him saying 'Peace, peace, peace'. In 1212 Peter had become infamous for prophesying the death of King John; when John learned of this he had Peter chained in the dungeons of Corfe Castle for the best part of a year before being dragged behind horses to Wareham (a distance of around sixty miles) and hanged.

What all of this amounted to, then, was a society in which the Church loomed large and its spiritual power was taken extremely seriously. As a result, the imposition in 1208 of an Interdict by Pope Innocent had been a severe sentence on all of John's subjects. Interdict suspended all celebration of the sacraments with the exception of baptizing infants. Marriages could not be blessed. The dying could not receive communion or confess their sins and they could not be buried in holy ground. Churches were locked. Their bells went quiet.

England's collective soul was placed in limbo – and remained there for nearly five years. The sentence of Interdict had been relayed to the king by the bishops of London, Ely and Worcester, and it was incumbent on all the bishops present in England to forbid divine service to take place in their diocese.

John had reacted to the Interdict with a shrug. Immediately on being given final warning of the sentence he ordered his sheriffs to seize the lands and goods of any churchman who complied with papal orders. Since a very great number did so, John took over a vast amount of Church property, diverted most of its vast revenues into his treasury and became, as a result, one of the richest kings in English history. His profits from the Interdict reached perhaps £100,000 – the equivalent of about four years' royal income. Rather gallingly for the English Church, much of that wealth was spent in diabolical ways: large parts of the revenues of Christ Church, Canterbury, which were redirected into the royal pocket, were spent on lavish clothes and jewels for John's household, huntsmen and hounds, new costumes for the king's lion and its keeper and two thousand crossbow bolts and military uniforms.[79] The Pope responded by adding a personal element to John's sentence: he was excommunicated in 1209. Still, for a time, he carried on unperturbed.

✝

Mauclerk, standing before Innocent III in February 1215, knew all of this just as well as the Pope did. What both of them also knew, however, was that since the dark days of the Interdict, relations between John and the Pope had been transformed. Indeed, from being the blackest sheep in Innocent's whole flock, John had, quite improbably, become the Pope's favourite. The pressure of excommunication had finally told in 1213 when Innocent had encouraged Philip Augustus of France to launch a full invasion of John's kingdom, on the basis that he was an enemy of the Church. Eager to avoid this, and busy preparing for what would become the ill-fated Bouvines campaign of 1214, John had finally submitted – literally and brilliantly. Not only had he accepted Langton as his archbishop and permitted him to return to England, but on 15 May 1213 he had also placed his kingdom in the hands of Rome – accepting the Pope as master of the English Church and as his feudal overlord. More or less in an instant John graduated from being one of Innocent's most intractable opponents and became a favoured son, whose realm in theory now belonged to Rome and was as such under the closest possible papal protection. As Innocent had put it at the time, 'Lo! You now hold your kingdom by a more exalted and surer title than before, for the kingdom is become a royal priesthood ...'[80] John was forced to cease pillaging the wealth of the English Church. In late 1214, following his return from Bouvines, he had also seen fit to issue a charter of liberties guaranteeing the rights of the English Church to freely elect those whom it chose.[81] Around the same time he had offered individual English churchmen grants of land and authority as a form of peace offering. All this was valuable, but nothing was so useful as being able, in a time of crisis such as the one he faced in the early months of 1215, to regard Pope Innocent III as his staunchest and most powerful ally.

It is in this context that we can understand Mauclerk's description of his meeting with Innocent on 17 February. 'I found the Lord Pope at the Lateran and that same day went to him, saluting him with due reverence on your behalf and presenting your letters to him,' wrote Mauclerk to John. The Pope's reaction was exactly as the king desired. 'Receiving these with beneficence he asked diligently about you and the peace of your realm. As soon as he understood, thanks to my answer, that all went well with you, he rejoiced, giving thanks to the Almighty.'[82] Mauclerk went on to tell the king that baronial representatives were lobbying Innocent to complain about the bad-tempered meeting that had taken place at the New Temple in January. They were claiming (fairly accurately) that 'in breach of your proper oath, you showed contempt towards conceding their ancient and customary liberties'. Mauclerk advised the king to send more men to Rome to ensure that the royal side of the argument was both up to date and strongly pressed. Otherwise, however, his letter fairly bubbled with confidence about John's prospects of securing papal approval for his position. 'Your lordship should know... I have acquired much grace for your reverence,' he wrote, 'both in the sight of the Pope and in the eyes of all the cardinals, so much so that it is said in the curia that there was never anyone from your land who found greater favour.'[83] Mauclerk was right to be positive. Innocent stood squarely behind John, his vassal, and would remain a staunch supporter for the rest of the year that followed. The fact of John's earlier submission alone would probably have guaranteed this. But John had gone further still. And what was about to happen back in England would render him more certain than ever of papal favour. Within two weeks of Walter Mauclerk's happy audience with the Pope, John took another step closer to the holy father's heart. On 4 March he followed in a long Plantagenet tradition and swore an oath promising to go on crusade.

✝

By 1215 the crusading movement was more than one hundred years old, but enthusiasm in the west for travelling to the Holy Land, often known by the French name of Outremer, burned as hot as ever. Gerald of Wales provided a neat summary of the mood of an entire century when he wrote that 'the whole of Christendom ... is excited to battle and to vengeance, so also are all the nations of the heathen and the people of the infidels excited to resistance and rebellion; from which causes there arose so great a disorder upon the Earth and so great a concussion in the world as had not been heard of for many ages before.'[84] Under Innocent III the Church had asserted its power to remit the sins of men who went on crusade. This was a direct and very attractive spiritual pact. Pain and suffering on earth could be written off against the far greater tortures that awaited in Purgatory.

Pope Urban II had preached the First Crusade in 1095. It led to the capture of Jerusalem four years later and the establishment of a Christian kingdom in the near east, which stretched at its peak along the whole length of the Levantine coast. Since then the peoples of western Christendom (known generally as 'the Franks') had been engaged in a sporadic but basically ceaseless war to defend this kingdom from attack by Islamic forces around the eastern Mediterranean. In the summer of 1187 that struggle met with calamity. Christian forces were slaughtered at the battle of Hattin, where they lost a precious wooden relic believed to be the remaining part of the True Cross on which Jesus had been crucified. Months later Jerusalem had been recaptured by forces under the great sultan and founder of the Ayyubid dynasty Ṣalāḥ ad-Dīn Yūsuf ibn Ayyūb, better known in the west as Saladin. To the Muslims of the region, this was 'a magnificent triumph to Islam' and proof of 'the grandeur of Mohammad's law ... [whose] might exceeded that of the Christian religion'.[85] To Christians both in Outremer and at home in the west, it was a scarcely fathomable catastrophe.

The Third Crusade, in which John's brother Richard the Lionheart had been a prominent leader between 1191 and 1194, had failed to recapture Jerusalem. No successful attempt had been made on the city since. In his first year as Pope, Innocent III had stated his intention to 'arouse the nations of Christendom to fight the battles of Christ', but the Fourth Crusade, launched under his authority, had been a comprehensive failure, achieving only the embarrassing sack in 1204 of Constantinople, another Christian city. The Pope was disappointed but not deterred. In 1213 he issued a papal bull known as *Quia maior*, in which he claimed personally to have foreseen the collapse of Islam, writing that Muhammad had 'seduced many from the truth' and reassuring the Christian faithful that God had given him a sign that 'the end of this beast approaches'.[86] This marked the beginning of the Fifth Crusade, and although in 1215 no troops had yet departed for the east, Innocent still regarded the organization of another assault to be a matter of urgent, near-apocalyptic importance. All the same, it was one thing for a Pope to predict the eradication of the heathen enemies of Christ; it was another thing entirely for the secular forces of the Christian west to travel three thousand miles to the eastern Mediterranean and see that it actually happened.

John had good reasons for taking his crusader's vow. There was a long Plantagenet connection with the crusading movement. John's great-grandfather, Fulk V of Anjou, had been king of Jerusalem from 1131 to 1143, and many of the subsequent kings were John's cousins. As well as earning further personal affection and respect from Innocent, as a crusader he would also be allowed remittance from debts and a three-year period of grace to fulfil secular obligations. In other words, any concessions that might be wrung from him by his irate barons during the spring of 1215 could be deferred until at least 1218 on the grounds that a crusade represented a king's highest priority. Yet at the same time, John knew full well what crusading involved, and understood that the personal and political costs of fighting God's enemies could be extremely high. It is fair to wonder if John took his crusader's vow with the real intention of going to the east like his brother Richard, or whether, like his father, who had taken the oath but died before getting around to the journey, John was simply embracing the mood of the times for his own short-term ends. The English barons certainly thought they knew: according to the Crowland chronicler they believed the king was behaving 'not out of piety or for the love of Christ', but rather that the whole thing was a fraud.[87]

Those who made a commitment to go on crusade generally did so amid scenes of high public drama and emotional intensity. The best crusade preachers roused huge crowds to a frenzy. People were encouraged to make a private oath to God, declaring that they intended to travel to the east and fight the infidel, but the main drama of the public gatherings involved the 'taking of the cross': cloth strips were cut or torn into the shape of a cross, and this was sewn onto the right shoulder of the would-be warrior's cloak or tunic, marking him out from the rest of society.

A sense of the fervour that could greet crusading drives is captured in an account of Bernard of Clairvaux preaching the Second Crusade in the presence of King Louis VII of France at Vézelay in Burgundy:

> The Abbot ... was there at the time and place appointed together with the very great multitude which had been summoned ... a wooden platform was built for the Abbot in a field outside of Vézelay, so that he could speak from a high place to the audience standing around him. Bernard mounted the platform together with the King, who wore the cross ... [After Bernard had preached] the people on all sides began to clamour and to demand crosses. When he had ... passed out the parcel of crosses which had been prepared, he was forced to tear his clothing into crosses ... He laboured at this task as long as he was in town.[88]

The level of enthusiasm displayed by some crusaders came close to a form of mania. The most zealous would forgo merely wearing a bit of cloth and would cut the shape of the cross into their skin, keeping the wound fresh by applying herbs.

One clergyman was even recorded as having branded a cross onto his forehead.[89] Of course, there were those who found themselves possessed by the crusading spirit only to regret it later on. The thirteenth-century poet known as Rutebeuf wrote sardonically about the motives of some who went to the east. 'When your head is swimming with wine by the fireplace, you take the cross without a summons. Then, you intend to go to inflict great blows on the Sultan and his people . . . When you get up in the morning, you have changed your talk.' Changing one's talk, however, was a problem. Reneging on a crusading oath was frowned upon. Gerald of Wales heaped scorn on John's father, Henry II, for substituting the foundation of three monasteries for his vow to journey to Jerusalem. (Gerald quoted St Augustine: 'you can lie to God, but you cannot deceive God.') In 1196 a monk of Evesham called Edmund had a vision in which he saw the sufferings in Purgatory of a young knight who had discarded his cross: he was forced by demons to endure every night all the pains he had avoided in life.[90]

John took the cross in London on Ash Wednesday, 4 March 1215, while he was staying at the Tower. It was a highly symbolic moment: the first day of Lent, a day of overt penitence, when Church liturgy fittingly allowed for the marking of a cross of ashes on believers' foreheads. We do not have a record of John's ceremony, but it probably followed the form laid out in a contemporary text known as the Lambrecht Pontifical.[91] According to this, those taking the cross first heard mass, then lay on the floor of the church or chapel with their arms spread in the shape of a cross, before placing their outer clothing near the altar and listening to psalms sung by the congregation.

After this came the *Kyrie eleison* and the Lord's Prayer, followed by more prayers. The priest asked God to free the would-be crusaders from their enemies, to grant them 'bodily health and protection for their souls' and a smooth path towards Heaven, and to preserve them from 'every diabolical attack' and 'enemy ambushes upon the way'. Then the cloth crosses were sprinkled with holy water and perfumed with incense, while the congregation sang an antiphon celebrating Christ's own wooden cross, the 'wondrous sign through which the Devil is vanquished', which would enable the crusaders to 'frustrate the impious deeds of our adversaries ... that we might be able to seize the port of salvation [i.e. Jerusalem]'. Next blessings and prayers were offered for the crusading ship and for the staffs and purses which were the ceremonial ornaments carried by all crusaders to indicate that they were pilgrims as well as soldiers. Finally, the priest called on God to 'help your servants ... through all the ways in which they will be travelling ... so that no adversary may harm them, no difficulty hinder them, but rather everything be salutary, everything prosperous for them, so that ... whatever they might strive after with righteous desire, they might attain with speedy accomplishment.' This, surely, would have been music to John's ears. Certainly it was music to Innocent's. He had been informed of the king's intention to take the cross, and on the day of the ceremony in London the Pope was already preparing a letter in Rome commending John for his devotion and addressing him as 'glorious king'.

As far as we can infer anything of the king's mood around the time that he was promising to wager his immortal soul on the war in the east, he had matters on his mind other than purely devotional ones. He continued with his domestic tasks, particularly those that involved his favourite pastime of hunting. John arranged for horses and grooms to be moved around the country, paid expenses run up by the keepers of his greyhounds, bloodhounds and beagles, settled the bills of his fishermen, who needed new nets, and made careful instructions for the keeping of his falcons and hawks, which were to be guarded by mastiffs and fed on 'plump goats and sometimes hens' and once a week 'the flesh of hares'. He gifted his brother William, earl of Salisbury, one hundred pike to stock one of his fishponds, redecorated the chapel altar at the manor of Kingshaugh in Nottinghamshire and commanded a refitting of the royal travelling kitchens, with a new linen tablecloth, new bread-baskets, fresh leather and canvas coverings for the pantry carts and new kitchen vessels, which were to be delivered to the scullion, Robert.[92]

Clearly, though, he believed that war was coming. Throughout January and February he had been keeping up negotiations with his rebellious barons through William Marshal, earl of Pembroke, and Stephen Langton, archbishop of Canterbury, while simultaneously mustering continental mercenaries under captains such as the experienced Poitevin soldier Savaric of Mauléon, and sending crossbowmen, horses, light weapons and heavy artillery in the form of giant wooden catapults known as *ballistae* to his castles. These were mixed messages indeed. Marshal and Langton were explaining to the rebels that the king was willing to come to terms and to review the 'evil customs' that had developed during the past sixty years of Plantagenet rule. But at the same time, royal fortresses at Nottingham, Colchester, Hertford, Winchester and elsewhere were being heavily reinforced. A large team of professional diggers was hired to enlarge the moat at Corfe Castle.[93] John's visit to the Tower to take his crusading oath prompted him to order structural – probably defensive – works in London's main royal bolthole. (Ten oaks were felled in the woods of Essex to provide timber for the job.[94])

Once he had taken the cross John stayed busy. He travelled around London, Surrey and Kent during the first half of March, before heading north around 18 March to spend three weeks in and around Nottinghamshire. In April he went back down to the Thames Valley, moving between Oxfordshire and Berkshire. By now, Easter week was drawing close, and with it the deadline for coming to terms with his fractious barons. John was waiting – increasingly anxiously – for news from his men in Rome, including Walter Mauclerk. He had done everything within his power to cloak his realm with the protection of the Church. Now all he could do was hope that the word of Innocent III, whenever it came, would be enough to dissuade his barons from going to war against him.

1. King John hunts in the royal forest: an idealized image from the fourteenth century, but a delicious image of a Plantagenet king in his splendour.

2. Pope Innocent III was one of the most formidable churchmen of the middle ages. By turns opponent and staunch supporter of King John, he would make his mark on 1215 by preaching the fifth crusade and undertaking root-and-branch reforms of the church at the Fourth Lateran Council.

3. Matthew Paris' map of England, Wales and Scotland is remarkably accurate and geographically complete. Paris also produced a detailed road map of the pilgrim routes from England to Rome.

4. Saladin's forces slaughter the Franks at the Battle of Hattin in 1187, during which the True Cross was captured by the Muslims. This catastrophe launched a new age of crusading fervour in Europe.

5. To make a crusader's oath in 1215 was as solemn an undertaking as ever, and God looked unkindly on those who did so in bad faith.

6. Château Gaillard, Richard the Lionheart's fortress on the River Seine. Captured by King Philip Augustus of France in 1204, it became a monument to Plantagenet failure in Normandy.

7. The Battle of Bouvines, 27 July 1214. Battles were rare and unpredictable events. The humiliation of John's imperial and Flemish allies reverberated painfully throughout England during the following year.

8. Englishmen and women who found themselves imprisoned in the dungeons of Corfe Castle were lucky to see daylight again. Matilda de Briouze and her son were starved to death here on King John's orders.

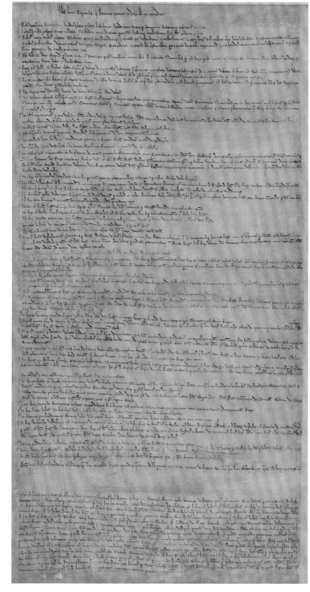

9. The Articles of the Barons, an advanced draft of the agreement that became Magna Carta, laid out many of the grievances afflicting John's divided realm.

10. Magna Carta. A failed peace treaty that emerged from the chaos of 1215 would eventually become a touchstone for ideals of liberty, limited government and justice.

11. The rebel leader Robert Fitzwalter, depicted here on his seal die, was a typical baron of his age: belligerent, grandiose and chivalrous.

12. The Ankerwycke Yew on the banks of the Thames, opposite Runnymede, may be more than 2,000 years old: a living link between early Plantagenet England and us.

Wisdom, health . . .
and beauty

Western Christendom in 1215 was in the throes of a revolution in learning. A community and culture of international scholarship had been developing during the course of the previous hundred years and by the early thirteenth century it was flourishing. Universities had sprung up in cities such as Paris, Bologna and Modena. Bright young men who had acquired a good knowledge of Latin during childhood were flocking from around Europe to study in them. And this trend had found its way to England. A tradition of scholarship had existed in Oxford since shortly after the Norman Conquest, if not before. In 1167 there was something resembling a university there, and in 1209 a group of scholars had fled attacks by the townsmen to found a new learned institution in Cambridge. So by 1215 in England communities of highly intelligent clerics were teaching, studying, living and bickering together, and investigating a wide variety of disciplines. These were taught in Latin and organized into three main groups. The trivium consisted of logic, rhetoric and grammar.

The quadrivium tested students on astronomy, music, arithmetic and geometry. These subjects were known as the seven liberal arts; once they had been tackled it was possible to advance to the highest disciplines of all: theology, law and medicine.

Different universities specialized in different subjects – Paris was the centre of theological investigation, whereas aspiring lawyers tended towards Bologna. There was no shortage of Englishmen at either. Paris in particular swarmed with brilliant Englishmen: and, of course, one of the cleverest was a central player in the political dramas of John's reign. Before the Interdict crisis of 1206–13 Archbishop Stephen Langton had been a star theologian at the university of Paris, delivering hundreds of lectures and developing theories about the limits of royal power that would feed into the thinking of the rebellious barons and ultimately into the text of Magna Carta. The universities were not simply a refuge for crusty dons poring over arcane spheres of knowledge: they were flourishing schools, bustling with human activity, which maintained an interest in the greatest issues of the day, and churned out highly learned clerks, many of whom took their place in the governments of Europe, advising and opposing their kings in roughly equal measure. Then, as now, this was seen as one of the rare routes to power for the low-born. Thomas Becket, while hardly a peasant, nonetheless had modest roots as the son of a textile merchant, but had risen to the greatest heights thanks to the basics of a liberal education, first in a London grammar school, followed by a year's study in Paris. Walter Map, reporting remarks by John's tutor Ranulf de Glanville, wrote that 'the gentry of our land are too proud or too lazy to put their children to learning ... the villeins on the other hand ... vie with each other to bring up their ignoble and degenerate offspring to those arts which are forbidden to them; not that they may shed vices, but that they may gather riches.'[95] Map's snobby reasoning here was that the liberal arts were literally thus – meant solely for the edification of free-born men.

✝

Knowledge was intimately associated with the Church, since both teaching and learning were the business of clerics. Yet the subject matter studied in the early Plantagenet years was by no means wholly governed by scripture. Indeed, the age was characterized by a blending together of Christian learning and influences from beyond, most notably the works of the ancient Romans and Greeks, and disciplines that had emerged from or been finessed in the Muslim world.

By 1200 many of the writings of Aristotle had been translated from ancient Greek into Latin, and thus the work of one of the greatest and most influential natural philosophers in human history was available to students and academics across Europe. His *De anima* ('On the Soul') opened up fundamental questions about the nature of the human spirit, the order of beings (from plants to animals to humans) and the real working of the senses. An attempt was made in 1210 to ban Aristotle and various commentaries upon his work on the grounds that he was a pagan but this prohibition, which centred on the Arts faculty at the university of Paris, failed. Indeed, it damaged the university by allowing the rival institutions that emerged during the early thirteenth century to advertise themselves to students as places where Aristotle might freely be read and debated. There was no getting away from it: the business of understanding and analysing Aristotle in particular and squaring the thinking of the ancients with the basic tenets of Christianity (particularly as they had been written about by St Augustine of Hippo) was now the starting point and the goal of European scholarship.[96]

Besides Aristotle, students might expect to encounter the titans of ancient Rome: Cicero and Ovid, Virgil and Horace. In studying the heavens, men turned to writers such as the second-century Alexandrian astrologer and mathematician Ptolemy. Meanwhile, Islamic scholarship was spreading into Europe, particularly in the fields of science, where it was embraced by men like Adelard of Bath and Daniel of Morley, who translated important works into Latin – in Adelard's case, an Arabic version of Euclid's *Elements* – and contemplated theories of natural philosophy that had found their way into Arabic scholarship via the ancient Greeks. The works of polymaths like the eleventh-century Persian writer Avicenna (Ibn Sīnā) and the twelfth-century

Muslim Córdoban Averroës (Ibn Rushd) circulated in the west, and Islamic scholarship was fundamental to improving Christian understanding of mathematics (much more easily addressed using Arabic rather than Roman numerals) and astronomy. The astrolabe – a device used to measure and predict the positions of the heavenly bodies – had been used in the classical world, but owed its arrival in medieval Christendom to its development and deployment by Muslim astronomers.

Yet of course, for all the expansion of learning by association with other cultures, Christian texts and Biblical study were at the core of western intellectual inquiry in the early thirteenth century. Theology was regarded as the highest branch of knowledge and the Bible was ultimately understood to hold all the answers to all life's great questions, whether it was interpreted literally, as a history or as a rich source of moral lesson and allegory: a text which held cryptic answers to be unfolded and applied by those who had sufficient training and wisdom to do so. Seen in that light, Archbishop Stephen Langton's greatest achievement was arguably not his painful midwifing of Magna Carta (for which he would be ultimately rewarded with nothing but suspension from ecclesiastical office by the Pope) but his time spent at the university of Paris organizing the books of the Bible into the chapters by which they are still divided today.

✝

One of the most interesting, practical and useful aspects of medieval learning was medicine. By our standards life expectancy in 1215 was short and medical treatment not always effective. Surgeons had failed to save Richard the Lionheart from a painful death from blood poisoning in 1199, and John's doctors could not help him when he suffered his fatal illness in 1216. Clearly, anaesthetics and antibiotics were many centuries away. Much, therefore, was entrusted to the healing power of prayer, pilgrimage and the mysterious potency of saints' relics. Yet working alongside and in harmony with the spiritual side of treatment, thirteenth-century surgery and medicine were mature and developing fields of practical science with a complex body of theory and a code of practice.

If Paris was the place to learn theology and Bologna the city to study law, then Salerno, a city south-east of Naples on the Italian coast, was renowned as Europe's unrivalled centre of medical study. (Its one-time archbishop Alfanus claimed that 'no illness was able to settle there'.[97]) There doctors learned the theories of the ancient Greek writer Galen and combined them with newer understandings of practical diagnosis and treatment. Salerno produced the leading medical textbooks and was the prime destination for health tourism among those wealthy enough to travel to be cured of their ailments.

The best physicians, whether in Salerno or in monasteries and hospitals across Christendom, had an extensive working knowledge of herbal remedies, which were prescribed in accordance with Galenic theories of the four humours – in bodily terms these were yellow bile, black bile, phlegm and blood. Treatments also involved insects and animals, ranging from leeches, which were used then as now in blood-letting, to lions (eating the flesh of a lion was thought to cure 'those who suffer apparitions'[98]). Other medical ingredients were sourced from far and wide and were very expensive: the red clay known as Armenian bole, for example, would have to travel more than two thousand miles to reach a doctor in England who might wish to use it to treat diarrhoea or dysentery.

Surgeons operated with a variety of carefully manufactured tools. Tourniquets staunched blood flow, cupping was used to drain blood by creating a vacuum around a wound, and clyster pipes were inserted to apply enemas. Cauteries of various shapes were heated and used to burn suppurating or rotting flesh. Speculums could hold open incisions. Surgical needles were used to stitch wounds with silk thread. The most ambitious operations were undertaken in accordance with manuals like Roger Frugard's *Surgery* – one thirteenth-century French manuscript of this book survives with detailed instructions and illustrations explaining the six stages involved in attending to fractures of the skull, from draining an external wound with a marine sponge and a feather to trepanning and chiselling open a skull which had suffered a depressed fracture and from which bone fragments had to be removed.[99]

Women's medicine was also an advanced field of specialization. The works of the mysterious eleventh- or twelfth-century author (or authors) known as Trotula of Salerno circulated throughout western Europe. The *Trotula*, as the work is now known, addressed every conceivable female complaint, including late or heavy menstruation, an ulcerated womb, swollen feet during pregnancy, gallstones, sunburn, lice, scabies, bedwetting, excessive freckles, loose or blackened teeth, 'stench of the mouth', vaginal and anal prolapse and cancer. Contraceptive advice included carrying next to the flesh a weasel's testicles or 'the womb of a goat which has never had any offspring'; conversely, women who could not conceive because in the doctor's opinion they were too fat might be smeared in cow dung mixed with very good wine, then put in a steam bath – a process to be repeated 'two or three or four times a week and she will be found to be sufficiently thin'.[100]

Besides conventional medical remedies the *Trotula* also offered recipes for cosmetics, such as one for hair removal cream concocted from ingredients including cucumber leaves, almond milk, quicklime, mercury, arsenic, oil, wine, frankincense and cloves. The burning sensation this caused was relieved with two moisturizers, one made of bran and the other of henna and egg whites.[101] Teeth could be whitened with a powder made from the mineral natron, red tile, salt and pumice, which was rubbed onto the teeth with a linen cloth. A potion to ensure 'that a woman who has been corrupted might be thought a virgin' included tree-sap, red clay, oak apples and plantain juice, and was applied by means of a pessary. The *Trotula* observed that this would also cure a nosebleed.

4

Lords and Masters

King John had promised his barons he would meet them in Northampton at Easter to settle their long list of grievances. He did no such thing. Instead he spent Easter in London, staying at his favoured spot, the New Temple.

Holy Week was the most solemn festival in the whole church calendar. It began on Palm Sunday, when processions into church marked the passage of Christ into Jerusalem. The week that followed was a swell of ritual and liturgical ceremony, churches bursting into colour and song after the austere solemnity of Lent as they prepared for the awesome occasion of the Passion and resurrection. John was the first English king to mark Maundy Thursday by washing the feet of a few (carefully selected) paupers, who had in years past been presented with robes and cash gifts as a symbol of royal penitence. Elsewhere in England, men busied themselves having their hair and beards trimmed before the festival.[102]

On a typical Good Friday England's parishioners would come to church to hear a reading of the whole Passion as recounted in the Gospel of St John, after which a crucifix would be unveiled by the high altar so that the clergy and congregation could crawl barefoot to kiss its base in the ceremony known as 'Creeping to the Cross'.[103] King John entertained himself on Easter Sunday 1215 just as he had done at Christmas: by hearing a performance of *'Christus vincit'*. This time the chorus was led by Master Henry of Cerne and Robert of Xanton, one of them from Dorset and the other from near Poitiers in France, although both were described in the chit for payment that was issued a couple of days later as simply 'clergymen in our chapel'.[104]

John's choice of music was as traditional and triumphant as ever, and it matched his bullish mood. His military preparations continued at pace: towns were barricaded, castles staffed with extra soldiers, catapults and crossbows ordered and mercenaries continued to muster. Tens of thousands of square-headed crossbow bolts were supplied to royal strongholds.[105] The royal forests of Essex, Northamptonshire, Hertfordshire and Yorkshire groaned with the sound of trees falling to provide timber for defensive building works.[106] A couple of weeks before Easter John ordered from London five new tabards and five banners with the Plantagenet royal arms of three lions embroidered on them in gold. Yet for all the king's magnificent bluster, his grip on his kingdom was far from secure.

In Rome on 19 March, Innocent III had finally decided to give his response to the month of lobbying by English representatives of king and barons, sealing three letters explaining his thoughts on the issues between them. The letters were addressed in turn to John, to Archbishop Stephen

Langton and the rest of the English bishops, and to the magnates. The tenor of all three was almost painfully favourable to the king. To the barons, Innocent wrote that the news of their rebellion was the source of 'grievous trouble to us' and that their dissatisfaction with John's rule would 'cause serious loss unless the matters are settled quickly by wise counsel and earnest attention'. He continued:

> By apostolic authority we denounce as null and void all leagues and conspiracies set on foot since the outbreak of dissension between the kingdom and the priesthood, and under sentence of excommunication we forbid the hatching of such plots in future – prudently admonishing and strongly urging you to appease and reconcile the king by manifest proofs of your loyalty and submission ... if you should decide to make a demand of him, you are to implore it respectfully and not arrogantly, maintaining his royal honour. [107]

To Stephen Langton and England's churchmen, the pope was even blunter. 'We are forced to express surprise and annoyance', he thundered, '[that] you have until now ignored the differences between [the king] and certain barons, magnates and associates of theirs, wilfully shutting your eyes and not troubling to mediate for a settlement ... some indeed suspect and state that ... you are giving help and favour to the king's opponents.'[108]

To John it must have seemed that all his careful wooing of Innocent had finally paid off. He had secured judgment entirely in his own favour. Yet although Innocent's letters were sympathetic, they were not in any way conciliatory. As a result, the ire of the English barons was not doused: it was stoked up. John's vision of peace was his boot on his barons' throats as they croaked out miserable apologies. The papal letters made it abundantly clear that there was absolutely no prospect of bringing the king willingly to terms. Assuming about four weeks for their transmission from Rome, Innocent's letters probably arrived in England at or immediately before Easter.[109] From this point on, a large number of English barons decided that they had no alternative left but to make war on their king.

✝

There were just over two hundred barons in England in 1215, of whom the most senior twenty were known as earls.* Entry to the baronial class was not an exact science: some men were born into it, some came to it through marriage or canny acquisition of lands, and some found themselves propelled into noble life by the favour of the king. What was clear, however, was that in a very broad sense the English barons recognized themselves as a class with close family relations, similar interests, agreed standards of behaviour and a collective role to play in the political life of the realm. Even more clearly, the barons owed their position in society specifically to the sponsorship of the king, recognized in a ceremony of homage. In this, the baron

---

* The title of earl had arrived in England with the Norman Conquest. At the time of Domesday Book in the 1080s there were seven earls – over time the ranks had expanded, with the most recent creation in 1208 when John appointed Saer de Quincy earl of Winchester.

knelt with his hands clasped inside the king's and promised that he would be a faithful servant. This ceremony was the ritual glue that bonded England's political society. Once made, this promise of fealty could only be unmade in the direst circumstances.

Once recognized by homage, however, a baron could comport himself like a mini-king. He held court in a castle, kept a large household of male and female servants, took counsel from knights and lesser barons, made judgments in his private courts, sponsored religious houses, commissioned fine chapels in which he and his family would eventually be buried, authenticated documents with his special seal, and identified himself at war, in tournaments and on the move with a heraldic shield and flag, emblazoned with his personal coat of arms. Since the upper classes were inevitably involved in warfare, a baron would be dubbed as a knight, usually at a young age, and would be aware of (even if he did not always observe) the emerging code of chivalry, designed to give spiritual, social and ethical guidance to men of great means. Ramon Llull, the thirteenth-century author of *The Book of the Order of Chivalry*, wrote that the duties of a chivalrous man included upholding justice, guarding the highways, defending peasants and 'persecuting traitors, thieves and robbers' as well as 'going about armed, taking part in tournaments, holding Round Tables, fencing, hunting deer, bears, wild boars, lions and other things similar'. He was to reject stealing, gambling, boasting and sleeping with other lords' wives. [110] These values were also transmitted by some of the most popular stories of the day: the tales of King Arthur, which had been popularized by the gripping, if essentially fanciful, pseudo-history of Geoffrey of Monmouth.[111]

Barons lived a life of obvious wealth and luxury. To do otherwise was shameful. They and their families wore fine, fur-trimmed clothes of imported silk and embroidered cloth. The men and boys wore expensive armour and could wield a variety of weapons: swords, maces, lances and daggers. They had sufficient leisure time to enjoy the entertainment of minstrels and acrobats and to play dice, bowls or chess.* They ate a varied diet, and a lot of it. Beasts, birds and fish were brought to the barons' tables alongside cheese, fruits, rice and milk. Imported wine was mixed for the table with honey, nutmeg or exotic spices such as the peppercorn-like dried berry known as cubeb, imported from the east. Much of April 1215 was taken up with the long Christian period of Lent – seven weeks of religious fasting, when fish was the only animal protein permitted. But even then the great baronial households could not be said to have gone hungry: one thirteenth-century account book shows that during Lent the household of the earl of Leicester consumed between four hundred and a thousand herrings every day, brought on carts from North Sea ports like Great Yarmouth and often cooked in pies flavoured with ginger, pepper and cinnamon.[112] Before a baron ate such a pie he might wash his fingers with water poured from a bronze aquamanile – a small table jug cast in

* The Lewis Chessmen, made from walrus ivory and probably imported from Scandinavia, suggest the opulence of chess sets around the turn of the thirteenth century. The Lewis Chessmen are split between the National Museum of Scotland in Edinburgh and the British Museum in London.

the shape of a horse, a unicorn or a knight on horseback.[113] Compared to the lives of most ordinary people in England – for whom Lent was often a time of cold, starvation and toil, and whose fingers were seldom if ever washed by the trickle of clean water from a bronze figurine – the barons were almost unimaginably privileged.

Not all of the barons – perhaps not even a majority – went into open opposition against the king at Easter in 1215. Nevertheless, what John experienced following the publication of the letters from the Pope was the worst baronial rebellion against the Plantagenet crown since the Great Revolt of 1173–4 that had very nearly cost his father his throne. The barons at the forefront of it had been identified by chroniclers of the time as 'the Northerners' since hostility first emerged towards the king in 1213 – 'Most of them came from the northern parts, so they were called the Northerners,' wrote the Crowland Chronicler – but this was not strictly true.[114] Many were from Lincolnshire, Nottinghamshire and Derbyshire as well as the counties further north, towards the Scottish border. Eustace de Vesci, who was the lord of the massive coastal fortress at Alnwick in Northumberland, had substantial interests in the north, as did others who were named in the *Histoire des ducs de Normandie et des rois d'Angleterre* as being of the rebels, including Robert de Ros, Richard de Percy, William de Mowbray and Roger de Montbegon.[115] Equally, however, there were many whose estates lay in other areas of the realm – not least in East Anglia. It was from here that one of John's most prominent opponents came: Robert Fitzwalter, lord of Dunmow. Fitzwalter's son-in-law Geoffrey de Mandeville was also a man of the south and east, as was Giles, bishop of Hereford, a son of William and Matilda de Briouze, who had suffered at John's hands earlier in the reign.

Robert Fitzwalter's silver seal die, which survives today in the British Museum, shows the lord as he wished himself to be imagined. He is mounted on a large horse draped in heraldic trappings. He is heavily armed, with a solid, square-topped helmet on his head, a shield carried in front of him and chain-mail covering his entire body, from a padded collar around his neck down to his wrists and ankles. His outstretched hand brandishes a sword as long as his arm, with a tapering, double-edged blade. As he kicks the horse forward Fitzwalter is also preparing to swing his sword in the direction of a long-necked, curly-tailed dragon. Understandably, the dragon is cowering. In front of the horse is another shield, with different heraldic devices. These are the arms of Saer de Quincy, earl of Winchester, Fitzwalter's friend and brother-in-arms (who also included a dragon in his armorial bearings). There was no mistaking from his seal die the fact that Fitzwalter wished to appear as the very paragon of early thirteenth-century valour and nobility. And that vision chimed with the view of the author of the *Histoire des ducs de Normandie et des rois d'Angleterre*, who thought Fitzwalter was 'one of the greatest men in England, and one of the most powerful'.[116]

Fitzwalter certainly had the land and personal history to prove it. Great lords' lands were measured by the unit of the knight's fee: an inexact unit, depending on location, but which was reckoned to provide enough income to sustain a single knight for one year. The 'knight's fee' was a crucial measure of political, feudal and fiscal accounting, which is why the term is prominent in Magna Carta. For each fee held, the baron was obliged to render the service of a knight (or money to the same value) when the king demanded it.* In Plantagenet England, only around 130 men held more than ten knight's fees – a level of landholding that would mark them out as barons.[117] By inheritance and by his marriage to Gunnora, the daughter of a Norman baron, Fitzwalter was in possession of ninety-eight knight's fees, a massive landholding which placed him very comfortably in the noble elite. His baronial seat at Dunmow sat on the border between Essex and Suffolk, but Fitzwalter had been recognized as the keeper of several impressive castles, most notably Hertford and Benington in Hertfordshire and Baynard's Castle in the city of London. He had served King Richard and King John in Normandy, and although his incompetent defence of Vaudreuil in 1198 had ended with that castle being taken unopposed by the French king and Fitzwalter himself imprisoned, he had managed to pay the ransom and return to England midway through John's reign.

Until the early years of the thirteenth century, then, Fitzwalter had pursued a fairly conventional baronial career. Like the rest of his class, his interests lay primarily in attending

---

* From the term 'fee' we derive the word 'feudal' and the notion of the 'feudal system' which describes the theoretical relations between all of the free and landed men in England in this period of the middle ages. The king was, in theory, the sole 'owner' of all land in the country. His barons held land in return for feudal services. They then sub-leased it to other men, either for cash or further feudal service. There was thus a pyramid of landholding, with the king at the top.

to his estates and fighting. Unlike the very best of his class, however, he had a hair-trigger temper and even by the standards of the age was notable for his quick resort to violence. Worst of all, in 1212 he had become embroiled in a conspiracy against the king that would both mark him for the rest of his life as a rebel and bring him to the fore of the dramatic events of 1215. While John was attempting to raise an army before his doomed Bouvines campaign, he had learned of a plot by Fitzwalter and Eustace de Vesci. Details are somewhat hazy, but it seems that Fitzwalter, de Vesci and their accomplices – who included at least four clerks of the royal Exchequer, the Scottish earl of Huntingdon and another northern baron by the name of Richard of Umfraville – had planned to have John assassinated while he was in Wales, after which they would invite the fierce French baron and heretic-chaser Simon de Montfort to come and rule in his place. John had taken the plot very seriously and Fitzwalter and de Vesci both fled the realm, to France and Scotland respectively. In his absence Fitzwalter's lands had been taken over by the crown and his most important castles were slighted: a process of deliberate damage in which teams of engineers and labourers pulled down walls and fortifications and removed valuable timber and stone for use in buildings elsewhere. For his part, Fitzwalter told the king of France that John had attempted to seduce his daughter.[118] Relations were normalized in the summer of 1213, but even then it was clear that the king and Fitzwalter still regarded one another with some suspicion, and by the spring of 1215 Fitzwalter was back at the head of the rebel movement.

Instead of meeting John at Northampton at Easter week, this

group mustered in arms (and here we can picture Fitzwalter as he displayed himself on his seal) at the great tournament field of Stamford in Lincolnshire. They may well have been there when the letters arrived from Innocent instructing them to 'appease and reconcile the king by manifest proofs of your loyalty and submission'. They did nothing of the sort. According to the chronicler Roger of Wendover, 'in their army there were computed to be two thousand knights, besides horse soldiers, attendants, and foot soldiers'.[119] Even if Wendover was exaggerating, this was still a large army and it headed en masse to a second tournament ground at Brackley in Northamptonshire, which was land held by de Vesci. The barons were now in righteous mood and they marched under a righteous banner. Fitzwalter had decided to confront the Pope's condemnation of the baronial cause head on and began calling himself 'Marshal of the Army of God and the Holy Church'. His men were in Brackley by Monday 27 April, and together they began to concoct a list of demands that they were determined John should concede if he were to avoid being violently deposed.

✝

On Monday 27 April John was a long way from Brackley. He was travelling from his sprawling flint-stone hunting lodge of Clarendon, in Wiltshire, to the mighty castle of Corfe in Dorset: a fortress with a deep moat, huge towers, elegant new Gothic royal apartments and the most secure dungeons in England. Here, undoubtedly, John felt safe. And 130 miles north-east the job of negotiating with the barons was left to two very capable representatives: Archbishop Stephen Langton and a loyal earl of even greater status than Fitzwalter: William Marshal, earl of Pembroke.

By his own reckoning – and that of many others – Marshal was the finest knight of his day, and his long life in service to the Plantagenet crown had also seen him rise to the top rank of the aristocracy. He was born the younger son of a minor baron around the time of the mid-twelfth-century civil war known as the Anarchy and his life was dramatic from the start: as a five-year-old boy he was given by his father as a hostage to King Stephen, who had to be dissuaded from hurling the child from a trebuchet when Marshal's father double-crossed him. Spared this fate, Marshal grew up to excel at horsemanship and earned his fame as a young man on the tournament fields of France, where he fought in teams assembled by John's glamorous, treacherous eldest brother, Henry 'the Young King'. Marshal visited Jerusalem on the Third Crusade, where he took secret vows to end his life as a Templar knight. On his return he became a useful ally to Richard the Lionheart, fighting at the king's side in the defence of Normandy between 1194 and 1199. Although his relations with John had at times been fraught, Marshal had nevertheless secured for himself marriage to an heiress of the hugely wealthy Clare family, and through it the earldom of Pembroke, which brought lands in Wales and Ireland. Although in 1215 he was approaching his seventieth birthday, he was still one of the most energetic and formidable men in England.

The *History of William Marshal* (or simply the *History*), written in verse after his death, gives us a colourful and invaluable picture of the baronial milieu around the turn of the thirteenth century.[120] It includes Marshal's strident views about the way a knight and a baron ought to behave, elaborated through long accounts of war, bravery and derring-do. At the centre of all his beliefs was the idea that a chivalrous man ought to display largesse and loyalty. Even the casual phrases and details of Marshal's biography burst with illustrations of the aristocratic culture of the day. A successful mercenary captain has 'the luck of the dice' (*A cui si chaïrent li dé*) when he captures a bishop during a siege. Prisoners seen bound together with ropes are 'like greyhounds on leashes' (*comme levriers en lesse*). Particularly fine wines are either 'clear, soft on the palate [or] sparkling, some with cloves, some spiced,' while a dinner is judged excellent because at the end of it 'pears, apples and hazel nuts' are served.[121] But what Marshal most admired was feats of physical strength, examples of rough or natural justice and good, old-fashioned war stories.

His best anecdotes, retold at length in the *History*, have the feel of fireside yarns designed to educate as well as entertain young men in the pursuit of nobility and chivalry. A typical account of a tournament includes the claim that 'those present on the field said that never had they seen a tournament in their lives marked by such great feats of chivalry ... and uniformly they spoke such words of praise about the Marshal's valour that those who were present on both sides awarded him the prize [for best combatant]'.[122] The tale of a siege directed by Richard the Lionheart against the town of Milly in Normandy features Marshal climbing a ladder from a castle's ditch to the top of its battlements while wearing full battle armour and carrying a sword, before singlehandedly fighting off or scaring away every defender, defeating the constable of the castle in combat and sitting on him 'to hold him firm' until reinforcements arrived. But perhaps Marshal's best story of all – told at very great length in the *History* – was one from his days as a young knight working as a bodyguard for John's mother, Eleanor of Aquitaine. Attacked by a large group of his French enemies, Marshal became embroiled in a skirmish against heavy odds. He fought as fiercely 'as a boar does before a pack of dogs' until he was wounded by another knight who crept up quite unchivalrously behind him, drove a lance through the fleshy part of his thigh and took him prisoner. Tied to the back of an ass and given no proper dressings to swab 'the blood which welled up from his body and his veins', Marshal was facing death until he managed to charm a 'noble-hearted, kind lady' into smuggling some 'fine linen bandages' to him inside a loaf of bread. The wound was healing nicely until one evening Marshal watched some of the knights and young noblemen among his captors playing a strength game in which the object was to heave a stone as far as possible. Inevitably Marshal got involved; just as inevitably he hurled the stone 'a good foot and a half further' than the best of his opponents. Unfortunately he strained so hard in doing so that he reopened the gash in his leg and thus remained both a prisoner and in terrible pain for a long time, until Queen Eleanor, whom he had been protecting, got together the money to pay his ransom and rewarded him with 'horses, arms, money and fine clothes ... for she was', Marshal conceded graciously, 'a very worthy and courtly lady'.[123]

Queen Eleanor's youngest son, John, had given Marshal a number of reasons to despise and fear him during his sixteen-year reign. But no man in England prided himself more on being considered a paragon of loyalty. He had been working as the king's proxy in negotiations with the barons throughout the weeks preceding Easter. And even if Marshal's task in winning round the rebels at Brackley in late April 1215 was an extremely daunting one, there could have been no more seasoned and dependable English baron to be negotiating on behalf of his king.

✝

What passed between Fitzwalter and Marshal at Brackley during the week commencing 27 April is not fully known. It is likely that the meeting was at best tense, and probably hostile. According to Roger of Wendover, 'the barons delivered to the messengers a paper, containing in great measure the laws and ancient customs of the kingdom, and declared that, unless the king immediately granted them and confirmed them under his own seal, they would, by taking possession of his fortresses, force him to give them sufficient satisfaction ...'[124] It is not certain what that 'paper' was, but several baronial documents drawn up in the spring of 1215 still survive and serve as a very useful guide to the issues of the day. Among these is a draft schedule of royal concessions, produced by someone with good access to the king's enemies, and known by the unfortunately dreary title of the Unknown Charter.[125] It is not a formal document, and is better thought of as a statement of a bargaining position that was drawn up early in the year.

The parchment on which these concessions were written up contains a copy of Henry I's coronation charter of 1100 followed by twelve articles, which are introduced as having been 'conceded by King John'.

The Unknown Charter tells us that the barons who assembled at Stamford and Brackley were concerned with four key areas of royal government: justice, inheritance law, military service and the policing of the royal forest. 'King John concedes that he will not take a man without judgment, nor accept anything for doing justice and will not do injustice', reads the first clause. This rather sweeping statement addresses the most personal features of John's rule – his notorious slipperiness in his dealings with his greatest subjects, the arbitrary fashion in which he treated them, the dubious company he kept and his dreadful behaviour towards families like the Briouzes, who had been hounded to death without anything like fair treatment under the law.

The next five clauses are much more specific and deal with the process by which men and women received inheritances after the death of a father or husband. The charter attacked John's policy of charging astronomical sums for heirs to come into their inheritances. It set out a policy by which the lands of underage heirs would be managed effectively in trust by 'four knights from among the more lawful men' of the fee, and that when the heir reached his majority, the king would not charge an inheritance tax. The Unknown Charter also demanded that the king observe men's wills and that he should allow widows to remarry according to the wishes of their families (rather than according to the wish of the king, who would auction off the bride to the highest bidder, regardless of social status). A widow should be entitled to live in her marital home for forty days after her husband's death 'and until she has had her proper dower'. Heirs were not to be responsible for interest on debts owed to the Jews by their fathers.

Following the statements on widows, two clauses dealt with foreign policy, granting that the king's men 'should not serve in the army outside England save in Normandy and Brittany' – and not, therefore, in Poitou, where John had been on campaign in late 1214. It also limited the king's right to charge the military tax of scutage to 'one mark of silver' – two thirds of a pound, i.e. thirteen shillings and four pence – on each knight's fee held. Together these two clauses amounted to a radical restriction of the king's ability to raise armies and deploy them where he chose, or to milk his barons in order to pay for mercenaries to fight in their place. A baron such as Fitzwalter, with his ninety-eight knights' fees, would in theory have a maximum liability to scutage of just over £65, rather than the £196 he had been liable for in the scutage of three marks on the fee that John demanded in 1213–14 before the Bouvines campaign.*

John had levied scutage on his men eleven times in the sixteen years of his reign – his father and brother had levied it eleven times between them in forty-five years. For the king to accept such a strict limitation on his ability to levy military

* With the usual caveats, a scutage payment of £65 might today be the equivalent of a one-off tax of £55,000, whereas £196 might be £165,000. These numbers reflect the *historic standard of living* value of income, as calculated by measuringworth.com.

taxation effectively meant that he would never be able to afford another war of conquest outside the British Isles. This was very probably the precise intention of those rebels who really were northerners, for some of whom the county of Poitou was further away (and of little more concern) than the kingdom of Norway.

The rest of the Unknown Charter was taken up with statements on reforming the royal forest, an area of perpetual concern throughout the early years of Plantagenet rule. Much of the English countryside was designated as forest (which could mean moorland and agricultural land, as well as thick patches of trees). The forest was the king's personal property, reserved for his hunting and subject to a separate body of law from the rest of the realm. It was a mark of royal favour to permit men the privilege of taking a deer from the forest; those Englishmen who killed animals in the forest, gathered firewood or felled trees were subject to either heavy fines or mutilation, in the case of the poor and socially insignificant. It was a bugbear of much of English society that the Plantagenet kings had expanded the boundaries of the forest since this put men at the mercy of a much more stringent and expensive code of law with no means of protest. The Unknown Charter aimed to force John to 'disafforest all the forests which my father and my brother and I have made'.

All this was, of course, in addition to the restatement of Henry I's coronation charter, which also emphasized the importance of reasonable payments for inheritance, marriage and widowhood, promised not to expand forest land, and made broad-ranging statements of good intent with regard to peacekeeping and the freedom of the Church. Perhaps most importantly, Henry I's charter acknowledged in its first clause that the king ruled not only 'by the mercy of God' but also 'by the common counsel of the barons of the whole kingdom of England'.[126] Besides all the terms of their increasingly specific and detailed programme of opposition to the king, this idea was in the minds of those barons who took to the field in the spring of 1215. Yet if they thought the king was about to roll over, they would soon be disabused of the notion. According to Roger of Wendover, when William Marshal and Archbishop Langton relayed back to the king the details of the barons' demands at Brackley, he flew into a rage.

> The king when he heard the purport of these heads, derisively said, with the greatest indignation, 'Why, amongst these unjust demands, did not the barons ask for my kingdom also? Their demands are vain and visionary, and are unsupported by any plea of reason whatever.' And at length he angrily declared with an oath, that he would never grant them such liberties as would render him their slave.'[127]

At length he calmed down and offered an entirely vague and perhaps deliberately insulting solution: he would abolish evil customs and take the counsel of 'faithful men' – which naturally seemed to preclude any involvement from men who mustered in military harness on a tournament field in the midlands.[128] This would be subject, in any case, to the approval of the Pope, whose letters had by now quite comprehensively shown that he was on the side of the king.[129]

Mediation, let alone reconciliation, looked to be impossible. On 5 May Fitzwalter and the barons sent a messenger (an Augustinian canon, according to the author of the Annals of Southwark and Merton Priory) to find the king at Reading and formally defy him by delivering news of a final break.[130] There could be no more ambiguity. The barons had unilaterally defied their lord and unbound themselves from the oath on which their relationship with the king and the whole of political society depended. They were outlaws, rebels and enemies of the realm. On 9 and 10 May John issued two documents: first, a charter addressed to 'all those faithful in Christ' arguing that it was for the Pope to arbitrate the dispute between king and barons. This led nowhere, for obvious reasons. Nor did the letters patent issued the following day, in which John promised not to attack his barons by force while they remained in negotiations, but to proceed by 'the law of our realm'.[131] Did John really believe that this was enough to mollify barons who had developed such a detailed and specific critique of his rule? If so, it was naïveté of the most unlikely sort. Far more likely, then, that this was cynical posturing. John was disingenuously framing himself as the penitent son of the Church and the voice of reason; by implied contrast he was setting up the barons as ungodly and seditious. And if anyone was taken in, they were not forced to wait long for John's true colours to show.

On 12 May, John sent out orders to his sheriffs commanding them to 'take in our possession our enemies' lands ... take for us their things and movables found in those lands'.[132] The barons, meanwhile, left Brackley, marched twenty miles to the nearest royal castle – which happened to be in Northampton – and laid it under siege. The war had begun.

Justice, law ... and outlaws

On the king's great seal the Plantagenet ruler was presented on one side as a warrior and on the other as a judge. The message was plain. If one of the king's duties was to fight battles and defend his realm, then the other – inseparable from his martial role – was to provide justice and uphold the law. In a practical, day-to-day sense this could mean anything from settling complex land disputes between his greater subjects to lending his authority to the justices who travelled England on the grand circuit known as the eyre, hanging thieves. Clearly, the barons who rebelled in 1215 thought that with regard to justice, John had failed on every score: the first clause of the Unknown Charter anticipated forcing a statement into the king's mouth that conceded a full repudiation of his tyrannical and unjust methods. 'King John concedes that he will not take a man without judgment, nor accept anything for doing justice and will not do injustice.' By the time Magna Carta was granted, this promise had become the basis for many clauses that addressed both the philosophy and the procedures of the Plantagenet judicial system.

One of those was clause 18, which demanded that the king should send out two royal judges to each county of England four times a year, where they would hear cases brought under three important writs, known as mort d'ancestor, novel disseisin and darrein presentment. These were legal processes that had been standardized and made widely available during the reign of Henry II, which is why Henry is often described as the father of the Common Law. All three writs related to land disputes, allowing them to be settled by royal judges. To start one of these processes, it was necessary to go to the royal chancery in Westminster and obtain a writ: physically, a chit of parchment with orders to the relevant sheriff to instigate legal proceedings. The sheriff then had to ensure that the case was brought before judges travelling on the eyre, with a jury empanelled of reputable local men – ideally, knights. Together these men would settle, or at least advance, the case, although litigation was frequently expensive and took a long time, which is why clause 18 of Magna Carta is somewhat unusual in demanding more action and intervention from the king, rather than less.

Besides the civil law, England in 1215 had a highly developed system of criminal justice. Since there was no police force, at the village level, responsibility for detecting crime lay with everybody in the community. Anyone who suffered or witnessed a crime was obliged to raise 'the hue and cry' – literally, making sufficient noise to rouse every able-bodied man in the neighbourhood, who would then try to apprehend the criminal. Various officials were involved in this process. Villages had constables who were the closest thing in existence to a local policeman. Villages were grouped into larger units known as hundreds, and each hundred held regular courts, organized by a bailiff. If a crime was too serious to be dealt with at a meeting of the hundred court, it could be sent up to the sheriff who oversaw the county court.

People could be brought before the royal judges on criminal charges by two principal means. Traditionally a private prosecution (known as an appeal) could be made, in which the supposed victim of a crime could have the supposed perpetrator brought before the judges. But from Henry II's reign onwards, there was a public system of prosecution too. Juries of presentment were assembled, which did not determine cases, but rather identified those which needed prosecution. Suspects were then brought forward to the judges to answer charges.

In an age before forensic investigation, it was naturally rather difficult to prove criminal cases in which there were no witnesses. The best judge in this case was God, and there were several means by which his opinion could be tested. The ordeal of fire or water could test the guilt of a suspect, and although this practice was challenged by Henry II's legal reforms, it still took place regularly during John's reign. Judicial duels might be fought by the two parties or their appointed champions – this practice was retained for centuries afterwards, particularly in the case of disputes between noblemen. Another measure used was compurgation, in which the accused was challenged to assemble a set number of worthy men who would swear to his innocence. Perhaps the best way to see the law in action in this regard is to examine two cases which came before the royal courts, both of which show the intersection of rational process and blind faith in the supernatural that characterized the working of the legal system in this age.

✚

During the summer of 1214 the king's justices had assembled in Middlesex to hear and pass judgment on crimes committed in the county. They were presented with two alleged criminals whose guilt they could only determine by ordeal. The first was Walter Trenchebof, who was accused of complicity in a bloody crime. One Guy Foliot had been stabbed to death by Ingeram of Fardingestorp, and Walter was accused of having supplied Ingeram with the knife used in the stabbing. More than these facts we do not know. What we do know is that the court ruled that Walter's guilt would be decided by the ordeal of water.[133]

The ordeal by water was conducted according to a traditional, if complex ritual that was naturally rooted in communion with the Almighty – who was believed to be taking as keen an interest in proceedings as the defendant. According to a twelfth-century account, Walter's experience would have proceeded like this:

on a Tuesday evening he would have gone to vespers barefoot and dressed in woollen clothes. There he remained for a three-day fast, eating only unleavened bread, watercress and salt, and drinking only water. On Friday, he was stripped of his clothes, given a small loincloth and a cloak, then led in solemn religious procession to a pit dug for the occasion, measuring twelve by twenty feet, filled to the brim with water and overlaid with a wooden platform on which a priest could stand in order to bless the water. Around the pool would stand the judges and the defendant's accuser. Both Walter and his accuser would have sworn oaths, then Walter's hands would have been tied tightly behind his bent knees, and a length of rope attached to his waist. A knot in the rope marked 'the length of his longest hair' – perhaps twelve inches above his head. Slowly, so as to make minimal disturbance to the water's surface, Walter would have been lowered into the pit, where he would either sink or float. To sink to the depth of the knot in the rope was a sign of innocence; to float was a mark of guilt.[134]

Walter floated, and thus the case was decided. He was pulled out of the water – presumably shaken and short of breath. Then sentence was pronounced. God had spoken. Walter had clearly supplied the knife that killed Guy Foliot. He was hanged.

It has been argued by modern researchers, who have simulated the experience of the ordeal by water, that it should have been possible for about four out of five men in the middle ages to pass the ordeal, assuming that they were not grossly overweight, fasted sufficiently in the build-up and made sure to blow as much air out of their lungs as possible before they took the plunge.[135] And indeed, what records we have suggest that it was much more common for people to sink than to float. Walter's unlucky buoyancy, therefore, quite reasonably suggested to eyes looking for a sign from the divine that he was guilty.

Indeed, this is borne out by the second case that the judges heard in Middlesex during the summer of 1214. This case also went to ordeal: a young man simply known as Simon, son of Robert, had been arrested and imprisoned on the grounds that he had been hanging around with a gang of thieves. According to the court records, he was 'purged' by the water – in other words, he sank – and having been fished out, he was allowed to live, on condition that he left the realm and never returned. (In another case heard during John's reign, the king intervened personally to give permission for a man called Eudo de Iselham, who had purged himself of guilt in the matter of William Coc's death and been banished, to return to England, his reputation insured by pledges of good conduct.[136])

Other forms of ordeal existed across Europe during the early thirteenth century, including the ordeal by fire, in which the accused would hold a red-hot ingot of metal for a prescribed period of time, and guilt would then be proven if the resulting burn became infected.

Yet when Walter Trenchebof and Simon, son of Robert, underwent their ordeals in 1214, they were taking part in a legal process that was on its way out of fashion. In 1215 the Fourth Lateran Council turned its attention to judicial matters and the role of churchmen in sanctioning the bloody capital and corporal punishments handed out by secular powers. 'No cleric may pronounce a sentence of death, or execute such a sentence, or be present at its execution,' ran canon 18. 'Neither shall anyone in judicial tests or ordeals by hot or cold water or hot iron bestow any blessing.'

Stripped of its essential sanctified purpose, the trial by ordeal rapidly fell by the wayside. Meanwhile, as Magna Carta placed the onus of judgment on a man's peers, the ancient, purgative methods of determining guilt were replaced in England with a reliance on the word of the community, as spoken by a jury, to decide legal cases. The ordeal would certainly return – not least in witch-hunting during the early modern period. But for medieval England 1215 was the point at which the chilling process of seeking justice at the bottom of a twelve-by-twenty-foot water pit began to disappear.

✝

In a time when the judicial process could be physically painful and punishments for crimes ranged from monetary fines to gouged eyes, hacked-off lips, ears or hands and ultimately death – many suspects simply ran from the law. In their absence they became outlaws, and it was permissible for anyone to kill or capture an outlaw. The process of outlawry could be applied to men of any station – William de Briouze and Robert Fitzwalter were both treated effectively as outlaws during John's reign. Of course, it was easier to be an aristocratic outlaw than a poor one, and the chances of surviving outlawry among the rich were substantially greater.

In popular culture today, outlaws have become deeply embedded in our imagination of the early Plantagenet years. Some outlaw legends do, indeed, have their roots in the reigns of King John. The tale of *Eustache the Monk*, written some time between 1223 and 1284, tells in rhyming couplets the dramatic story of Eustache Busquet, a Boulonnais nobleman's son who fell foul of the count of Boulogne's judicial system and became a freelance soldier, seafarer and pirate. He served King John for a time, but sided with the rebel barons in 1214. During the war that followed the failure of Magna Carta, Eustache controlled the Channel and was instrumental in guiding the French prince Louis onto English soil. Eustache was captured during the battle of Sandwich in 1217 and beheaded at sea. 'No man who spends his days doing evil can live a long life,' was the conclusion of the poet who recorded Eustache's exploits.[137] Likewise, the tale of Fulk Fitzwarin (see above), which survives in a single manuscript at the British Library, embellishes the story of the real-life marcher lord from John's reign. It describes the king, who exiles Fulk to Brittany, France and Spain, as 'all his life ... wicked, spiteful and contrary ... a man without conscience ... hated by all good people. In addition he was lustful: when he heard described any fair lady or damsel he wished to have her at once, either to entrap her by promise or gift, or to ravish her by force.'[138]

Of course, this image of King John is today a hoary old trope in the many reinventions of the Robin Hood legends which are still a mainstay of film and television. Yet, the original ballads of Robin Hood, which exist in manuscript and printed form from the fifteenth century, seem to have their origins in a different age of Plantagenet rule. They are apparently set in the early part of the fourteenth century, when the ruling monarch was neither John nor Richard the Lionheart but 'Edward, our comely king', as he is described in 'A Gest of Robyn Hood' (printed in London around 1495). This is most likely to have been either Edward I or his grandson Edward III.

5

London

The siege of Northampton was going badly. The rebellious barons had been camped outside the castle for more than two weeks. They had freed themselves of their oaths of loyalty to the king and now they had to show him they meant business. In the words of the Crowland Chronicler, 'After closing the gates and putting guards at the gate and along the wall, they started to attack the garrison that was in the stronghold.'[139] Yet it was looking increasingly as if they had chosen the wrong target. After fifteen days in the field, wrote Roger of Wendover, the barons had gained 'little or no advantage'.[140]

Northampton Castle was a fine, spacious and extremely well-defended royal fortress, first erected in the aftermath of the Norman Conquest, that stood in the north-west corner of the busy market town.[141] It was originally built by Simon Senlis, the first earl of Northampton, but had been permanently taken over by the crown when Henry II seized it in 1154, the year of his accession to the throne. The castle had flourished in Plantagenet hands. Its doorways had been topped with elegant arches and decorative stone corbels (Thomas Becket fled through one of those arches after his decisive showdown with Henry in 1164) and no expense had been spared on its upkeep. It was a crucial strategic stronghold – a great stone sentry guarding access to the midlands. The townsmen advertised their allegiance to the crown with a seal bearing a Plantagenet lion.[142] The king was a regular visitor to the castle, coming on average twice a year and spending £300 over the course of his reign to maintain it.*

He had come most recently in late February, hunting in the local chases, but also putting his mind to the state of the castle's defences. John had issued careful instructions concerning the guarding of Northampton's prisoners.[143] In the weeks before Easter, he had sent further orders, asking that the fabric of the castle be made as secure as possible against potential attack. Northampton Castle was surrounded by a moat filled by the river Nene; earthworks protected its main gate and a stout wall encircled a three-acre bailey, or courtyard. To make it safer still, royal foresters were commanded to provide 'timber and wood to fortify and wall our castle', while ten thousand crossbow bolts were purchased to fill the armoury. As a precaution against possible siege the pantries were stocked with 'forty quarters of wheat and twenty-four hog carcasses'.† Northampton was well prepared to survive more or less anything that might be thrown at it. In the first weeks of May

---

* Perhaps £240,000 ($370,000) today. This is the *historic opportunity cost*, as calculated by measuringworth.com.

† A quarter was eight bushels – so forty quarters was a great deal of wheat to order. Converting volume to mass is not a precise science when measuring grain, but the 320 bushels the king sent to Northampton in April 1215 might have been as much as 9,000 kg of wheat.

the English barons, led by Fitzwalter, were finding this out the hard way.

Leading the defence of the castle was Geoffrey de Martigny, a relative of one of John's most trusted lieutenants, the veteran mercenary Gerard d'Athée.[144] De Martigny and d'Athée were originally from Touraine, where the latter had manned the garrison at Loches, the last Plantagenet castle to fall during Philip Augustus's campaign of conquest in 1203–4. De Martigny was, therefore, no weak-willed royal flunkey, but a man closely connected to one of the most experienced soldiers in John's employment, who had been brought to England specifically for his ability to serve the king in times of crisis. Yet de Martigny could just as well have been an elderly woman with no experience of siegecraft and still held Northampton Castle, for although Fitzwalter and his army had come in numbers, they did not possess a single siege engine. John had spent much of the last three months ordering catapults and large crossbows and sending them to castles up and down the country. His barons had nothing of the sort. There could be no clearer indication of the disparity in resources between a king and even his greatest lords. With no heavy artillery, Northampton's reinforced walls simply could not be breached. The only tactic open to the barons was blockade, in the hope of starving the garrison out – and they were not going to do that without a very long wait.

The longer they stood outside Northampton, the worse the barons' fortunes grew. Roger of Wendover recorded that several men were slain during the siege. Most embarrassingly, this included Fitzwalter's standard-bearer, who was 'pierced through the head with a bolt from a crossbow and died, to the grief of many'. When word arrived towards the middle of the month that the rebels would receive a warmer welcome if they travelled twenty miles east to Bedford, they hurriedly packed up the siege and left. They arrived in Bedford to be greeted 'with all respect' by William de Beauchamp, a sympathetic nobleman who held the castle in the town.[145]

At this point their fortunes turned dramatically for the better. No sooner had Fitzwalter and his men arrived in Bedford than messengers appeared from the city of London, 'secretly telling them, if they wished to get into that city, to come there immediately'.[146] If they moved fast, the messengers said, the Army of God could leave behind them the second-string castles of the south midlands and take England's capital. There was no time to lose. They rushed to London, in the words of one writer, 'with a view to doing [the king] mischief'.[147]

The barons marched through the night and arrived on the outskirts of London as the light of a spring morning was spilling over the city walls. It was Sunday 17 May. The bells of London's one hundred churches were pealing, for the 'inhabitants were performing divine service'.[148] The timing could not have been better. Fitzwalter's men had been advised that they would be welcomed into the city without the need for any further military action, because 'the rich citizens were favourable to the barons, and the poor ones were afraid to murmur against them.' With the city still and most Londoners at prayer, the rebel barons simply marched in, aided by their sympathizers, who helped them scale the walls. 'They placed their own guards in charge of each of the gates, and then arranged all matters in the city at will,' said Roger of Wendover.[149] They had arrived in London ahead of John's half-brother William Longuespée, earl of Salisbury, who had made a vain dash for the capital with a band of Flemish mercenaries in the hope of holding it for the crown. Longuespée was beaten to the city gates. His failure was of great importance. Then, as now, holding London was a major step towards controlling England.

✝

The London in which Fitzwalter and his allies arrived in 1215 was a thriving place whose population was growing rapidly and which had long since overtaken Winchester, Norwich, York and the other major cities of England in size, influence and international recognition. It was a place fit for comparison with Paris or any of the other burgeoning European capitals. At its thirteenth-century peak the population would number some eighty thousand.[150] William Marshal's biographer called London *'la bone vile'*: 'that fine city',[151] and many of his contemporaries would wholeheartedly have agreed.

William Fitzstephen, an acolyte and biographer of Thomas Becket, can help us picture London as it might have appeared at the time. The preface to Fitzstephen's *Life of Thomas Becket*, written in 1173–4, took the form of a passionate, rhetorical, romantic paean to the city he called home. Fitzstephen declared that the English capital was chief 'among the noble and celebrated cities of the world ... which extends its glory farther than all the others and sends its wealth and merchandise more widely into distant lands. Higher than all the rest does it lift its head.'[152] Forget Paris or Constantinople, Venice or

Rome. London was, in Fitzstephen's eyes at least, a paradise of healthy air, Christian belief, military might, topographical good fortune, enlightened citizenship, female virginity and male sporting prowess. In the streets of this great city students bantered brilliantly, hawkers sold only the finest jewels and furs, and 'the matrons ... are the very Sabines'.* It was the new Troy, 'the fruitful mother of noble men'.

In truth, there was more to London than the frolicking of rosy-cheeked men and virtuous maidens. The city, taken together with its suburban satellite towns of Southwark (on the south bank of the Thames) and Westminster (a couple of miles to the west), was the commercial, religious, political and military hub of the south-east. It was large, wealthy and sophisticated: a human jumble of merchants and ministers, politicians and tradesmen, with a developed sense of its own communal character and a heartfelt wish among its leaders to be free and independent of royal interference. It had its own well-developed systems of internal rule and was in theory (if not in practice) democratic. The freemen of the city attended courts known as folkmoots and hustings to hear city business transacted. The city's merchants were members of regulated guilds and the city itself was divided geographically into administrative units called wards. These were run by aldermen, who tended to be appointed from elite, wealthy

---

* The Sabine women of classical history were famed for their beauty, honour and feminine wisdom. In 750 BC they threw themselves between the lines of their warring fathers (the Sabine men) and husbands (the Romans, who had abducted the Sabine women for the purpose of marriage). Thus, through the imperilment of their own lives, they successfully brokered a peace.

families well practised in holding office from generation to generation. Sixteen families, all connected by marriage and business, dominated London's political offices in the twelfth and thirteenth centuries.[153]

Every colour and smell of human life could be found intermingling within the old Roman walls that curved three miles around from west to east, enclosing a space of around 330 acres, in which palaces and markets jostled up against more modest houses, hospitals and taverns. The author of *Eustache the Monk*, the romanticized account of a real-life mercenary and pirate set around this time, characterized London as a place where magnificent palaces could be built, knocked down and re-erected in even greater finery.[154] Yet this was also the place where, in the popular pseudo-histories of King Arthur by Geoffrey of Monmouth, the legendary British king Constantine had slaughtered the son of his enemy Mordred, who was taking sanctuary in a monastery.[155]

The roads converging on London gave it rapid access to Dover and Canterbury in the south-east, to Colchester, Cambridge and Norwich in East Anglia, to the corridor between Oxford and Winchester in the west, and to Lincoln and York via the old Roman road known as Ermine Street. By water it was connected upstream to well-to-do royal settlements like Windsor and downstream to the estuary towns of Essex and Kent. Beyond these lay shipping routes to the continent, and thus eventually to every other bustling port of the known world.

The southern boundary of the city was formed by the Thames, deep and wide and dangerously rapid as it rose and fell with the tide over the course of the day. When the city was founded as Londinium in Roman times, it owed its existence to its position as the lowest point downriver where the Thames could safely be crossed. Even so, the river was a broad and occasionally lethal waterway. The huge stone edifice of London Bridge, nearly a thousand feet long and forty wide, was its only foot-crossing. London Bridge was densely populated, with shops and houses crammed side by side around a chapel dedicated to Thomas Becket. Hundreds of boats thronged the waters below, taking passengers up and down the banks, from the mansions on the Strand (the road that linked London with Westminster) to the wharfs and ports that stood further east, allowing access to the city from the bankside. The building of the stone bridge had begun in 1176 and been completed in 1209, with some of the work overseen by one Isenbert, a master builder who had previously worked on fine bridges in Saintes and La Rochelle in Aquitaine.[156] A fire had done significant damage to the new bridge in 1212, killing a large number of citizens in the process, and although rebuilding was underway it was still far from complete.

To the west of the city was another river: the Fleet, which emptied into the Thames at a place that would later be known as Blackfriars. A third waterway, known as the Walbrook, had once partitioned London, but it had silted up long ago, leaving a marsh, or moor, which covered a large area outside the northern walls.

In the centre of the city, on Ludgate Hill, stood the cathedral of St Paul's. By 1215 the Norman cathedral had been under construction for more than a century. Although it would not have a steeple for another six years, it nevertheless loomed over the city around it – at least as big as the great cathedral in England's former capital, Winchester. Inside, a long nave was supported on both sides by huge fluted stone pillars.[157] Outside in the churchyard Londoners gathered to gossip, protest and bear witness to all manner of political pageantry. Alongside the Guildhall, which was the centre of London's mercantile and administrative life, St Paul's was the most important building within the city walls. It marked the geographical mid-point of the city, where the main thoroughfares crossed, and was the spiritual centre too: dozens of smaller parish churches dedicated to saints such as Magnus and Margaret clustered around it, with one every few hundred yards at least. There was also a small but prominent Jewish population: near the Guildhall was one of several synagogues and outside the entrance known as the Cripplegate was the oldest Jewish cemetery in England.[158]

Across the river at Lambeth, the archbishops of Canterbury and Rochester had houses. Other churchmen had started to build inns, temples and mansions outside the walls on the Strand. There was a large Cluniac abbey at Bermondsey and several hospitals both inside and outside the city walls, including the great priory and hospital of St Bartholomew, at Smithfield. As the hundreds of church bells all ringing together on the morning of Sunday 17 May would have suggested, this was a city where the ritual and power of religion was uppermost in the fabric of life.

Yet if London was a spiritual hive, it was also very much a place of commerce. Two large markets dominated the town:

the Eastcheap and the Westcheap, where one could barter for life's staples, brought in on carts along the highways that connected London with the countryside, and by boat up the Thames estuary. By 1215 London had trading contacts with every corner of the earth. The wool and cloth trade with Flanders boomed, and claret flowed from Bordeaux, whose links with the English crown had been direct since John's mother, Eleanor of Aquitaine, had become queen in 1154. In 1138, a papal legate had visited London and been disturbed to see nuns going about in cloaks trimmed with exotic furs such as gris, sable, marten and ermine, most of which would have originated in the Baltic.[159] In his biography of Becket, William Fitzstephen also mentions gold, spices and incense from the middle east, arms from Scythia, jewels from the Nile valley and purple silk from China. Even if he is plainly guilty here of rhetorical exaggeration (the 'Scythians' had not ridden the plains of what is now Iran for about eight centuries by this point, so it seems unlikely that they were trading bows and arrows with the English), we know that the trading networks of the capital stretched for thousands of miles.

Yet the barons who piled into the city on 17 May would have known that for all its wealth and glamour the underbelly of London crawled with unpleasantness. Set against Fitzstephen's adoring description is that of Richard of Devizes, who left an account of the city from the perspective of an imaginary, rather stiff-necked Jew who had been to London and did not like it. 'All sorts of men crowd together there from every country under the heavens,' he wrote. 'No one lives in it without falling into some sort of crime ... Whatever evil or malicious thing that can be found in any part of the world, you will find in that city.' He went on to list the iniquitous places of the city: crowded eating houses, theatres and taverns. Of its underclass, he wrote, 'you will meet more braggarts here than in all France; the number of parasites is infinite. Actors, jesters, smooth-skinned lads, Moors, flatterers, pretty boys, effeminates, pederasts, singing and dancing girls, quacks, belly-dancers, sorceresses, extortioners, night-wanderers, magicians, mimes, beggars, buffoons . . . if you do not wish to dwell with evil-doers, do not live in London.'[160]

Even Fitzstephen admitted that the splendour of urban life was occasionally disrupted, although the worst he would acknowledge was 'the immoderate drinking of fools and the frequency of fires'.[161] In fact, the fire of July 1212 which damaged London Bridge had also devastated Southwark and the city proper.[162] And fire was not the only problem facing London's homeowners at that time. Sanitation and waste management were constant challenges. The Assize of Buildings – a set of detailed planning regulations passed in 1189, at the beginning of Richard I's reign – laid down the height and position of pavements, gutters, arches, walls and doorways, and ruled that an unwalled cesspit could not be dug closer than three and a half feet from the land of a neighbour.[163]

Mass popular unrest was relatively frequent. In 1196 William Fitzosbern – a brilliant and well-educated public speaker, famous for his long beard – had led a rebellion of poor Londoners, imploring them to rise up against their masters. This ended badly: having threatened the crown, Fitzosbern was trapped in a burning church, stabbed when he tried to escape, dragged to Tyburn behind a horse and hanged. (The spot beneath the gallows where the rebel leader died became a site of veneration for the poor, who scraped up handfuls of the dirt until there was a large and unsightly hole in the ground.)[164]

One of the richest sources of anecdote concerning London's darkest side can be found in the records of royal judges who visited the city to try criminal cases on the eyre circuit of 1244. These hearings date from a generation later than 1215, but the behaviour and the small tragedies they describe are both timeless and utterly typical of life in a medieval city. In the sad records of the courts, a world away from tales of skating on the frozen marshes or sniffing exotic spices, we learn of 'Elias le Pourtour, who was carrying a load of cheese' when he 'fell dead in Bread Street', and John Shep, serjeant of the sheriff of London, who threw a prisoner 'so violently into the deepest part of the prison that he broke his neck and died'.[165] The justices were told that a madman called William de Godeshalve killed himself with a knife, that William Gambun fell into the Thames while clambering from one boat to another and drowned, that John de la Neuwelonde bit Laurence Turpyn's right thumb off, that Robert of Kingston murdered 'Adam, son of Alice' with an axe, and that 'a girl about eight years old was found dead in the churchyard of St Mary Somerset. It was believed that she was thrown there by some prostitute', presumed to be her mother.[166]

✝

Of everything that could be found in the vast, varied and teeming city of London, perhaps the most valuable to

Fitzwalter and his 'Army of God' was its fortifications. There were two significant castles within the walls of the city: the Tower of London and Baynard's Castle. Both of these sat on the banks of the Thames. The Tower, which belonged to the king, was a fat, fierce, thick-walled monster and a potent symbol of royal authority that had loomed over the city ever since it was erected by William the Conqueror. (Fitzstephen tells us that the Tower's walls 'rise from very deep foundations and are fixed with mortar tempered with animals' blood'.) Baynard's Castle, which controlled access to London from upriver, was Robert Fitzwalter's personal power base in the capital. John had slighted the castle in January 1213 as punishment for Fitzwalter's faithlessness and plotting.* But it had been returned when he was pardoned six months later, and its custody, together with Fitzwalter's links in the city to trading interests, meant that from a position of some desperation, the baronial party were now transported to a place of great strength.

According to the Crowland Chronicler, Fitzwalter's party had attracted a large number of younger men of noble blood: the 'children or grandchildren of magnates', who had come to join the rebels in search of adventure and to make their name through fighting.[167] But this was far from an invading party consisting solely of noble interests. For London itself had a long and somewhat fractious history with the Plantagenet kings, and in the last weeks of May 1215, Londoners saw their

* Less than two years had passed since Baynard's Castle had been slighted. It had been returned to Fitzwalter in July 1213, so in 1215 it would probably have been something of a building site.

opportunity to take a stand against King John and perhaps force him to make concessions in a moment of weakness.

Wringing special privileges and promises of independence from kings was a speciality of London's citizens. In 1130 Henry I had been paid one hundred marks to confirm that the city could choose its own sheriffs. When King Stephen was embroiled in the war known as the Anarchy, he gave the capital its freedom in return for financial and military support – a relationship that was rewarded in 1141 when Stephen's enemy, the empress Matilda, was driven out of the city before she could be crowned there. During Richard I's early reign, when the king was absent and his ministers were willing to consider almost any proposal in exchange for silver to pay for his crusading, London even managed to secure permission to elect its first mayor. Henry Fitzailwyn served from 1191 until his death in 1212 and began a long tradition of independent power wielded by a locally elected leader – a tradition which continues today.[168] John himself had confirmed this right shortly after Fitzailwyn died, when he had granted to the citizens of London all their ancient liberties. Thus by 1215, when one Serlo the Mercer was elected mayor, London was a place that knew how to turn a royal bind to its own advantage. The city would exact a good number of concessions from John in the months that followed the barons' arrival in May.

Once the rebels had secured their position in London, they decided they needed to assure themselves of allies further afield. According to Wendover, they 'sent letters throughout England to those earls, barons and knights who appeared to be still faithful to the king ... and advised them with threats, as they regarded the safety of their property and possessions, to abandon a king who was perjured and who warred against his barons, and together with them to stand firm and fight against the king for their rights and for peace; and that, if they refused to do this, they, the barons, would make war against them all, as against open enemies, and would destroy their castles, burn their houses and other buildings and destroy their warrens, parks and orchards.'[169] Their actions in London were just as uncompromising: they attacked houses belonging to Jews, robbed the owners and stripped stones from their buildings to improve the city's defences.

The effect of the barons' defiant occupation of the capital was to bring about a stalemate. For all the ordnance, artillery and men at John's disposal there was no realistic possibility of his besieging London successfully. He had lost access to two of his key sources of wealth: the royal treasury at Westminster and the Tower of London. He remained in control of a number of castles and manors in the nearby area and retained the support of many heavyweight English earls and barons: among them his half-brother William Longuespée, William Marshal and the earls of Chester, Cornwall, Warenne and Albemarle. The king buzzed around between Winchester and Windsor, monitoring his enemies' actions in the capital. Before very long it became clear that, with neither side able to crush the other, the only way to bring some semblance of peace to England would be by negotiation.

From late May into the early days of June, messengers travelled back and forth between the king and the rebels holed up in and around Baynard's Castle. Slowly but surely they began to feel out the basis for a peace treaty that could be granted by the king in exchange for his enemies' dispersal. Between the king and the rebels – although clearly leaning toward the latter – sat Stephen Langton, the archbishop who had been at the root of so many of John's earlier problems. Langton would be an important mediator, and would subsequently make a profound intellectual contribution to the final charter that appeared in June 1215. By 10 June the outlines of an agreement had taken detailed form, and King John was ready to meet his rebellious barons in person. The stage that was chosen was a broad, green meadow alongside the Thames twenty-three miles upstream from London. Magna Carta would describe it as '*in prato quod vocatur Ronimed inter Windlesoram et Stanes*': 'the meadow which is called Runnymede between Windsor and Staines'.

Language, legends ...
and names

In 1215 England was a multilingual realm. The three main languages in use were Latin, French and English, although in small pockets of the country there were others in use, among them Welsh, Cornish and Hebrew. How all these tongues interacted tells us much about the way that society itself was divided.

Latin was the language of the Church and the law, and an international tongue in which the educated elites could communicate across the whole of Christendom and beyond. An education in Latin was the sign of a clerk, and a mastery of Latin marked a superior intellect from an ordinary one. Latin was the language of church services and Biblical texts. Legal proceedings – in church courts at least – were conducted verbally in Latin, and records were made in Latin by government officials. Anyone without a functioning knowledge of the language of the ancients was by definition excluded from intellectual and bureaucratic discourse – and even within literate circles there was considerable snobbery about proficiency.

Latin was furthermore the language of almost all the chronicles and grand treatises of the age, and writers like Gerald of Wales and Walter Map, Roger of Wendover and Matthew Paris prided themselves on both the quality of their Latin and often their ability to cram their accounts with familiar phrases from the writings of classical authors and Biblical texts. The frequency of these references suggests that many of these court-associated authors were writing on at least two levels at once: simultaneously giving a straightforward narrative account of events and building a web of in-jokes and historical allusions that were accessible at the time only to their most cultured readers, and which are now mostly lost even on a scholar.

Latin was, therefore, both a tool of official business and of social and cultural elitism. Naturally, Magna Carta was written in Latin. Like most official documents the Latin was heavily abbreviated with shorthand marks indicating sections of words (particularly word endings) that had been skipped to save space. This truncated way of writing was quite unremarkable for thirteenth-century scribes, all of whom would fill in the missing letters mentally when consulting an official text. However, to those unschooled in the peculiarities of official shorthand, writs, charters and letters would have appeared dispiritingly dense and incomprehensible.

If Latin distinguished clerks from laymen, it was the use and comprehension of French and English that divided rich and poor. Since the Norman Conquest

in 1066 French had been the language of kings –
although not the only language. Henry II was said to
have understood most of the tongues used between
the English Channel and the Holy Land, although,
according to Walter Map, 'he spoke only French and
Latin'.[170] By John's time French was still the spoken
language of the court, and this was hardly surprising.
Both John's parents had been French speakers, as were
his brother Richard and his wife Isabella of Angoulême.
This is not to say that the French spoken in England was
the same as that spoken elsewhere. Just as the dialects
and accents of northern and southern France differed
significantly (they were known respectively as the *langue
d'oïl* and *langue d'oc*, after the different words for 'yes'),
so English French sounded rather unlike that spoken
in Paris. Walter Map, whose great work was a gossipy
account of court politics, records that the way to insult
faulty francophones was to accuse them of possessing
'Marlborough French', since in Marlborough 'there is
a spring of which they say that whoever tastes it speaks
bad French.'[171] This perceived linguistic pecking order
reflected the supposed cultural superiority of those
born and bred across the Channel. It is not surprising
that the young William Marshal was sent to serve
his eight years as a squire not in another part of the
kingdom of his birth, but across the sea, in Tancarville
in Normandy. Neither, for that matter, is it surprising
that Marshal's biography, written to exemplify and
celebrate a man who considered himself the paragon

of English knighthood and nobility, was composed in Norman French.

It was not until the mid-fourteenth century that Plantagenet England embraced English as the language of those pleading in legal courts, debating in parliament or writing poetry for court patrons. Yet if French was the linguistic currency of England's elite in 1215, it was not very highly regarded or widely used by the majority of the population. These people spoke English, and since the Norman Conquest had destroyed any 'national' standard for the native language, they spoke it in a wide variety of dialects, which differed sharply even between neighbouring counties.[172] People from distant counties may have been mutually incomprehensible. Nevertheless, among the general population English survived as a spoken language throughout the middle ages, and its resilience meant that almost everyone, from serfs to princes, would have required a working knowledge of it, even if snobbery dictated that some of them chose to deal whenever possible in Latin and French.

Where English had suffered most by 1215 was in its use as a written language. Old English, the language of the Anglo-Saxons, had been supplanted as the language of administration and bureaucracy, of chronicle and history. Some writers continued to put saints' lives and narrative verse down in their local dialect, but these were the exceptions in a period of domination for Latin and (to a lesser degree) French. As one historian has pointed out, around two hundred medieval copies survive of Geoffrey of Monmouth's mid-twelfth-century Arthurian epic, the *History of the Kings of Britain*, which was written in Latin; fewer than two hundred English manuscripts of any description survive from the same age.[173] All the same, as a language of serious scholarship and even of entertainment English was not entirely dead. Some time between 1190 and 1215 the English priest Layamon completed the epic sixeen-thousand-line poem known as the *Brut* – similar in character and content to, and indeed, drawing ultimately upon Geoffrey of Monmouth's work, but written in the vernacular.

✝

So England in 1215 was a land of many languages – not quite Babel, but certainly a place where men and women were divided and defined by the words they used. And nowhere can we see how language reflected social stratification more starkly than in the field of names. Without exception, the names of the men involved in making Magna Carta on both the royal and the baronial side had a continental flavour. The king is named in Magna Carta as Johannes, although he would have been more familiar to his companions by the French version, Jean. He was the son of a Henry and his brothers had been called William, Henry, Richard and Geoffrey. In 1215 these were all distinctively French-sounding names, as befitted a dynasty that had its roots in Anjou, Normandy and Aquitaine, rather than in England.

Around the king too were rich and powerful men with uniformly un-English names. The archbishop of Canterbury was a Stephen; the two most prominent leaders on the rebel side were Robert (Fitzwalter) and Eustace (de Vesci). With them, arrayed on either side, were more Roberts and Richards, Henrys and Geoffreys. Even the few unusual names whom we find connected to the Great Charter – men like Saer de Quincy or Serlo the Mercer, mayor of London – came originally from across the Channel. Of traditional Anglo-Saxon names – Edmunds and Edwards, let alone Edwigs and Ethelstans – there are none. This shows how complete the Norman colonization of English aristocratic life had been since 1066.

Beyond the charter, though, it is a different story. The Curia Regis rolls, which preserve the activities of the royal court, show us that for ordinary people in England, the world sounded rather different.[74] In one case Edmund of Hastings comes before the court in Sussex with his wife Petronilla.[75] And Edmund is far from the only archaic name among the same records. We also hear of Ailnoth and Edric, Odgar and Ughtred, Gunilda and Forthulf. Even more strange and wonderful names abound besides: Pupelin, Hamelin, Spendora, Chilleluve, Ermengarda, Buiamond, Goldhauec, Dierana and Hemfrid.

Besides forenames, of course, most people who appear in historical records from 1215 have what we would now call a surname. These could be created in various ways, and were usually connected to the forename by a joining article such as 'de', 'le', 'atte', 'Fitz', 'wife of', 'daughter of' and so on. As one modern writer has put it, 'medieval names, whether noble or plebeian [were] derived from location, occupation, characteristic or patronym.'[176]

For baronial families in 1215, surnames tended to be hereditary: reflecting an illustrious ancestor, a place of origin or an office. Some of the great medieval noble dynasties had already established their surnames by this date – they were represented among the twenty-five enforcer barons by men such as Robert de Vere, earl of Oxford, and Roger Bigod, earl of Norfolk. For the lower orders, however, things were much looser, and fixed surnames were far less common.

Women might simply append the name of their husband to their own, as in the case of Edmund of Hastings and Petronilla, mentioned above, who appear in the records as *'Edmundo de Hasting et Petronille uxori sue'* ('Edmund of Hastings and Petronilla, his wife'). This worked for children too: they would often be referred to simply as John, son of Robert – or, by the same logic, Hamlin, son of Theoric. (The system could occasionally get complicated: John son of Amicia wife of Robert de Beaumes must have grown up hoping to achieve something in his own life that would make it simpler to identify him.)

Other surnames tell us a bit about the people who bore them. 'Foreigners' were easily identified: those who had surnames such as Breton, Fleming and Daneis or, closer to home, people like Thomas de Lincoln and Marjory de Evesham. But in an age in which people seldom migrated very far, many more surnames referred to jobs: Archer, Butler, Carpenter, Clerk, Constable, Cornmerchant, Mayor, Monk, Shepherd and Vintner. As time went by, these 'occupational' names themselves became hereditary, so it is not possible to say for certain whether a man called Archer spent his days shooting arrows, or whether perhaps that had been the job of his father.

Basic family status was reflected in names such as 'the Bastard' and 'the Widow', while some surnames were simply epithets. It does not take much imagination to work out why a man might be called Walter Pure, John the Simple, Robert Perjure or John Prikehard, let alone Roger the Deaf or Geoffrey the Bald. And of course the habit of giving men nicknames was not limited to the English peasant classes. After all, King John had to suffer the indignity in his youth of being called *Jean sans Terre* ('John Lackland'), and, after the loss of Normandy in 1203–4, as *Johannem molle gladium*: John Softsword.

6

Runnymede

The lush meadow called Runnymede, about twenty-three miles west of London, is a low-lying, damp, green field cut through and watered by the river Thames, lined by trees and rising gently on its western side to form what is now known as Cooper's Hill. Since Saxon times Runnymede had been considered a liminal space: a threshold, a boundary and a sort of no-man's-land; an ancient political meeting point where two sides in dispute had traditionally come to work out their differences on neutral ground. This role was etched into its very name, which derived from three old English words: *rūn*, *ēg* and *mǣd*, referring in turn to the concepts of a place of council and counsel, an island surrounded not by water but by marsh or low hills, and, simply, a meadow.[177] It was quite literally a wetland on which a king might take advice. This was well known in 1215. The Latin term normally used to describe it was *pratum* – a large grassy meadow. But Matthew Paris wrote that its name was earned because from 'ancient times' it was a place for meetings concerning the peace of the kingdom.[178]

Making political deals in liminal spaces like Runnymede was an important tradition in English history. In 1016 the rival kings Cnut and Edmund Ironside had met on Alney Island in the river Severn to swear oaths agreeing to divide the kingdom between them; it has been argued that the 'Hursteshevet' where Edward the Confessor came to meet the thegns of England in 1041 and agree terms for his accession to the crown was the sandy spit at Hurst Head, which sticks out into the sea between Hampshire and the Isle of Wight.[179] A conference on peace held at Runnymede could have been a nod to this tradition. Equally it could have been reasoned that in the summer of 1215 Runnymede was simply a good practical place for John to meet the rebel barons. It was partway between Windsor to the north-west and rebel-held London. The barons could arrive at the meadow by way of a town called Staines; it lay on the opposite bank of the Thames from Windsor, and the road that joined them was the only means of approach. There could, then, be no trickery from either side: no ambushing the meeting spot from an unexpected direction and no surprise attacks on one another at their base camps. The ground of Runnymede itself was too soft to be considered a sensible place to do battle, if either side was thinking of anything so rash.

In the second week of June 1215 the water meadow was filled with hundreds of people. The chronicler Ralph of Coggeshall wrote that the barons 'gathered with a multitude of most famous knights, armed well at all points'.[180] They erected tents across the field. It is likely that many of these would have displayed the arms of the chief baronial rebels: Fitzwalter, his brother-in-arms Saer de Quincy, earl of Winchester, Geoffrey de Mandeville, Eustace de Vesci and two of the other greatest lords in England, Roger Bigod, earl of Norfolk, and Richard earl of Clare, all of them protected by royal letters of safe-conduct. The king's party camped on the other side, in large semi-permanent pavilions. Above these John might well have displayed the royal banners that he had ordered in the spring: the Plantagenet lions stitched in gold thread.[181]

The king himself did not camp out at Runnymede, but spent most of his time in his apartments within the imperious round keep of Windsor Castle, perched high on a chalk cliff overlooking the river.[182] He received visitors at the castle – Hugh, the prospective abbot of Bury St Edmunds, found the king there when he was seeking confirmation for his election – and rode or travelled by barge downriver when his presence was required at Runnymede. His chief advisers were churchmen – Archbishop Langton, Henry archbishop of Dublin, William bishop of London and others – and a handful of loyal barons, including his half-brother Longuespée, William Marshal, the earls of Warenne and Arundel and others.* John's private thoughts at the time of the discussions are lost to us. It is unlikely that he was thrilled to be having to deal civilly

---

* John's advisers at Runnymede, as named in the preamble to Magna Carta, were: 'Stephen, archbishop of Canterbury, primate of all England and cardinal of the holy Roman church; Henry, archbishop of Dublin; Bishops William of London, Peter of Winchester, Joscelin of Bath and Glastonbury, Hugh of Lincoln, Walter of Worcester, William of Coventry and Benedict of Rochester; Master Pandulf, subdeacon and confidant of the lord Pope, Brother Eymeric, master of the Knights Templar in England; and the noble men William Marshal, earl of Pembroke, William, earl of Salisbury, William, earl of Warenne, William, earl of Arundel, Alan of Galloway, constable of Scotland, Warin fitzGerald, Peter fitzHerbert, Hubert de Burgh, seneschal of Poitou, Hugh de Neville, Matthew fitzHerbert, Thomas Basset, Alan Basset, Philip d'Aubigny, Robert of Ropsley, John Marshal, John fitzHugh, and others of our subjects.'

with men such as Fitzwalter and de Vesci, who had relatively recently been plotting to have him murdered. But he did not have much choice. Matthew Paris, although writing later in the thirteenth century about events that had occurred when he was only fifteen, still conjured a striking and plausible image of the king during the negotiations. While John was charming in public, wrote Paris, behind the scenes he 'gnashed his teeth, rolled his eyes, grabbed sticks and straws and gnawed them like a madman'.[183] And well he might have. The treaty that was being thrashed out in early June would propose devastating new restrictions on every future king of England's ability to govern as he pleased.

✝

The news reaching John from around his realm during the second half of May was not encouraging. Besides the barons barring the gates of London to him, rebellions had also broken out in Lincoln and Devon. The Welsh under their leader Llywelyn ap Iorwerth were agitating in the west and had moved to take Shrewsbury. Similar foreign opposition could be expected in the north, where Alexander II of Scotland was ready to ally with the English northerners. And it would not need very much imagination to see Philip Augustus licking his lips in France, enjoying every second of his Plantagenet enemy's discomfort.

It had therefore taken only a week after the fall of London for John to open negotiations with the rebels, suggesting that they come to meet him under the protection of letters of safe-conduct. One of these was issued to Saer de Quincy on Monday 25 May. Two days later, another safe-conduct was issued to Archbishop Stephen Langton, permitting him to come to Staines 'to entreat for peace between us and our barons'.[184] John was now in direct contact with his enemies, and their negotiations had a mediator in the archbishop.

To start with John did not give himself wholly over to the idea of peace and reconciliation. The archbishop of Dublin was instructed to prepare 'two good galleys well equipped and with good crew' for the use of William Marshal. William Longuespée was provided with four hundred Welshmen to defend Salisbury.[185] In Winchester John was also amassing a large number of foreign mercenaries brought over from Poitou. The first week of June marked the lead-in to the festival of Whitsun and John took the opportunity to travel to Winchester and spend several days inspecting his troops. At the same time he was also taking direct and provocative action against his baronial enemies: manors belonging to the rebels Geoffrey de Mandeville and Hugh de Beauchamp (the castellan of Bedford, who had received the rebel barons in early May) were stripped and reassigned to John's friends Savaric of Mauléon and Hasculf de Suligny.[186] Yet for all this, John was beginning to feel the financial pinch of losing access to his treasury. A letter sent to Scarborough on 11 June showed the king desperately shuffling money from debtors to creditors in order to pay his servants and crossbowmen their back-wages.[187] Every day that went by made it more likely that the king would come to terms with the rebels and buy himself time to regroup.

The terms that were being demanded were, by the second week of June, very well fleshed out. We know a surprising amount about the drafting process, because as well as the Unknown Charter (which represented baronial demands at some point during the early spring of 1215) there also survives a remarkable working draft of the charter that the king's enemies sought. It is known as the Articles of the Barons. The parchment on which the articles were written was authenticated with the royal seal and most likely taken for safekeeping by Archbishop Langton, since it ended up in the Canterbury Cathedral archives.

By the time the Articles of the Barons were drawn up, the baronial vision of peace with the king had developed significantly. 'These are the articles which the barons ask for and the lord king grants,' it began, and there followed forty-nine clauses of demands ranging across a wide variety of topics, from inheritance and marriage to merchants' rights and the power of the king's officials to arrest his subjects.[188] The king was to exile his foreign mercenaries from the realm and eject a named group of foreign advisers from his service. He was to be forbidden from imposing the military tax of scutage except with public consent, 'by common counsel of the kingdom'. Welsh and Scottish hostages whom John had taken were to be returned.

No longer was there any reference to the coronation charter of Henry I. Instead, this was a document that looked firmly towards the establishment of a final and binding agreement which the king was evidently soon to announce. The very first clause committed the king to setting a limit to payments for heirs to receive inheritances, and explained that the precise value 'is to be pronounced in the charter' ('*exprimendum in carta*'). The final clause again referred to 'his [i.e. the king's] charter' and made reference to a certain period of time 'to be determined in the charter' ('*determinandum in carta*'). In other words, it was drawn up on the understanding that very soon John would be making some larger gesture of conciliation in which all the matters of contention outlined in the Articles would be definitively addressed.

No date was recorded in the Articles of the Barons, but there are grounds for supposing that the version that survives, sealed by John, was drawn up on Wednesday 10 June.[189] Already a long process of negotiation had gone on – and the concessions in the Articles to Londoners, the Welsh and the Scots suggest that the list of baronial demands had expanded as they drew new allies into their fold. So too had they begun to account for the interests of the social rank below the barons: clauses guaranteed that the king would not allow his barons to exploit feudal obligations owed from their own men; another clause set limits on the service due to barons from their knights. A welter of interests was creeping into negotiations. There were some significant gaps in the draft: for instance there was little mention of John's obligations to the Church, which was surprising since Archbishop Langton had been such a prominent figure in negotiations, and since John had made such a public show of his penitent Christianity and alliance with Rome. Overall, though, the Articles of the Barons showed that by the second week of June John was being pressured into making concessions in which the whole political community of England – indeed, of Britain – might potentially have at least some small claim.

Yet manifestly the Articles of the Barons were not the finished agreement. The Articles show us the peace treaty as it nearly was: tantalizingly close to realization. They were thrashed out by royal and baronial representatives during early June. Between Monday 8 and Thursday 11 June the barons were permitted to come to 'Staines' – which almost certainly meant Runnymede – under further issues of safe-conduct.[190] On Wednesday 10 June John came down from Windsor to Runnymede in person and was evidently deep in discussion with his advisers and opponents all day, for when the abbot of Bury came to try and find him there, he was forced to wait 'for a very long time'.[191] And five days later it would have its final form, as the treaty that history has come to call Magna Carta.

✝

On Wednesday 10 June King John had dinner with Abbot Hugh of Bury St Edmunds in Windsor Castle. Afterwards the two men sat together on his bed within the royal chamber, 'conversing privately about many things'. The chronicler who recorded the account left it, frustratingly and cryptically, at that, although he suggests that John was short on patience, for he flew into a rage at one of the abbot's companions, screaming at him for an innocuous remark, until the poor man 'became amazingly red' and fled unbidden from the royal presence.[192] What more passed in the abbot's private conversation with John we do not know. But it is not too fanciful to think that at some point their discussions concerned events downriver at Runnymede. Hugh had been there waiting for John that very day. He had seen the barons, their knights, their servants and their clerical staff milling around the meadow, some locked in discussions with the king over the terms suggested by the Articles of the Barons, and others, presumably, hanging around much as he was doing. If he did not know already then he would have heard directly from John that the Articles had been sealed, and that the final stage of the peace process was drawing near: a fully developed treaty was almost ready to be confirmed, formally granted and promulgated to the realm. He may well have learned that this was going to happen soon. From Windsor on that same day John had extended his grant of safe-conduct to the barons for a further four days. They would come back to Runnymede to meet him once again on Monday 15 June. Then, in all likelihood, the deal would be done.

And so it came to pass. On 14 June the royal household would have celebrated Trinity Sunday. At the church service to mark the day they would have heard a lesson read from the fourth chapter of the Revelation of St John.[193] If any among them – including the king – were looking for portents of the week that was to follow, then they might have found them in the lesson's strange, apocalyptic vision: twenty-four elders wearing crowns bowed before an enthroned, divine being the colour of deep red gemstones, whose throne was surrounded by a rainbow that shimmered like an emerald. John's fondness for bright jewels was well known; his interest in the lesson may have been further piqued by its last verses, which described the elders bowing before their master's throne and throwing away their crowns.[194] Was this a metaphor for what was to come at Runnymede? Or would it be John whose crown was cast, as it were, to the floor?

On that Monday the delegations of king and barons met once again at the usual place. There were still minor disagreements about details, but the time had come to make peace or abandon the process. Both sides chose peace. A long list of reforms was first sworn to by the king's and barons' representatives and then – in the words of the agreement, voiced in the royal third person – it was 'given by our hand' (*datum per manum nostram*). In other words, the terms of a deal were formally granted and sworn to by the king himself, before the clerks of his chancery set to work making identical copies of the full agreement. Each copy that was made was called an engrossment, and each was certified and given demonstrable legal authority by the attachment of the royal seal: a double-sided piece of coloured wax connected to the parchment with a silk cord.* What was written on the parchment above that seal had been a long time in the making.

'John, by the grace of God, king of England, lord of Ireland, duke of Normandy and Aquitaine, count of Anjou, to his

---

* Despite what is often thought, written, drawn and believed, Magna Carta was never 'signed'. In 1215 kings and other lords only used impressions of their seals and would never stoop to so lowly a task as writing, even if they were able. Writing was the business of royal clerks. Sealing was the job of a royal official known as a spigurnel. It was a matter of huge importance, for it was the indisputable symbol of royal approval for a document. Harsh penalties fell upon those who meddled with the royal seal: the chronicler Walter Map relates a story of 'a clever workman' who created a fake copper seal die to imitate that of Henry II. The king ordered the workman to be hanged, and although he subsequently took pity on the man's family and commuted the death sentence, the forger was instead confined to a monastery, 'lest his pity should appear over-indulgent'. M. R. James (ed. and trans.), revised by C. N. L. Brooke and R. A. B. Mynors, *Walter Map: De nugis curialium: Courtiers' Trifles* (Oxford, 1983) 494–5.

archbishops, bishops, abbots, earls, barons, justices, foresters, sheriffs, reeves, ministers, and all his bailiffs and faithful men, greeting,' it began. About four thousand more Latin words followed – a broad-ranging and occasionally bewildering critique and proposed correction of John's whole system of government, and nothing short of a full assault on his rights and prerogatives as king. It was more than twice the length of the Articles of the Barons, consisting of sixty-three clauses rather than forty-nine. In some places the charter was precise, measured and densely legalistic. In others it was vague and idealistic. Its clauses did not follow a completely clear, logical order – indeed, in parts the charter was a ragbag of adjacent promises on unrelated matters. In that sense it was a work in progress on which time had finally been called. What is more, Magna Carta would not gain its famous title until two years after Runnymede.* Yet there was no mistaking the fact that this was a 'great charter', the like of which had never been attempted before.

After a preamble naming John's advisers, Magna Carta started with the Church. 'Firstly, we have granted to God and confirmed by this, our present charter, for us and our heirs in perpetuity, that the English Church shall be free,' began the first clause, going on to explain that under the terms of

* After John's death the charter was twice reissued by his son Henry's minority government. On the second of these occasions, in 1217, a Charter of the Forest was also issued. Magna Carta then gained its famous name, to distinguish between the two. For clarity and convenience I have used the term 'Magna Carta' here to refer to the charter of 1215 as well. Although in theory anachronistic, this practice is usual among all modern historians of the reign.

John's earlier charter and his good relations with Innocent III, he would allow the Church to hold 'free elections, which are considered to be of the utmost importance and necessity'. No such grant had been made in the Articles of the Barons, and we can detect here Archbishop Langton's hand, late in negotiations, ensuring that John's late commitments to the Church as supposed defender (and crusader) were observed above everything else. Indeed, the clause on the Church was elevated above all the rest not merely by its position, but by its second half, which stated that 'We have also granted to all the free men of our realm … all the liberties written below.' The freedom of the Church was thus not merely the first clause among equals. It was a promise that was wholly boxed off by the language of the charter, so hallowed and elevated that after it had been made the charter effectively started again.

The way in which the charter was restarted was also extremely carefully worded. Magna Carta was granted, it said 'to all the free men of our realm' ('*omnibus liberis hominibus regni nostri*'). The freeness of the men was absolutely critical. On Monday 15 June 1215 the barons of England were divided into two categories. There were John's allies, who were his liege men and had all at some time sworn an oath to obey him as their lord. Then there were the rebels, all of whom had explicitly and unilaterally defied the king at Brackley, who had impertinently sent an Augustinian canon to tell him so in person at Reading, and who could in no sense therefore be considered 'free men' of the realm. They were outside the king's protection, his law and his favour, and would remain so until they relented and renewed their oaths of allegiance.

The liberties that would follow in the charter had been freely granted by John, but they could not be enjoyed by anyone who was not willing to obey him.

Next the charter dealt with one of the most bitter issues of dispute between John and his barons: the matter of reliefs for inheritance. The spiralling sums charged to the king's subjects were now to be strictly curtailed – no longer could barons like William FitzAlan be charged extraordinary sums like ten thousand marks to have their inheritance: the limit, said Magna Carta, was '£100 for the whole barony' or one hundred marks in the case of a knight. These were still substantial sums, but nothing like what the king was used to charging. Moreover, it would seriously blunt the king's ability to drive men into debt as a means of political control. Other clauses of the charter dealt with related issues. On debt, the king's bailiffs were to be forbidden to 'seize any land for any debt . . . so long as the debtor's chattels are sufficient to pay the debt' (clause 9). Two clauses carefully laid out the process for calculating dead men's debts – a block against royal officials arbitrarily naming a sum which could then be extracted aggressively.

Other areas of government which we would now loosely group under the heading 'tax' were also addressed. The sheriff's farm, which was a payment taken from the counties at a fixed level, was to be levied only at the 'ancient' rate (clause 25). The rate itself was not laid out: evidence of Magna Carta's unfinished status. Scutage – another major political issue – was also dealt with. The military tax was now to be 'reasonable'. As the Articles of the Barons had foreshadowed, it was only to be charged on exceptional occasions (on the knighting of the king's eldest son or the marriage of his eldest daughter), or else with the 'common counsel of our realm', which was to be taken according to a newly spelled-out procedure (clause 14). Although no one knew it at the time, this would have profound consequences for generations to come. Later in the thirteenth century these meetings of common counsel would come to be described as parliaments, in which the right to take tax was exchanged for the reform: the sort of political wrangling that underpinned Magna Carta would eventually become the routine mode of English government. (Eventually it would become sacred around much of the world.)

Other aspects of law and inheritance also came under scrutiny. Widows were not to be denied their inheritances, they were not to be forced into marriages that disparaged their status and they were not to pay the king to inherit what was owed to them (clauses 7 and 8). If inheritances were left to young men below the legal age of majority, they were to be excused fees to inherit when they grew up. The practice of granting wardships – custody of the lands and profits of underage heirs – would continue, for it was a normal part of feudal life. But those who were granted wardships were no longer to strip the assets in search of quick profit. Rather, the guardian was to take care of the 'buildings, parks, fishponds, pools, mills and other things pertaining to the land, and when the heir comes of age he shall restore to him all his land stocked with ploughs and growing crops, such as the agricultural season requires . . .' (clauses 4 and 5).

The issue of justice and judicial process loomed large in Magna Carta, just as its abuse had in John's reign. The Court of

Common Pleas – the highest court in England – would cease to follow John as he tramped his endless path around England's highways. Instead it was to be held in 'some fixed place' (clause 17). Again, precisely where this would be was left un-negotiated. County courts would be convened by the king sending 'two justices to each county four times a year', where they would hold the county assizes with four reputable knights of the local area to help them determine cases. Elsewhere the charter stated that judges and other legal officials ought to be competent (clause 45). Earls and barons should only be amerced (fined) for offences according to the judgment of their peers (clause 21). Yet it was in the grand principles of justice that Magna Carta issued what would become its most famous and long-lasting pronouncements, embodied in clauses 39 and 40. Together these stated: 'No free man is to be arrested or imprisoned or dispossessed, or outlawed, or exiled, or in any other way ruined, nor will we go or send against him, except by the legal judgment of his peers or by the law of the land. To no one will we sell, to no one will we deny or delay, right or justice.'

These ideas had been in gestation ever since the Unknown Charter was drawn up and probably before. Indeed, the first article of the Unknown Charter had envisaged John conceding that 'he will not take a man without judgment, nor accept anything for doing justice and will not do injustice'. Articles 29 and 30 of the Articles of the Barons had come up with almost identical wording to that which ended up in Magna Carta. A broadside aimed at the spirit, rather than merely the letter, of John's rule had been a consistent part of the baronial rebellion almost since its conception. Now it had its wording.

A slew of other issues ran through the charter around these ambitious central principles. Weights and measures were regulated for corn, wool and cloth. The despised practice of purveyance – by which royal officers could take goods and crops, horses and carts for the king's use without paying – was banned (clauses 28, 30 and 31). Bridge building was regulated (clause 23). The legal rights of women (other than widows) were curtailed: according to the charter, no man could be 'arrested or imprisoned because of the appeal of a woman for the death of anyone but her husband' (clause 54). A cluster of clauses took aim at legislation in the king's forests. The king promised not to try to enforce the harsh law of the forest on non-forest land (clause 44). He promised to investigate corrupt forest officials and to address the issue of afforestation. During John's reign and the reigns of Henry II and Richard I before him new swathes of the countryside had been designated as forest: the king's personal property, on which hunting deer and boar was forbidden, as was collecting firewood, felling trees to clear the land or erecting buildings. This became a burden on an increasing number of people, or as Richard FitzNigel, author of the 'Dialogue of the Exchequer', had put it: 'Those who have their homes in the forest may not take wood from their own woodlands for use in their own homes.'[195] In Magna Carta, John promised to review the creep of forest boundaries that had taken place since he came to the throne (clause 47). Crucially, though, he refused to countenance amending afforestation from any earlier. This was not the only area of reform where the king managed to wriggle.

The crusading oath that John had sworn on Ash Wednesday

served exactly the purpose the king intended, if not to the extent that he had hoped. In clause 52 of Magna Carta the king promised to restore 'lands, castles, liberties [and] rights' to anyone whom he had mistreated in England or Wales. But in the cases of people who claimed ill treatment during the reigns of Henry II or Richard I, John would only say that 'we will have respite during the crusaders' term'. The same applied in the matters of forest creep in England before 1199 and to any injustices committed in Wales during the same period (clauses 53 and 57). In other words, while John was prepared to hear complaints dating back to the start of his reign immediately on the granting of Magna Carta, anything that touched on matters before he was king could be kicked into the long grass for three years. Indeed, if John really was to go east to teach the Muslims of the Holy Land the sort of military lessons he had singularly failed to teach the king of France, that period could conceivably be even longer.

Yet given the length and scope of Magna Carta there was only so much that even a practised backslider like John could achieve. So many interests collided in the charter that he found himself making grants covering matters both within his kingdom and beyond. In clause 13 the city of London extracted a promise of almost full autonomy, granted 'all its ancient liberties and free customs both on land and on water'. This freedom was extended, moreover, to 'all other cities, boroughs, towns and ports'. (Clearly, jealousy of the Londoners' proposed special privileges had seeped into the debates at Runnymede, and the other townsmen present had demanded that the king treat them all in the same fashion.) Merchants were granted almost total freedom of movement: 'to be safe and secure in leaving and coming to England and in staying and travelling in England . . . to buy and sell without any evil tolls . . .' (clause 41). Fish-weirs – wooden fish-traps that obstructed river transport – were to be removed from the Thames and Medway, two of the London area's major waterways (clause 33).

Elsewhere there were provisions for knights, who were not to be 'distrained [i.e. forced] to do more service for a knight's fee . . . than is owed for it' (clause 16). The Welsh were promised justice for any 'lands or liberties or other things' that had been taken from them 'without lawful judgment of their peers' (clause 56). Prince Llywelyn himself was named: he would have hostages returned (clause 58). So was Alexander, king of Scots, whose sisters were being held at John's court: they would be returned, along with other hostages. In the case of any of Alexander's liberties and rights that had been affronted, John promised to act 'in accordance with the way we deal with our other barons of England' (clause 59).

Taken together, all this amounted to a vast set of new obligations for the king to observe. It also raised an important question. It was all very well for John to agree to Magna Carta, and for his scribes to set to work copying out engrossments of the charter on large pieces of parchment (each made of a single dried, bleached and scraped piece of sheepskin, written upon with quill pens cut from the finest wing-feathers of geese, applying ink made from crushed oak-galls). But how was the king to be made to obey it?

The answer was provided at the end of Magna Carta, in a clause just as far-reaching as anything else attempted within the charter. This was known as the security clause (clause 61), and in its way it was perhaps even more significant than the more famous clauses 39 and 40 which enshrined the right to liberty and due process before the law. For the mechanism it suggested to enforce the terms of the charter was nothing short of revolutionary.

Since the Articles of the Barons had been formulated it was recognized that John was temperamentally unsuited to the sort of radically constricted kingship that the charter suggested. A security clause had been envisaged there. In Magna Carta it was developed. If the king should 'transgress against any of the articles of peace', it read, a panel of twenty-five elected barons was legally entitled to 'distrain and distress us [i.e. the king] in all ways possible, by taking castles, lands and possessions and in any other ways they can ... saving our person and the persons of our queen and children.' Who these twenty-five men should be was not explained – probably because at the time no one had decided. We know the identity of these twenty-five barons only because other sources recorded their names. What was clear, however, was that in essence Magna Carta provided the barons with a licence to start a civil war.

In theory, this made some sense. It provided a third way between obedience to a tyrannical king and the legally dangerous option of throwing off homage and attacking him from beyond the bounds of the law. In practice, however, the security clause was a recipe for disaster. Magna Carta had been drawn up precisely because no one in England really wanted to end up in a war with the king. It was a peace treaty. And yet it was a peace treaty that advocated war as its means of enforcement. The contradiction ought to have been obvious to all, and perhaps on Monday 15 June it was. All the same, on that day Magna Carta was granted by the king. His officials – and helpers specially drafted in for the task – began copying it out into engrossments to be distributed to the country, probably via the bishops and religious houses.*

Finally, a date – 19 June, the Friday of the same week – was set for the final ratification of the charter. For although the king had granted Magna Carta, it remained the case that the rebel barons were not entitled to enjoy its many rights and privileges until they renewed their homage to him and returned to the status of 'faithful men'. The question was: were they prepared to do so?

✝

Taken in the round, Magna Carta was an extraordinary agreement. It was much longer, more detailed, more comprehensive and more sophisticated than any other statement of English law or custom that had ever been demanded from a king of England. Its scope ran from the minute to the massive and from the profound to the particular. It demanded everything

---

* Today four copies of the 1215 Magna Carta survive. Two are held in the British Library in London – one in a good condition and the other badly damaged by fire and a botched nineteenth-century attempt at preservation. (The latter copy once belonged to Canterbury Cathedral.) Another copy is owned by Lincoln Cathedral and is displayed in a gallery at Lincoln Castle close by. A fourth is owned by Salisbury Cathedral. The Salisbury Magna Carta is in a notably different pen-hand from the chancery cursive script of the other three. This suggests that at Runnymede the volume of work engrossing the charter demanded that other, non-chancery scribes were co-opted to help.

from the removal of specific foreign henchmen in John's employment to the cosmically grand assurance that John would not 'deny justice'. It did not employ the same crude hankering for past laws that had been the basis for the Unknown Charter. It looked to the past by demanding ancient customs and payments at their 'ancient' levels, but it was not simply a statement of laws as they used to be. It represented reform as well as retrenchment and it was not wholly conservative.

Pulsing beneath Magna Carta were two profound ideas. The first was that the English barons could conceive of themselves as a community of the realm – a group with collective rights that belonged to them en masse rather than individually. The second was that the king was explicitly expected to recognize in himself two duties. He was still the man who made the law. Now, he had to obey it as well. The theologian John of Salisbury, writing in Henry II's day, had stated that the difference between a prince and a tyrant was that while both made and enforced laws, the prince also *subjected* himself to the law.[196] In granting and sealing Magna Carta, John was promising to be a prince and not a tyrant.

Not everyone, however, believed him. In the days following Monday 15 June several attempts were made to reopen negotiations on certain points in the charter. Some barons were not happy that the rate for inheritance reliefs was £100, rather than a hundred marks. There was an attempt to harden the language of the security clause.[197] John was forced, outside the terms of the charter, to dismiss his justiciar, Peter des Roches, bishop of Winchester – a man unpopular in the country. A secondary agreement was made with the rebel barons including Fitzwalter over London: in it John accepted that his enemies (still calling themselves the Army of God) could continue to hold the city for two months, until 15 August, with the Tower of London being supervised by Archbishop Langton.[198] This had the convenient (and to John outrageous) effect of keeping the king cut off from his capital and his best sources of revenue. Yet for some barons, it was still not enough to compel them to trust John. According to the Crowland Chronicler, during the days that followed the charter's granting 'some of the magnates from beyond the river Humber' left Runnymede 'and under the pretext that they did not attend [the granting of Magna Carta], they resumed hostilities.'[199]

For those who remained, Friday 19 June was a day of ceremony and reconciliation. The rebel barons were received by the king and granted the kiss of peace. They made their homage anew and then ate and drank with John at a feast to mark the occasion.[200] Some – including Eustace de Vesci – were persuaded to witness official documents, which was a clear sign of royal favour. John's clerks, meanwhile, continued to copy out the agreement, and his sheriffs were instructed to make its terms known far and wide about the country. Those who were not busy with that laborious task were put to work writing letters to John's castellans, sheriffs and constables, ordering them to restore possessions that had been taken unlawfully either during or before the outbreak of hostilities. A typical letter was sent to William Longuespée on 19 June, when the king was back at Windsor following the reunification banquet: 'You must know that peace has been re-established between our Barons and us and that we give back immediately all the lands, castles and properties we seized from someone without a trial and unjustly.'[201] On 23 June he even ordered the return of some of his foreign soldiers to Poitou.[202] John was on his best behaviour. Yet beneath it all he was scheming. Matthew Paris's image of him frothing at the mouth and gnawing sticks during negotiations may have been fanciful, but a wide gap certainly existed between John's public and private demeanour.

The weeks that followed the break-up of the conference at Runnymede were messy and marked by increasing distrust. Although Fitzwalter had extracted from the king a promise to keep London in baronial hands for two months, he was loath to leave the capital for fear that it would fall in his absence. He tried to encourage as many of his allies as possible to remain in the south and in the saddle by organizing a summer tournament not far from Runnymede, at which the grand prize was a bear.[203]

John, meanwhile, had far more to concern himself with than tournaments and bears. In the immediate aftermath of the charter's confirmation, he received a flood of demands from all over the country, insisting that he give back lands, castles and privileges that he had confiscated in the previous years. In the ten days that followed the feast of 19 June, he was forced to make fifty restorations to the rebels. Fitzwalter, Saer de Quincy and Eustace de Vesci all directly profited, receiving respectively Hertford Castle, Mountsorrel Castle in Leicestershire, and the right to run dogs in the forests of Northumberland.[204]

John kept this up for about four weeks. But before long, the effort or the humiliation became intolerable. A meeting was held at Oxford between 16 and 23 July at which the king and his enemies came together to address issues arising from the enforcement of their agreement. Six freshly drawn-up engrossments were handed out and a few more concessions were made but at this point John embarked on a political manoeuvre that swiftly eroded the peace. Through Archbishop Langton and a group of other high-ranking churchmen he issued an open letter to his barons, asking them to supply *him* with a charter acknowledging the fact that they were 'bound by oath' to defend him and his heirs 'in life and limb'.[205] They refused. Indeed, on one day of the conference, when John was laid up in bed with painful feet, likely caused by gout, they refused even to obey his orders to meet him in his chamber.[206] According to Matthew Paris, John's own mercenaries now mocked him, sniggering that there were twenty-five other monarchs in England and that John was a disgrace to kingship.[207] From that point on, what little trust had existed between the two sides evaporated. As the Oxford conference broke up in rancour, John made a move that would flush all remaining goodwill away for ever. He wrote to Pope Innocent III, explaining what had happened in his realm and asking him to annul the charter and release him from his oath to obey it.

The fragile peace of Runnymede had lasted, wrote the chronicler known as the Dunstable Annalist, 'only for a little time.'[208] This was quite an understatement. In late August Pope Innocent III wrote back in a state of righteous anger that he could summon better than any other man in Europe. The situation in England, he wrote, was the work of the devil:

> Although our well beloved son in Christ, John illustrious king of the English, grievously offended God and the Church ... the king at length returned to his senses ... But the enemy of the human race [i.e. Satan], who always hates good impulses, by his cunning wiles stirred up the barons of England so that, with a wicked inconstancy, the men who supported him when injuring the Church rebelled against him when he turned away from his sin.[209]

The Pope went on to rehearse his prior instructions to the English barons, noting that he had explicitly told them 'to strive to conciliate the king by manifest proofs of loyalty and submission'. They had ignored him, he noted. 'And so by such violence and fear as might affect the most courageous of men he was forced to accept an agreement which is not only shameful and demeaning but also illegal and unjust, thereby lessening unduly and impairing his royal rights and dignities. '... We refuse to ignore such shameless presumption,' thundered the Pope. 'For thereby the Apostolic See would be dishonoured, the king's rights injured, the English nation shamed, and the whole plan for a crusade seriously endangered.'

What came next left little room for interpretation: 'We utterly reject and condemn this settlement, and under threat of excommunication we order that the king should not dare to observe it and that the barons and their associates should not require it to be observed ... we declare it null, and void of all validity forever.'

The letter was dated at Innocent's home town of Anagni, near Rome, on 24 August 1215. The minute it left the Pope's secretariat, Magna Carta was certifiably dead. In practice, it was dead already. On 5 September Peter des Roches, John's loyal bishop of Winchester, and Pandulf Verraccio, the papal legate, excommunicated the baronial leaders by name. In response, in early September the barons wrote to Louis, the heir to the crown of France, inviting him to come and take John's place as the new ruler of England. Two weeks later, John sent an order to his men to start seizing Robert Fitzwalter's lands. The arrival of Innocent's letters in England towards the end of September merely confirmed what everyone knew.

The country erupted into war.

Wives, widows . . . and children

Women in the middle ages were regarded through the prism of two conflicting Biblical models: the Virgin Mary and Eve. The model of Mary – miraculously chaste yet maternal – provided the basis for courtly romance, chivalry and religious reverence. Yet the analogy of Eve characterized women as morally weak and inherently sinful, and encouraged men to regard them as lesser beings, defined entirely by their sex: fair game to be scorned, ignored, traded for political gain, put to work, excluded from the process of law, demonized and beaten.

The conflict between these two images of femininity underpinned the contradictory and at times grossly abusive ways in which women were treated in society at large throughout the middle ages. In the fourteenth century Geoffrey Chaucer poked much fun at confused English attitudes towards the female half of the population. The Wife of Bath's Tale is a masterfully layered joke on the subject, developed around the story of an Arthurian knight's quest to understand what women most desire; he learns that it is to have 'sovereignty as well over their husband as their love, and for to be in mastery above him'. The tale ends with a plea by the narrating wife of Bath that 'Jesu Christ us send/Husbands meek, young and fresh abed ...', a line which must have amused listeners in the late fourteenth century as much as it would have done in 1215.[210]

The basic truth of medieval society that underpinned Chaucer's humour was that in reality almost every woman's position and status in life depended on her relation to a man, or several men. Since marriage and childbearing were the main bonds that tied families within their broader community, most women married in their teens, frequently without having much say in the choice of their husband, and were thereafter expected to devote themselves to his service and the maintenance of a good household, be it in a nobleman's castle or a villein's shack. Women were pressed into and bound by their relationships with men, and even those aristocratic women who entered nunneries were sent with a dowry, as a sign that they were now a bride of Christ.

The need for women to be attached to men was both theological and practical. The inferiority of women was decreed in the Bible – the letter to Timothy traditionally credited to St Paul declared that women should 'adorn themselves in modest apparel, with shamefacedness and sobriety, not with braided hair or gold or pearls or costly array ... Let the woman learn in silence with all subjection ... I suffer a woman not to teach, nor to usurp authority over the man, but to be in silence.'[211] The thirteenth-century French theologian Jacques de Vitry wrote that 'Between Adam and God in Paradise there was but one woman and she had no rest until she had succeeded in banishing her husband from the garden of delights and in condemning Christ to the torment of the Cross.' On the basis of these, and plenty of similar texts, women were not permitted to fight in battle, nor to celebrate the mass, nor to pass judgment in court. It is true that on occasion women could govern (usually in temporary place of a man), take part in legal proceedings, distribute land and alms, trade in markets and run households great or small. But most of these activities could only be undertaken with male approval. In widowhood, some women were granted a little more freedom, but they remained vulnerable without close male patronage. Peasant women were in a bleak sense granted a degree of equality with their men, but only insofar as they were expected to undertake the same hard physical toil in the fields. This was not the case at the other end of society. The ideal noblewoman, according to another thirteenth-century writer, Robert de Blois, was a cultivated but essentially passive and genteel figure, who 'could carry and fly falcon, tercel and hawk ... knew well how to play chess and tables, how to read romances, tell tales and sing songs'. She would also, naturally, bear children and keep a lavish household to impress her husband's associates.

Of course, there were women who bucked these traditional roles, although they were uncommon. One such was John's mother, Eleanor of Aquitaine, who went on crusade, married two kings, fomented a massive rebellion against her husband, survived fifteen years under house arrest, acted as regent for Richard I and involved herself heavily in the politics of John's early reign until she died in her early eighties. For others – even the most headstrong – life was restrictive. Hawise, countess of Aumale, was described by the chronicler Richard of Devizes as 'a woman who was almost a man, lacking nothing virile except the virile organs'.[212] But in 1212 when her third husband, Baldwin de Béthune, died, John forced her to pay the outrageous fine of five thousand marks just to come into her inheritance and her dower and thus secure her freedom not to remarry.

In aristocratic literature, even that which tended towards a more chivalrous and worshipful idealization of women, there lingered an implied scorn for the perceived stain of femininity. In the legends of King Arthur it is Queen Guinevere's infidelity that starts the cycle of events leading to Arthur's death in battle with Mordred. The twelfth-century courtesy poem known as the *Facetus* ('The Courteous Man') warned those seeking a good wife to avoid the daughters and widows of 'celibate priests and canons, torturers, beadles malicious [i.e. overbearing officials], actors, or those who lend money'.[213] The author compared an ill-bred woman to a leaking roof or smoke-filled room: all, he suggested, were nuisances and bothersome.

Since aristocratic women such as Hawise of Aumale had been among the victims of John's most egregious abuses, Magna Carta took a passing interest in their affairs. Widows' rights were carefully spelled out by clauses 7 and 8: a widow was to have 'her marriage portion and inheritance at once and without trouble' and the king was no longer allowed to demand a fine to allow her to inherit what was rightfully hers from her marriage. She had the right to remain in her marital home for forty days after her husband's death, and 'no widow shall be compelled to marry, so long as she wishes to remain without a husband.' However, as we have seen, clause 54 of the charter severely limited women's rights with regard to the criminal law. 'No one shall be arrested or imprisoned on the appeal of a woman for the death of any person except her husband.' Even here it could not have been clearer that women were persons defined almost entirely and solely according to a man, be it a father, brother or the one who had seen fit to marry them.

Certainly, Magna Carta did not herald any great female emancipation, as one small example from a generation after 1215 suggests. In 1244 royal judges visited London and scores of citizens were summoned before them to answer accusations of criminality, or simply to provide information about recent deaths in the city. Towards the end of the proceedings, a woman called Isabel, wife of Serlo, appeared before the judges and alleged that a man called William Bertone had come into her house at Easter 1242 and 'beaten and ill-treated her' so that she had given birth prematurely to a stillborn, malformed male child. The city sheriffs were asked if they had seen any evidence of this, and said that they hadn't, but another royal official testified 'that he saw [the baby] with its head crushed and its left arm broken in two places and its whole body blackened by that beating'. William then came to the court and denied having anything to do with it. It was her word against his.

During the thirteenth century there were several means of determining guilt in a case where there were no witnesses. Yet the ordeal had now been condemned by the Church, and trial by combat would plainly have been unsuitable here. So the court settled on a method called compurgation, which involved the accused getting together a given number of citizens of good standing, and having them swear to his innocence.

That is what William Bertone agreed to do and a week or so later he came back to court to 'defend himself thirty-six-handed, eighteen compurgators being chosen from one side of the Walbrook and eighteen from the other side'. (The Walbrook was the ancient river that divided the city of London north to south – it no longer flowed, having silted up, but it was still a symbolic line through the city.) With the mayor and the aldermen of London before him, and Isabel facing him, William swore 'he had never beaten Isabel so that the child of which she had been prematurely delivered was nearer to death and further from life'. Then six of his compurgators swore 'that to the best of their knowledge his oath was a true one'. William then swore his oath again – and so did a further six of his compurgators, and so on. After everyone had sworn their oaths, the court made its judgment. William had proven himself innocent. Isabel, meanwhile, for making a false accusation, was carted off to jail.[214]

✝

The first task of almost every wife was to provide her husband with children. (Failure to do so could bring problems: John's childless marriage to Isabel of Gloucester was annulled at the time of his accession.) It used to be thought that the concept of childhood did not exist in the middle ages as it does today.[215] But in 1215 there was a clear distinction between those who were adult and those who had not yet become so. Children could not or did not make confession to a priest, take communion, enter into a fully binding marriage or pay church taxes. Neither, in law, could they hold land in their own right – which was one of the most important issues dealt with in Magna Carta, in clauses such as clause 4 and 5, which concerned reliefs and wardship. The age at which childhood ended was not entirely simple – children were deemed to pass into maturity at different ages in different areas of life. Infancy ended at seven; childhood at fourteen. Adolescence could be interpreted in some cases as lasting until the age of twenty-eight.

Since child mortality was high, babies were mostly baptized on the day of their birth – or as soon as possible. It was a sin, punishable with penance and a fine, to let a child die unbaptized: the souls of such infants were later portrayed by Dante as being trapped in limbo along with the virtuous pagans of antiquity. Those who lived were cared for by their mother (or a wet nurse for the upper classes) for their early years, after which they tended to follow one parent – boys watching and copying their father's work outdoors and girls remaining in the household with their mother.

Children played and bathed, enjoyed toys like whipping tops, skittles and dolls, and learned nursery rhymes and songs. Even if they did not take school lessons, all were still expected to know basic prayers including the Paternoster, the Creed and the Ave Maria in English. Children of wealthier parents would and did learn very much more, up to and beyond full literacy for those destined for life in the Church. From around the age of seven, though, peasant children would be helping with adult work, while noble boys were sent to the households of other barons to learn the business of lordship. At the same age, children could be betrothed. By twelve (for girls) or fourteen (for boys), they were ready to marry. Childhood was nearly over.

7

England under Siege

The first the English knew of the shipwreck was when the soldiers' bodies washed up on the beaches. The men came first: knights and their companions who had until recently been living in Flanders were now thrown up on a foreign shore by the cold lap of the North Sea, which had carried them to Great Yarmouth, the formidable walled town famous for its herring trade, a few miles to the east of Norwich. Behind them came the corpses of their families: women and children had been piled onto the boats with the promise of a new life and fortune. Their hopes had been violently dashed.

The soldiers had been recruited by Hugh de Boves, one of John's most experienced military contractors. Described by the incorrigibly judgmental Roger of Wendover as 'a brave knight but a proud and unjust man' (and loathed by at least one other chronicler, the Dunstable Annalist), Boves had been sent to north-west Europe to help raise an army with which John could strike back against his rebel barons.[216] For the most part the recruiters had succeeded: convoys of troop carriers had been arriving in Dover from the continent for days, and John had been present in the town to watch his hired swords disembark.

But as all sailors knew, an autumn crossing of the Channel carried risks. When gales blew up from September onwards, the lurch of the waves could easily overwhelm vessels better suited to hugging the coastline than venturing into open water.

And that was precisely what had happened. A storm had risen during the crossing, smashing Boves's boats to pieces, and everyone aboard was lost. Boves was one of the many who washed up dead at Great Yarmouth. According to Wendover, 'at each of the ports on that part of the sea coast there was found such a multitude of bodies of men and women that the very air was tainted by their stench'. He wrote of children who had been drowned as they slept in their cradles; once cast into the ocean, the flesh had been nibbled from their little bones by 'the beasts of the sea and the birds of the air'. [217]

When John learned of Boves's death he was said to have flown into one of his temper tantrums. 'He was dreadfully enraged and took no food that day, but remained until the evening as if he were possessed by madness,' wrote Wendover. [218] Still, this was a king quite used to seeing men around him perish and he had more pressing concerns than a few boatloads of dead Flemings. Those who had survived the crossing made up the core of a formidable army, bolstered by fighters from Poitou and Gascony in the south, Louvain and Brabant in the north. By the end of September the time had come for this fierce body of men to mobilize.

The key to controlling England remained the possession of London. Thanks to the continued support of Mayor Serlo, the capital was still in rebel hands, but it was certain John would march on the city as soon as he felt strong enough to do so. The king's mercenary army was growing larger and more dangerous every day. By the end of September the barons decided to stall him by occupying the best-defended stronghold between London and Dover: Rochester Castle. The battle for control of this imposing fortress would become one of the most famous sieges of the middle ages.

✝

Castles had been erupting like great craggy molehills across the English landscape ever since the conquering Normans had imported the science of castle-building in 1066. For more than 150 years the castle had been the most important piece of military technology in England. Strict laws set out who could and could not build castles, and laid down the conditions governing which buildings could be crenellated and turned into fortresses. This had been the case since at least the days of Henry I, whose law-code, the *Leges Henrici Primi*, stated that the king had 'jurisdictional rights ... in his land solely and over all men ... [over] fortifications consisting of three walls', and that 'construction of fortifications without permission' was an offence that would 'place a man in the king's mercy'.[219] Kings and barons paid dizzying amounts to erect and maintain these fortresses: Dover Castle, one of the finest and most formidable in the realm, had gobbled up £7,000 of royal expenditure over the eleven years it took to build.*

---

* Spending £7,000 on a public capital project like Dover Castle in the thirteenth century would be the equivalent of spending at least £1.7 billion ($2.7 billion) today. This value represents the *relative economic cost*, according to measuringworth.com.

Men who knew how to put up a strong castle were known in the records as *ingeniator*, or 'engineer', but were likely to have combined the roles of architect and foreman. Maurice the Engineer – also known as Maurice the Mason – was paid a shilling a day to oversee work on Dover Castle and the keep at Newcastle-upon-Tyne in the 1170s. Fortinus the Engineer was paid in clothes: he earned a robe in 1203–4 for helping to repair Colchester Castle for the king. The best engineers could remain in royal service for generations. John had inherited from his father and brother the services of Master Elias of Oxford, who had built or renovated everything from royal houses and hunting lodges to the Tower of London. Castles were an indispensible tool of kingship, and the men who made them were highly prized.[220]

Ever since Henry II, successive Plantagenet kings had sought to increase the number and strength of the castles under royal control. Some were built from scratch. Others were repaired or refortified. Many more were simply seized from their owners. From the time of the great war of 1173–4, when large numbers of castles were taken into the king's possession as punishment for rebellion, around fifty percent of the fortresses in England were held by the crown.

John controlled well over one hundred castles in England. They ranged from relatively modest and simple military bases to the huge edifices of Dover, Corfe, Odiham, Kenilworth and the Tower of London. He spent vast sums on improving his castles, particularly in the frontier regions of the south-east, the Welsh marches and the northern borders with Scotland. He invested £2,000 in Scarborough, and more than £1,000 in Kenilworth, Knaresborough and Odiham. Castle-building was at times the greatest single cost that the crown's revenues had to bear.[221] To John, as to his brother and father, the massive expense was more than just a matter of bravado and status. Castles were the hard currency of politics. They served as royal houses, prisons, treasure-stores, garrisons and centres of local government. To possess a castle was to control the area around it, and to hold a castle with the king's permission was a mark of royal favour. To hold a castle against the king was an outright declaration of war.

Who exactly had the right to keep Rochester Castle was a matter of some disagreement. It had been erected for the king by Gundulf, bishop of Rochester, between 1087 and 1089 in lieu of payment of a debt, and it consisted, like most castles of its age, of a huge, squat, rectangular stone keep surrounded by powerful walls and an 'outer bailey': a well-defended area containing outhouses, workshops, servants' quarters and animal sheds. The walls were built from the local hard blue-grey Kentish limestone known as ragstone. Like any good castle, Rochester was well situated: set inside a curve of the river Medway, and further protected to the south by a hill and to the north and east by a ditch.

More significant than any of this, however, was the matter of Rochester's custody. In 1127 Henry I had granted it to the archbishop of Canterbury, William de Corbeil, and a condition of the gift was that it would remain in the custody of his official successors in perpetuity.[222] Thus it had come into the keeping of Archbishop Stephen Langton, who had arranged for it to be maintained day-to-day by Reginald Cornhill, sheriff of Kent. Since 9 August John had been trying to arrange for the castle's transfer to one of his own followers, Peter des Roches, bishop of Winchester. But Langton, increasingly unable to hold his neutrality in the war between king and country, had resisted, and the matter was unresolved when the archbishop left England for Rome in mid-September, heading for the Fourth Lateran Council, Innocent III's grand ecumenical gathering to which almost every major churchman in Christendom had been summoned. The matter of the castle therefore rested with Sheriff Cornhill, and by the early autumn Cornhill had decided to throw his lot – and Rochester Castle – in with the rebels.

In the second week of October a force estimated between ninety and 140 knights had poured out of London in the direction of Rochester. They were led by William d'Aubigny, Lord of Belvoir (pronounced 'Beaver') in Leicestershire, one of the council of twenty-five barons that had been named to enforce Magna Carta, who was also, according to Wendover, 'a man bold and tried in war'. They could scarcely have hoped for a better commander. D'Aubigny knew castles inside out. His own power base at Belvoir Castle was one of the strongest and most dominant in the midlands, and he was highly conversant with the conventions and craft of holding a fortress against an attacking force. Over the weeks that followed, he would exhaust every ounce of his skill and bravery trying to resist the waves of troops sent to reduce Rochester Castle by the indignant king of England.

✝

Besieging a castle was an undertaking theoretically weighted in favour of the besieged. By the early thirteenth century, most English castles were built in stone, not from timber (as had been the case before the Norman Conquest), and could therefore easily resist attack by fire, arrows, crossbow bolts, stones, spears, axes and almost every other small arms known to the Christian mind. Once a large and well-maintained castle was secured it could be held by a relatively limited number of men for a considerable length of time. Even if the outer walls were breached – itself no easy task – the towering stone keeps that were characteristic of Plantagenet castles were very difficult to assail successfully, defended as they were with ditches, thick-walled towers and tiny window slits from which missiles and arrows could easily be aimed but through which they could seldom be succesfully returned. The lowest doors on castle keeps were usually on the first floor, rather than at ground level. When a castle came under attack its defenders would simply haul up or even burn the wooden ladder that gave access to the door, so that it could neither be stormed nor battered down with a ram.* Stones, arrows, boiling liquid and red-hot sand could be tipped onto the heads of attackers, making any attempt to scale a castle's defences using ladders or scaffolds very dangerous. All of this meant that, more often than

---

* See, for example, the great square keep at Dover Castle, ninety-five feet in height, with a splayed base and original entrances on the first and second floors. Dover was constructed in the 1180s by Henry II and was subsequently improved by John.

not, a castle would fall to a siege not because its defences failed but because the will, the health or the stomachs of the defenders gave out first.

In autumn 1215 Rochester Castle was garrisoned by a relatively large band of knights, accompanied by their attendants and retinues.[223] This was a far greater defending force than the thirteen men who would manage the following year to hold off for eight days an attack on Odiham Castle in Hampshire. Yet the number of men inside Rochester was not necessarily helpful to its defence. When d'Aubigny and his men dashed into the castle they found it 'destitute not only of arms and provisions, but also of every kind of property'. Wendover, who clearly admired d'Aubigny, wrote that the rebels immediately lost heart and wanted to abandon the castle, but were dissuaded by their leader, who warned them of the chivalric humiliation that they would draw down upon themselves if they were to be thought of as 'knights-deserters'.[224] A scramble for supplies took place in which the town of Rochester was thoroughly plundered, but there was 'no time left for them to collect booty in the country around'. There were, in other words, many mouths inside the great square-towered keep of the castle, and perilously little with which to feed them. And John, with his army of mercenaries, was on his way.

The road between Dover, where John was based, and Rochester, where the rebels were frantically rounding up food and provisions, was known as Watling Street and had originally been built to move Roman armies about the country. According to Wendover, it took John's army – now an 'immense multitude of knights and soliders, [which struck] all who beheld them with fear and dismay' – just three days to decamp from the south coast and lay Rochester Castle under siege.[225] It was a daunting sight. Besides a large number of trained soldiers, including crossbowmen 'who thirsted for nothing more than human blood', the royal army brought with it large siege engines, including what Wendover called *petrariae* or stone-throwers: large catapults for hurling rocks.* These were set up within range of the castle and went to work; John 'severely annoyed the besieged by incessant showers of stones and other weapons'.[226] The dust and the noise generated as lumps of rubble smashed into the sides of the fortress would have been mightily impressive.

Siege warfare was the most important form of conflict in the middle ages, from western Europe to the frontiers of China and Mongolia. Whereas pitched battles were dreadfully uncertain affairs, as John had found to his cost at Bouvines the previous year, sieges were regular and somewhat

---

* Terms for medieval catapults were varied and vague, but there seem to have been several types in use. A trebuchet had a pivoted hurling-arm which was powered by a counterweight: modern tests have shown that a trebuchet with a one-ton counterweight could sling a fifteen-kilogram lump of rubble between 120 and 180 metres, with the accuracy of a mortar. (See P. V. Hansen, 'Reconstructing a Medieval Trebuchet', *Military History Illustrated Past and Present* 27, 1990.) A ballista was a giant crossbow powered by a winch. A mangonel threw stones, which were released from a fixed wooden throwing arm when it was hauled back then released to hit a cross-beam. These catapults were often given scary names, such as 'God's Stone Thrower', 'Malcousin', 'The Furious' and – in the case of the infamous catapult owned by John's grandson Edward I – 'Warwolf'. They had changed little in design since Roman times, as a glance at Vegetius shows: Flavius Vegetius Renatus, *De Re Militari*, 66.

more predictable. They proceeded according to centuries of military science and were governed (or semi-governed, at any rate) by a code of chivalric conduct, under which deals could be struck between besiegers and besieged to determine the terms of engagement. Pre-siege agreements would typically state the length of time that a siege would be held, in hope of relief, before the garrison either formally surrendered – to be treated with mercy – or else held out until it was stormed and slaughtered. The wisdom that informed the conduct of siege warfare in Europe dated from classical times, and writings such as those of the military engineer Vitruvius in the first century BC and the Roman Vegetius in the fourth century AD were collected and studied in the courts and royal libraries of medieval Europe.*

The fact that sieges were scientific and partially rule-bound, however, did not mean that they were civilized. Fierce and ingenious tools and tactics were employed on both sides and famous sieges tended to produce infamous tales of the ghastly privations inflicted on attackers and defenders alike. It was said that at the siege of Constantinople in 717–18, the Arab besiegers had been in such a sorry condition that they had been forced to eat human flesh and human faeces, pounded together into patties and cooked.[227] Perhaps this was a symbolic exaggeration designed to invoke the horror rather than the actuality of the siege, but similarly vile stories

* The Bibliothèque Nationale in Paris contains twenty manuscript editions of Vegetius's writings made in the eleventh and twelfth centuries. That there was a direct intellectual link between Roman and medieval siege warfare is beyond doubt. See J. Bradbury, *The Medieval Siege* (Woodbridge, 1992), 3–4.

abounded in history. Vikings besieging Chester in 918 had been driven back when defenders dropped boiling ale and water on the attackers and threw live beehives at them, so that their skin blistered and peeled from their flesh, and their hands and feet swelled up with painful stings. John's grandfather, Geoffrey Plantagenet, count of Anjou, was said to have created the legendary potion known as Greek Fire by mixing together nut oil and hemp flax, which he blasted from a catapult when he was attacking a castle at Montreuil-Bellay on the frontiers between Anjou and Maine. The great twelfth-century Holy Roman Emperor Frederick Barbarossa was especially adept at siege terror tactics: his troops were said to have played football with their enemies' severed heads and tortured captured defenders by scalping them or cutting off their hands and feet, to provide amusement and relief from the boredom that naturally accompanied such an attritional method of warfare.

Cruel and unusual devices were deployed to try and break sieges: beyond the conventional siege engines such as ladders, scaling towers, belfries, battering rams and catapults, there was a degree of biological and psychological warfare that could sink to great depravity. Rotting corpses – animal and human – were flung into castles to weaken morale, or dunked into water sources to spread disease. During sieges in which non-combatants had been ejected from the castle or town in order to reduce hungry mouths among the defenders, it was deemed perfectly acceptable under the rules of war for the besieging army to trap the unarmed civilians in no-man's-land, within view of the castle, and allow them to starve to death. Taunting, torment and creative displays of despicable cruelty were all used to grind down the minds and wills of those behind the walls and encourage them to give up as quickly as possible.

Even when the violence was not grotesque, siege sites were awful places for both sides, cursed by sickness and starvation. John's brother Richard had died at the siege of Châlus-Chabrol in 1199, after he was hit by a crossbow bolt fired from the parapets by a defender using a kitchen frying pan as a shield. Both John's men and the barons barricaded inside Rochester would have known, therefore, that what lay ahead was a dangerous and potentially deadly encounter.

'Our age has not known a siege so hard pressed nor so strongly resisted,' wrote the Crowland Chronicler.[228] For several days John's catapults pounded the walls of the castle, while archers and crossbowmen sent up a hail of arrows and bolts, but it soon became obvious that the fortifications were too strong simply to be smashed down with missiles. (There was a small irony here: John himself had provided £115 early in his reign to improve Rochester's defences when it had briefly been in royal hands.) On 14 October the king sent a writ to the nearby town of Canterbury demanding that his officials there saw to the production 'by day and night of as many picks [i.e. pickaxes] as you are able'. If the walls could not be knocked down, then they would have to be attacked from below. This was bad news for d'Aubigny and the garrison. Undermining – tunnelling under the walls of a fortress – was not likely to be a swift process, no matter how many picks the reeves of Canterbury managed to send.

Their best hope for a rapid end to the siege was going to be relief from outside.

On 26 October an armed band of barons rode out of London in the direction of Rochester intending to distract John's forces. The sortie included seven hundred horse – a substantial relieving party – but they got no closer than Deptford, twenty-five miles from Rochester, before they heard that John, whose numbers were far greater, was preparing to head them off. It was not a battle that the rebel leadership was inclined to fight, so – despite the fact that they had apparently sworn an oath to assist the garrison – they turned tail, scuttled back to London and hoped for the best. To Roger of Wendover, this was nothing short of cowardice. 'They turned their backs on the beseiged William and his followers and returned to their old haunt,' he wrote. Safe in London, the chronicler continued (probably fancifully), 'amusing themselves with the dangerous game of dice, drinking the best wines which they chose at their own option, and practising all other vices, they left their besieged companions at Rochester exposed to the danger of death, and enduring all kinds of misery.'[229] John worked his crossbowmen and catapult operators in shifts to keep up the bombardment around the clock, while d'Aubigny's followers defiantly threw back the rocks with which they were being assailed. Beneath the clatter of rubble against masonry, one could have heard the quieter but deadlier sound of picks and shovels cutting through the Kentish soil, inching their way beneath the fortress.

Sapping was a highly potent, if perilous, means of breaking a siege. It required men to dig tunnels below the walls of the castle, weakening the defences at the foundations. When the tunnel was big enough it was deliberately collapsed, in the hope that it would bring down a portion of the fortress with it. This could be an effective technique, even if it carried the unpleasant risk of the tunnel collapsing prematurely and crushing the miners or burying them alive. John himself had experienced the unwelcome results of skilled sapping in 1203–4, when Chateau Gaillard – the greatest Plantagenet castle on the banks of the Seine in Normandy, built by his brother Richard to be impervious to attack – had partially collapsed and ultimately been lost to the French thanks to the efforts of miners working close to the base of the walls, protected from bombardment by a sow, a large, moveable wooden shield.* During the course of the middle ages mining and countermining would become fine arts, and castle defences would stretch below the ground to include tunnels built to intercept offensive sappers, who could be fought off hand-to-hand if necessary.† At Rochester in 1215, however, the defenders had no way of keeping King John's tunnellers at bay.

The area of the castle that both artillery and diggers were targeting was the south-east corner, where the keep was positioned close by the castle's surrounding curtain wall. At some point, probably at the very end of October or the start

* The image intended was of a large mother pig protecting her suckling piglets, the miners, beneath her belly. Sows were also known as cats or weasels.

† Visitors to the medieval tunnels beneath Dover Castle can still see evidence of this aspect of subterranean warfare.

of November, the relentless assault from above and below succeeded in punching a hole through that wall. This was a significant achievement, testament to the effort and manpower John had devoted to the task. It meant that the royal forces now had access to the bailey. Still, there remained the matter of the keep itself, 150 feet high, rugged and thick, into which the garrison was now firmly backed. There was still plenty of work for John's men to do before they could hope to break in. Yet if there was one thing that the king of England never lacked, it was determination. He commanded his miners to keep digging.

And so they dug. Evidently they moved at a good rate, because on 25 November John sent a writ to Hubert de Burgh, his justiciar and loyal servant, asking him for a rather unusual service. He demanded that Hubert 'send to us with all speed by day and night forty of the fattest pigs of the sort least good for eating to bring fire underneath the tower'. This could only mean one thing: the tunnel below the south-east corner of the keep was considered to be deep enough to do its job. The shaft was ready to fall in – and with it, John hoped, one of the four towers, which was now held up only by the wooden struts inserted by the sappers.

Pig fat melts at around 45°C, smokes at around 120°C and ignites spontaneously when its temperature climbs up near 300°C. With the fat of forty pigs smeared all over the wooden struts of John's mine, it would have been a fairly straightforward matter to create a blistering fire beneath the south-east corner of Rochester's keep. This must have been a peculiarly disquieting experience for the hungry garrison inside, who by this point, according to Wendover, had been reduced to eating the flesh of their warhorses.[230] The scent of wood smoke mixed first with the fragrance of roasting bacon, followed soon after by the acrid tang of burning lard. This would presumably have been followed by a pause in the bombardment as the attackers watched eagerly to see whether their many weeks of mining had been successful; and finally, fatefully, the awful thundering sound of falling masonry. For when John's infernal mine collapsed, it took down a large chunk of the south-east tower. The attackers rushed the hole in the wall, and d'Aubigny's men were forced to scramble a retreat to the very last possible place of safety left to them.

The structure of Rochester's keep was such that a strong internal wall divided the building in two, which made it possible to seal off half of the rooms. Now a small rearguard from among the garrison took cover behind this wall. There was not room for everyone, however, so those who were thought to be the weakest were thrown out to the mercy of the king's men, who apparently treated them very badly indeed, cutting off their arms and legs for sport. Everyone realised that this was the end: according to Wendover the garrison knew that their choice was either to come out, gambling that the king would spare their lives, or remain where they were, secure behind a stone wall but certain to run out of food. Within days – or possibly hours – of the south-east wall falling, the remainder of the rebels packed behind the dividing wall made their decision. On 30 November they held counsel, where they agreed 'it would be a disgrace ... to die of hunger when they could not be conquered in battle'. Thus resolved, they came out from their final bolthole, bedraggled and undernourished, and surrendered themselves and what remained of their broken hideout to a triumphant, but extremely angry, King John.

The siege of Rochester Castle had lasted nearly two months. That it had gone on as long as it did was a testament to the fortitude of the rebel barons who had held it, allowing London and other strategically important parts of the southeast to be secured against the king. That it had been broken so comprehensively was a testament to the fixity of purpose that drove John as he fought to recover from his humiliations. The king was sufficiently riled by the difficulty to which he had been put that he wanted all the nobles strung up on the gibbet. In the end, however, calmer voices persuaded him that this would increase the chances of his own garrisons being dealt with badly when circumstances were reversed. In any case, the rules of war frowned upon massacring captives who had surrendered rather than being taken by force, and even if John's men had mined their way to the heart of the keep, it had still been the choice of d'Aubigny's garrison to give themselves up, in the expectation of being shown mercy. Presumably somewhat disgruntled by this anticlimax, John allowed his enemies to live – although he did not stretch to granting them freedom. D'Aubigny and his fellow noblemen were packed off to 'close custody' in the king's notorious dungeons at Corfe Castle. A few others – Wendover names them as Robert de Chaurn, Richard Giffard and Thomas of Lincoln – were kept by John's side.[231]

They joined the royal court as it finally moved away from the smouldering ruins of Rochester, heading north to the midlands, where the king would celebrate Christmas at Nottingham.

Birds, beasts ... and bloodsports

The relationship between man and animal in Plantagenet England was close and sometimes bloody. In a practical sense, animals provided transport, food, clothing and the power that drove agriculture. They were also the predators and the prey for hunting and bloodsports, both of which were keenly enjoyed by the European upper classes in this age. As pets they could be beloved companions. And on a psychological level, animals were also the stuff of deep human fascination – the subjects of myths, allegories and fables, the icons drawn on great families' coats of arms, and the inspiration for strange doodles that can be found littering the margins of medieval manuscripts.

The most common domesticated animal in medieval England was the sheep. The Domesday survey suggests that in the late eleventh century sheep made up as much as seventy-five percent of English livestock, and that number seems to have changed little by the early thirteenth century. Next came cattle, followed by goats and pigs. All of these creatures provided milk, meat or both, but only sheep supplied the wool that was a staple of the English economy. The booming cloth trade based across the North Sea in Flanders relied heavily on English wool exports; there was also a healthy homespun textile business, in which raw wool was spun into yarn, woven into cloth, fulled (i.e. soaked, cleaned and beaten to remove dirt and natural oils, and felted) and dyed to produce a finished product which was then sold at market. All of this depended on families up and down England tending large flocks of sheep, amounting to millions of animals in total.

Yet if sheep were plentiful, their importance was rivalled by an animal that existed in far smaller numbers. The most prestigious and indispensable beast, to kings, barons and knights at least, was the horse. Horses were the basic means of transport and an essential part of farming. Travelling on foot in 1215 was painfully slow, whereas a man on horseback could cover at least two dozen miles a day – longer if he changed his mount and travelled by stages. For the lower orders who worked the land and the upper classes who owned it, the horse was becoming a vital beast of burden for drawing goods and hauling the plough. It is no exaggeration to say that without horsepower, England's economy would have been nowhere near as sophisticated or productive as it was.*

* There was, however, still an important place for oxen in medieval agriculture. A generation after 1215 the monastic writer Bartholomew the Englishman, who lived and worked in Paris and Magdeburg, wrote about oxen and their herdsmen in his compendium known as *De proprietatibus rerum*, describing how a

It was not just in peacetime that horses were valuable. The strongest and fastest were the principal vehicles for military assault: a heavily armed knight on horseback was the thirteenth-century equivalent of a tank, and could wreak terrible damage when deployed against foot-soldiers. The wealthiest military men rode warhorses, which were classified as destriers (large, strong and best suited to jousting), coursers (swift and agile, so useful in battle) and rounceys (all-purpose horses well suited to pursuit, which could also be used as packhorses). A palfrey was a smaller, smooth-gaited horse suitable for everyday riding by both men and women. Smaller, stockier horses could be employed as packhorses or sumpters to carry baggage, or carthorses.

Besides horses, some of the most highly valued beasts in England were predators – primarily birds of prey and dogs. Hunting verged on an obsession for the early Plantagenet kings and their companions, and the popularity of the chase in the early thirteenth century was evident from the fact that writers had begun to produce practical hunting manuals, detailing the best ways to pursue game. According to a manual by Gaston Fébus, count of Foix, dating from the early fourteenth century, the principal game animals were red deer, roe deer, fallow deer and reindeer, wild goats, hares, rabbits, bears, wild boars, wolves, foxes, badgers, wild cats and

---

good oxherd was able to whistle and sing sweetly to his beasts, in order to persuade them to bear the yoke and pull the plough in straight and even lines.

otters – these being, according to Fébus, the only animals that dogs would willingly pursue.[32] The Holy Roman Emperor Frederick II, who took the imperial crown in 1220, would himself write an astonishingly detailed and scientific guide to falconry, entitled *De arte venandi cum avibus* ('The art of hunting with birds'), which describes in detail the habits and physiology of hunting birds and the methods best employed to train and fly them against their prey.

King John never produced any such text, but it was not for want of enthusiasm for the chase. He owned hundreds of dogs, including greyhounds and bloodhounds, which were kept at his houses and castles up and down England, so that he could hunt wherever he rested. Besides his dogs John was, like Frederick II, extremely concerned for the welfare of his birds. He kept falcons and hawks, which were trained to fight and bring down game birds, including duck, heron and crane. Indeed, the king's passion for hunting can be detected behind several clauses of Magna Carta. Game birds generally fed, nested and lived near riverbanks, and John's habit of fencing off watersides and designating them as his personal hunting grounds was a major cause of irritation to his subjects. Clauses 47 and 48 of the charter committed the king to restoring the free status of riverbanks he had enclosed, and investigating abuses by his officers that had taken place besides the water.

Not all dogs, of course, were bred for hunting, and ladies might keep lapdogs to amuse themselves. As for cats, archaeologists have found that by 1215 they were kept as domestic animals – and had been for around two hundred years. But the life of a cat was not that of a pampered companion: mostly they were kept as mousers, and expected to live off their catches. They also had to have their wits about them. Cats were not regarded as human food – the fact that they ate other animals made them as taboo as carrion-feeding birds – but cat fur was a cheap luxury, which social convention permitted the lower orders to wear. Good-looking cats were very often caught and killed for their skins.[233]

✛

Thirteenth-century Englishmen and women delighted in games and contests, and plenty of these involved animals in one way or another. For the baronial and knightly classes competition was designed to nurture the skills needed in war, and it found its manifestation in the tournament: a free-for-all sparring session contested between highly trained military men, all aiming to prove their superior horsemanship and combat skills. The tournament is a staple of modern fiction and film imagining the middle ages. Tournaments in 1215, however, were much rougher than the ritualized pageants they had become by the fifteenth and sixteenth centuries. In the age of Magna Carta a tournament was contested by teams gathered on large areas of open countryside – the field of competition might be a dozen or more miles across. Galloping across this land, knights competed to seize one another's horses and persons, which would, respectively, be confiscated by the winner or released on payment of a ransom. The losses could be spectacular, but so could the gains: William Marshal's youthful talent as a tournament knight was the basis for his wealth and political career in later life.

The lower classes would generally have encountered the hunt or the tournament as bystanders, but they had their own rough-and-ready versions of the most popular elite sports. Becket's biographer William Fitzstephen described the numerous sporting pastimes popular in London.[34] To visit Smithfield on a Sunday in Lent, he wrote, was to see 'a swarm of young men' riding their horses in races around a circular course and tilting at each other with blunted lances. 'On feast-days throughout the summer the young men indulge in the sports of archery, running, jumping, wrestling, slinging the stone, hurling the javelin beyond a mark and fighting with the sword and buckler,' wrote Fitzstephen, who mentioned games of football being played by each of the schools in London as well as the trading guilds. We also hear of cocks, bulls, boars and bears being baited into fighting one another for popular entertainment, and of citizens 'sporting with birds of the air, with hawks, falcons and such-like, and with hounds that hunt their prey in the woods'.

Even when animals were not directly involved, the sports enjoyed by ordinary people were militarily influenced. Fitzstephen described Londoners fighting one another while standing on the sterns of small boats below London Bridge, racing along with the current and aiming to strike a fixed wooden shield with the tip of a lance. When the marshland to the north of the city froze over in winter, young men made ice-skates out of animals' shin-bones and raced out to play on it. The braver among them would take part in ice-jousting, tilting against each other with lances. Bones were frequently broken, wrote Fitzstephen, 'and wherever the ice comes into contact with their heads, it scrapes off the skin utterly.'

✟

The thirteenth-century interest in animals was not wholly restricted to harnessing their labour or slaughtering them. Zoology was exotic and interesting in and of itself and John's reign saw the beginning of the use of the Tower of London as a royal menagerie. Henry I had kept an animal collection including lions, tigers, camels and porcupines at the royal house at Woodstock in Oxfordshire, but the establishment of the royal zoo at the Tower was significant, and it would last for more than six hundred years. From 1210 the Tower was home to several lions – appropriate to the house of Plantagenet, which bore three on its arms. A bestiary compiled around the time lions arrived in London explained what visitors to the Tower may have thought about them. Lions, it argued, exhibited the same ideal traits as human kings: ferocity tempered with mercy. 'The merciful nature of lions is confirmed by numerous examples,' wrote the author. 'They will spare men lying on the ground, and will lead captives whom they meet to their home. They will attack men rather than women. They only kill children if they are exceptionally hungry.'[235]

This seems more an allegorical than a literal description of a lion. Yet it is not as strange as some other medieval notions about animals. According to the same bestiary, beavers would bite off their own testicles when pursued, since they knew that humans valued them for medicinal use. A tigress could be deceived by throwing down a glass sphere, which the beast would confuse with its own cub and attempt to suckle. A panther's breath was so sweet that it enticed every animal on earth to follow it – except for dragons, who detested the smell and would hide. A hungry fox would smear its own belly in red earth and lie motionless, imitating carrion, until birds swooped down to peck at it, whereupon it would leap into life and devour them.

It is probably fair to say that the most exotic beasts of the age lived not in royal menageries but in the imagination of chroniclers. According to the Crowland Chronicler, the year before 1215 was notable for the appearance and capture in England of 'fish of strange forms' (*pisces insolatae formae*).[236] The pattern of their scales made them look as if they were armed with shields and helmets, like soldiers. Gerald of Wales travelled to the ends of the British Isles and beyond, and wrote of the many peculiarly behaved creatures he encountered. In his *History and Topography of Ireland* he recounted that 'I saw in Paris a lion which a cardinal had given when it was a whelp to [Philip Augustus]. This lion used to make beastly love to a foolish woman called Johanna.' According to Gerald, if the lion escaped from its cage it could only be calmed by this Johanna, using 'a woman's tricks'. Gerald also observed in Ireland a goat, 'remarkable for ... the length of its coat and height of its horns', which belonged to Ruaidri, king of Connacht. This goat behaved, if we believe Gerald, in the same way as Philip Augustus's lion, since it 'had bestial intercourse with a certain ... wretched woman'. Despite Gerald's obvious relish in these tales, he was careful to insert in each of his accounts heavy-handed assertions of his own disapproval. 'How unworthy and unspeakable!' he wrote of the Connacht goat. He thought it appropriate that the Parisian lion should be put to death, 'not for the guilt ... but to make the remembrance of the act a deterrent.'

13. The round tower of Rochester Castle, seen here in the foreground, was rebuilt after John destroyed the square-sided original, using a mine brought down with blazing pig-fat.

14. The tomb effigy of William Marshal – self-made knight, loyal baron and canny politician – at the Temple Church in London. His thirteenth-century biography tells us much about his life and times.

15. Eustache the Monk – pirate and soldier of fortune – was killed at the sea-battle of Sandwich in 1217. Unlike the (later and fictional) Robin Hood, Eustache was a real-life outlaw from the age of King John.

16. The Fourth Lateran Council of November 1215 was attended by more than 1000 churchmen. Its decrees would have a profound impact on the lives of millions of people, and would have seemed far more significant at the time than Magna Carta.

17. Archbishop Hubert Walter's gold mitre, found in his tomb at Canterbury, suggests the dazzling splendour of the thirteenth-century English Church.

18. The tomb effigy of King John at Worcester Cathedral. John was buried with a monk's cowl on his head and a sword by his side.

19. Tasting the wine for quality? Or siphoning off extra rations? Monastic life was supposed to be serious and austere, but not all monks met its high standards.

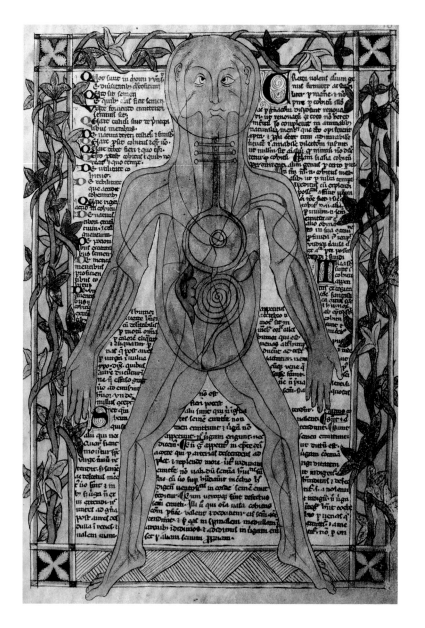

20 and 21. Medicine in the thirteenth century: *left*, a diagram showing the veins and flow of blood through the body; *right*, a surgeon operating on a man's eye and nose.

22. Horses were extremely valuable and needed careful attention, including regular re-shoeing.

23. A self-portrait of Matthew Paris from his *Historia Anglorum*. Monastic chroniclers left some of the most vivid, if sometimes skewed, accounts of Plantagenet England.

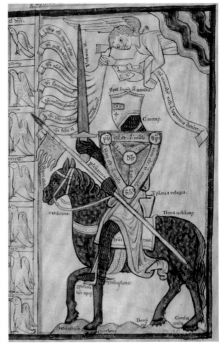

24. Chivalry in action: a heavily armoured knight on horseback has the virtues bestowed on him from Heaven.

25. Students listen attentively to their teacher. Medieval Europe had a thriving intellectual culture.

26. Dogs were highly prized animals, useful for tending sheep, hunting stags and hares, and guarding or avenging their masters.

lnid animal est imilo flumo qd
dicitur hydrus. phisiologus dicit
de eo quod satis est hoc animal inimicu
cocodrillo. & hanc habet naturam z con
suetudinem. bum uidet cocodrillum
in littoribus fluminis dormientem apto
ore uadit z inuoluit se in limum luci qd
possit facilius illabi in faucibus eius. co
codrillus igitur de subito excitatus uiuu
transgluttit eum. Ille autem dilanians
omnia uiscera eius per minus. exinseri
but eius. Sic ergo mors & infernus figura
habent cocodrilli. qui inimicus est domi

27. The thirteenth-century imagination conjured even more
extraordinary beasts than the natural world could provide.

8

'There Is No God'

It had been expensive and frustrating to keep an army of foreign troops and mercenaries in front of Rochester Castle for nearly two months, and in the weeks that followed the castle's collapse, John let his soldiers off the leash. They went plundering. Plenty of damage had been done to the area around Rochester during the siege. Now, as Christmas approached, the king gave his troops permission to expand their locus of terror far across the country.

This was bold. Then again, things certainly seemed to be going John's way. Bringing down Rochester was a huge military achievement and the barons' attempts to entice Louis to offer himself as a rival king had thus far come to little. Although Saer de Quincy and Henry de Bohun, earl of Hereford, had gone to France to urge the prince to make haste, Louis had only sent 140 knights to London, and otherwise seemed some way from coming to lead a full invasion in person.

Meanwhile in Rome, John's political case against the rebel barons was growing stronger. By an unholy coincidence, on the very day that Rochester's walls had fallen – 30 November – Pope Innocent III heaped further opprobrium on those who dared to oppose the English king. Innocent had spent the whole of November chairing the Fourth Lateran Council, which had been convoked to rally the Church behind his proposed fifth crusade, though its decrees would ultimately penetrate much deeper into the fabric of Christian life. The council gave Innocent a chance to remain personally involved in the affairs of England, as all but four of the English bishops were in attendance.

The seventy decrees, or canons, of the Fourth Lateran Council – preceded by a statement on the creation, the fall of man and the redeeming promise of belief in the Holy Trinity – offered up a wide-ranging reform of Church life. A council of this kind was at most a once-in-a-generation gathering: the Third Lateran Council had taken place in 1189 and the Fifth would not convene for nearly another three hundred years, in 1512. Innocent had summoned more than a thousand churchmen, including two of the four Church patriarchs, to lend approval to his muscular vision of Christian rejuvenation and to take back to their homelands the message that it was time to muster up a new crusade.

The issues touched upon were many and varied.[237] The Pope's long-running concern with heresy and irregular doctrines was at the fore: the council condemned 'every heresy setting itself up against this holy, orthodox and catholic faith' and threatened excommunication and anathema on 'all heretics whatever names they go under'. Uppermost in Innocent's mind were the Cathar heretics of southern France, against whom he had launched such a ferocious campaign, but heresy and heretical sects were not unknown among the English either.

Walter Map recorded one particularly salacious account of Cathars engaging in bestial orgies at the behest of a master who took the form of a giant black cat, before going on to say: 'To England . . . there have come no more than sixteen, who by order of King Henry II were branded and beaten with rods and have disappeared.'[238] This had taken place in the 1160s, and since then organized English heresy had been notable mainly by its absence. There was, however, a degree of popular scepticism about matters of doctrine. Around 1200 the London-based monk Peter of Cornwall had written that 'there are many people who do not believe that God exists. They consider that the universe . . . is ruled by chance rather than Providence . . . nor do they think that the human soul lives on after the death of the body.'[239] If John had been considering slackening his watch over heresy, the decrees of the Lateran Council might have given him pause: 'If a temporal lord . . . neglects to purge his land of this heretical filth he shall be bound', the document boomed, 'with the bond of excommunication.'

The Fourth Lateran took rigorous action to improve the quality and education of the clergy and had little patience for churchmen who fell into lust, drink or other frivolities. One sternly worded article banned churchmen from keeping their own furniture in holy buildings and condemned 'altar-cloths and communion-cloths so dirty that at times they horrify some people'. Clergy were forbidden to hunt or hawk, or to own hunting dogs or falcons. They were 'not to watch mimes, entertainers and actors', nor to wear fashionable or ornamented clothes. Sexual impropriety among the clergy was to be punished 'according to the rules of canon law', while drunkenness was now to be grounds for suspension from office. The council was especially concerned with drinking games, 'whereby in certain parts drinkers bind each other to drink measure of measure and he in their judgment is most praised who has made most people drunk and drained the deepest cups.'

It is arguable, of course, whether any of this fundamentally changed the reality or perception of a louche clergy: these same sins of pride and wantonness would underpin much of the anticlericalism that lay behind the sixteenth-century Reformation. In other areas of life, however, the Fourth Lateran Council would have a profound and long-lasting effect. Canon 18 stated that:

> no clerk may decree or pronounce a sentence of death; nor may he carry out a punishment which involves blood or be there when it is carried out ... nor shall any clerk write or dictate letters requiring a punishment which involves blood ... also let no clerk be put in command of mercenaries, crossbowmen or suchlike men of blood ... and none is to bestow any blessing or consecration on a purgation by ordeal of boiling water or of cold water or of the red-hot iron.

This brief decree redrew the boundaries between churchmen and the secular powers they served. For generations bishops had been able to ride into battle; now the days of the warrior bishop were numbered. The clergy would still attend battles and sieges – but in the centuries that followed their weapons were to be crucifixes, relics and prayer rather than clubs and maces. As we have seen, trial by ordeal would fall into disuse.

If the Fourth Lateran Council began a process by which the Church withdrew from its central role in determining and administering secular justice, in other areas it pushed Christian doctrine deeper into the lives of ordinary men and women. 'Every Christian of either sex after reaching the years of discretion shall confess all his sins at least once a year privately to his own priest,' read canon 21. After this, all should 'receive with reverence the sacrament of the eucharist at least at Easter'. Confession had become an increasingly important part of popular religious life during the twelfth century, and was encouraged on Maundy Thursday, which was known as the 'day of absolution'. Its inclusion in the decrees of Fourth Lateran emphasized its now central place among the sacraments of the Church. It also bound it closely to the Eucharist. This rite, which joined every single member of Christendom together in the miracle of bread and wine becoming the flesh and blood of Christ, was one of the central pillars of religious culture in the middle ages.[240] A generation after Fourth Lateran, the celebration of the Eucharist gave birth to a new festival: Corpus Christi. By the fourteenth century, Corpus Christi was one of the most important and raucous occasions in the Church calendar, celebrated on the Thursday after Trinity Sunday (a moveable feast falling between mid-May and mid-June) with parades, mystery plays and (ironically) the same orgies of gluttony, drunkenness and vice that the Fourth Lateran Council had taken such care to condemn.

When its conclusions were promulgated across Christendom in December 1215, the full implications of the Fourth Lateran Council were far from understood. According to Roger of Wendover, its articles seemed 'agreeable to some and tedious to others'.[241] But if anyone had been moved to speculate which agreement made that year would have the most long-lasting effect on English society, it is doubtful they would have thought of the short-lived and inconclusive treaty between John and his rebel barons. The peace of Runnymede had rapidly dissolved. Innocent's canons, compiled at comparable length, would have seemed to promise far more important changes.

In the immediate political context, too, events at the Fourth Lateran Council had a sharp effect on England. At the opening of the conference, on 4 November, Innocent confirmed the suspension of Archbishop Stephen Langton from his ecclesiastical duties as punishment for his failure to bring the rebel barons into line over the previous nine months.[242] During the final session the Pope confirmed the excommunication of all the barons of England 'and all who aided them' and sent his verdict back to England to be publicly declared in churches all over the realm on every Sunday and feast day. The sentence was to be accompanied with the ringing of bells. This was only a confirmation of the decisions that the papal legate had promulgated two months earlier, but news that the Pope remained squarely behind him must have been encouraging to John, who could now approach Christmas with confidence that his realm would soon be once more under his control.

✝

On Friday 18 December King John and his retinue arrived at the monastery of St Albans in Hertfordshire to thrash out the next phase in his war against the barons. On Sunday he assembled his followers in the chapter house of the massive, sprawling monastery. The monks were in attendance as the Pope's letters about the suspension of Archbishop Langton and the excommunication of the barons were read aloud. After this the king withdrew, along with his closest advisers, into the abbey cloisters, where, in Roger of Wendover's words, they 'devised plans for overthrowing his enemies, and arranged as to the payment of the foreigners who were fighting under him'.[243]

The plan with which they emerged was strategically simple and tactically pitiless. The royal army would split into two. John would take half his men north. William Longuespée, and John's foreign advisers and military leaders Falkes de Breauté and Savaric of Mauléon would remain in the south. Both halves of the army would 'ravage the whole country with fire and sword'.[244] Despite the counsel of loyalists like William Marshal, who remained with the king but who claimed to be 'sorely grieved by the outrages committed by both sides', this was total war, waged largely by professional soldiers from another land.[245] The prospects for anyone who stood in the way of the royal army were dire.

As word spread that John was about to let his army loose, spirits dipped among the rebels. 'They were downcast,' wrote the Crowland Chronicler. 'And struck with terror they gathered in London or in religious houses. Few now believed in fortresses.'[246] This was hardly surprising: Rochester Castle had been one of the most solid strongholds in England; what hope could there be for anywhere less stoutly defended, should the king appear with his forest of catapults and hordes of sappers bearing pickaxes and pig fat?

No one relished the prospect of facing an army composed predominantly of mercenaries given free rein to do their worst. A generation earlier, Walter Map had written that mercenaries were as depraved as heretics who avoided the mass. Map called them 'routiers', but they were also referred to as Brabançons, since the most bloodthirsty of them were popularly supposed to come from the Low Countries, and particularly from the region of Brabant. (Other good places from which to hire soldiers included Aragon, Navarre, the Basque country and Wales.) A mercenary fought for profit before loyalty, and operated generally outside his country of origin: such a person was assumed to have little regard for the wellbeing of anyone he came across or the customs of the territory he plagued.[247] Walter Map described routiers as 'armed from head to toe with leather, iron, clubs and swords' and accused them of leaving 'monasteries, villages and towns in ashes, and practising indiscriminate adulteries with force, saying with all their heart, "There is no God".'[248]

A church council of 1179 had sentenced mercenaries and all who maintained them to excommunication, for 'they respect neither churches nor monasteries, and spare neither widows, orphans, old or young nor any age or sex, but like pagans destroy and lay everything waste.' This view was shared by many of England's most honoured knights. William Marshal looked very dimly upon John's mercenaries. Not only were they disreputable men, he thought, they were poor allies too. His biography states that in the autumn and winter of 1215 the king's 'foreign knights and soldiers, who every day were set on pillage ... spared hardly a moment's thought on how to advance his cause in war, being bent instead on laying waste his land'.[249]

John instructed his sheriffs and military captains to confiscate lands from rebels and give them to loyalists, first doing 'what should be done to the land of a king's enemy and traitor'.[250] Scores of these ominous orders sped from the king's chancery, licensing his followers all over the country to start helping themselves to enemy land. From St Albans, he then began his journey north to the heart of rebel country. Roger of Wendover provided a vivid description of the damage that he left in his wake. The king, he said:

> spread his troops abroad, burnt the houses and buildings of the barons, robbing them of their goods and cattle, and thus destroying everything that came in his way, he gave a miserable spectacle to all who beheld it. And if the day did not satisfy the malice of the king for the destruction of property, he ordered his incendiaries to set fire to the hedges and towns on his march, that he might refresh his sight with the damage done to his enemies, and by robbery might support the wicked agents of his iniquity.
>
> All the inhabitants of every condition and rank who did not take refuge in a churchyard were made prisoners, and, after being tortured, were compelled to pay a heavy ransom.

The castellans who were in charge of the fortresses of the barons, when they heard of the king's approach, left their castles untenanted and fled to places of secrecy, leaving their provisions and various stores as booty for their approaching enemies; the king placed his own followers in these empty castles, and in this manner marched with his wicked followers to Nottingham.[251]

John reached Nottingham in time for Christmas, and spent several days in the area. According to the Crowland Chronicler he celebrated the festival 'not in the usual manner, but as one on the warpath'. His concerted effort to terrorize his realm showed no sign of abating. England was now in the grip of a war that bore down just as heavily on the ordinary men and women who made up the majority of its population as on the barons who had sparked it. These people were not touched by the promises of the Magna Carta, but they were certainly harmed by its failure.

✝

Most thirteenth-century Englishmen and women were peasants: rural smallholders for whom life was seldom easy. A minority were free men, at liberty to live and work where they chose, permitted to plead in royal courts and perhaps even fortunate enough to accrue enough land to rent some out or to employ their neighbours at busy times of the year. Most, however, were serfs – also known as rustics, villeins or neifs. These people effectively belonged to the lord of their land. As a condition of being allowed to live, eat, farm, marry, raise families and eventually die in peace, they owed the lord months of unpaid manual labour every year. They could not move away from his estate and were at the mercy of his officials. When a father died, his surviving family had to pay heriot – a tax that consisted of the best ox, cow or horse that they possessed. When a daughter married they had to pay the lord a fine called the merchet, and other arbitrary taxes known as tallages might be levied as the lord saw fit throughout the year. Serfs could be bought and sold along with the land on which they lived. They were, effectively, chattels.

Before the Norman Conquest England had maintained a busy trade in slaving – the practice of purchasing or kidnapping villagers and transporting them for sale elsewhere in the realm, particularly to Ireland. This had ceased in the early twelfth century, largely thanks to pressure from the Church. There was a significant difference in the condition of an eleventh-century slave and a thirteenth-century villein, in that a villein was at least associated with a plot of land and had a limited scope to live his life as he wished, even if major restrictions were placed on his freedom. Serfs could not be killed or maimed simply because the lord willed it and were not sold out of their families. But the difference between villeinage and slavery may not always have felt obvious to the persons concerned.

Peasants typically lived in small but sprawling villages the length and breadth of England. Villages were highly dependent on the interaction of neighbours, the benevolence and protection of the lords from whom they held their land, and the vagaries of the weather. Within them one could find a relatively wide range of prosperity. The best-off freemen might hold up to fifty acres, but for most serfs the amount of land they could cultivate varied between five and thirty acres.[252] Below this level families might scratch by on a couple of acres, perhaps even less, being otherwise totally reliant on charity from or employment by their neighbours.

Families dwelt in timber-framed buildings of twenty-five to fifty feet in length and twelve to sixteen feet in width. The best of these were built with walls of stone, clay or cob (a mixture of clay, straw and water) and shared with family members and animals. What the peasant family did to support themselves depended somewhat on the area of the country in which they lived. In much of England sheep-farming was big business. Otherwise, peasants raised crops, both for themselves and on their lord's land, working large fields by digging them in long strips with ploughs drawn behind teams of oxen and sowing corn, wheat, oats or barley in the spring for harvest at the end of the summer. Pigs and cows grazed pasture held in common, while gardens near peasant houses yielded useful domestic crops like onions, leeks, cabbages, peas, beans, parsnips, celery, garlic, parsley, apples, pears, plums, cherries and walnuts. In southern parts there were still occasionally grape vines; English wine was more common then than it is today. For peasants, however, the staple drink was not wine but beer. Thus the job of brewing was a vital one and bad brewers were harshly punished. (In Chester they were forced to sit in the 'shit-seat' – presumably a form of stocks.[253]) Brewing was not the only specialist job into which a peasant might enter: surnames found in early thirteenth-century legal records also tell us that in England there were Bakers, Butlers, Carpenters, Cooks, Dyers, Fishers, Porters, Millers, Smiths, Tanners and Weavers.[254]

A remarkable document written a generation or so after 1215 characterizes life for the English peasant in the thirteenth century.[255] It is a letter designed as a formulary to teach students basic composition, but it reveals how life for the majority of the English population was viewed. There is, no doubt, an element of exaggeration or caricature for rhetorical effect, but this suggests a life a world away from that of Magna Carta, whose provisions were shaped by barons, bishops and knights.

'A peasant to a peasant, greetings,' begins the letter.

> You have seen well we have a harsh lord, a sly serjeant, a wicked reeve, and almost barren land, and all these are adverse beyond measure. We almost entirely lack intervals of rest ... nor is there on earth anything while we live that revives our spirits ... And since men of free condition abhor both common manners and common people, were it not for our rational souls we would be held but as rabid dogs among them. In these things the ability to endure hardship is necessary for us, because if, complaining, we resist, our misery will be cut short for us. We have but one solace: we shall die, and at our death our servitudes will end.

What, then, did the war that followed Magna Carta mean for a peasant family? The months of deliberation and unravelling would not for them have represented a great turning of the wheel in English justice. Rather, the trouble between John and his barons meant the outbreak of misery of the sort that came around once in every generation. England in the twelfth and early thirteenth centuries was a more peaceful realm than France – where most of England's wars took place.[256] But when trouble did erupt, it was terrifying.

The twelfth-century Norman poet Robert Wace had written a dark description of the common experience of warfare in the age of marauding armies. 'What sorrow and what injury they did to the fine folk and the good land,' he wrote, recalling soldiers 'burning houses and destroying towns, knights and villeins, clerics, monks and nuns they hunted, beat and murdered ... you might see many lands devastated, women violated, men speared, babies disembowelled in their cradles, riches seized, flocks led off, towers brought low and towns burnt.'[257] This was more than just gloomy war poetry. 'The powerful shall suffer powerful torments,' went the old saying from the book of Wisdom.[258] But of course, the powerful never suffered in isolation.

✝

On New Year's Day 1216, traditionally a day for giving presents, John's men raided the abbey of Coggeshall in Essex and stole twenty-two horses.[259] It was an appropriately grim start to the year. Things did not get better after that. The first target of John's wrath was the north, and specifically the ginger-haired king of Scots, who had chosen to capitalize on his rival's difficulties by entering into a deal with his enemies. During the siege of Rochester Castle the northern barons, led by Eustace de Vesci, had agreed to recognize Alexander II as overlord of the three northern English counties of Northumberland, Westmorland and Cumbria. This expressly defied the terms of the 1209 treaty of Norham, under which Alexander's father, William the Lion, had been brought to heel. In mid-January 1216, John marched north with the intention, as he put it, of chasing 'the red Scottish fox from his lair'.[260] Just as the Scots had rampaged through England, so now John's mercenaries cut a swathe as far as the banks of the river Forth, pillaging from village to village. Then John turned back south and led a violent assault on East Anglia. For a few months it seemed that he was battling his way back to supremacy, forcing his defeated enemies to swear an oath against obeying Magna Carta. But as spring came, the tide began to turn. According to Marshal's biography the king was nearly broke.[261] Worse, John's enemies were buoyed by news from across the Channel. Having dallied for months, Louis the Lion, heir to the crown of France, had finally decided to cross the sea and join in the fighting on the barons' side.

On 21 May 1216 Louis made landfall in England, arriving at Sandwich on the Isle of Thanet in Kent with a considerable army behind him. And now the John of old – the man once mocked as John Softsword – returned. Faced with the threat of aggression from a man whom he had last confronted in Poitou with such disastrous consequences, he fell back. Between 1200 and 1214 this attitude had cost him most of his French lands: now it seemed likely that it would cost him his crown. Louis swept through Kent into London, and as news of his arrival spread, the men who had clung to John's side started melting away. Some who had been listed as his advisers in the Magna Carta, such as the earls of Warenne and Arundel, abandoned his cause. Seventeen of his household knights slunk away and, most hurtful of all, John's own half-brother, William Longuespée, now defected to Louis. Increasingly few men remained at the king's side – except, of course, that paragon of Plantagenet loyalty William Marshal. ('A man of loyal and noble heart, [Marshal] stayed with him in hard and difficult circumstances,' recorded Marshal's biographer proudly. 'He never changed that steadfast heart of his ...'[262]) To everyone else John was a lost cause. The would-be King Louis I held the future of England in his hands.

London rejoiced at Louis's arrival. The Welsh rallied against John's forces in the west and Alexander II regained some pride by sailing in person to Dover to pay homage to Louis for the Scots' gains in the north of England. Late in the summer the news arrived that on 16 July Pope Innocent III had died suddenly at Perugia, aged around fifty-six. John had lost his one remaining hope. He continued to move back and forth across his country, tamping down fires wherever he could, but by now the effort was starting to tell and his luck was running out.

On 11 October John found himself passing through the town of Bishop's Lynn – now King's Lynn – on the south coast of the large, square-mouthed estuary now known as the Wash, into which flow the rivers Welland, Nene and Great Ouse. This could be treacherous terrain. John skirted around the estuary and set off in the direction of Swineshead on the Lincolnshire side of the Wash, but as his baggage train followed, his servants misjudged the tide.* Many of John's carts, animals and men were soon sucked into quicksands. According to Ralph of Coggeshall, John 'lost his chapel with his relics, and some of his packhorses with divers household effects'. Roger of Wendover claimed the loss was more devastating still: by his account John lost 'treasures, precious vessels, and all the other things which he cherished with special care ... not a single foot-soldier got away to bear tidings of the disaster.'[263] At the very least this was inconvenient and embarrassing. But worse was to follow.

As his bags vanished into the heavy sands of the North Sea, John was himself deteriorating. He was forty-eight years old but in poor health: gout had hobbled him the previous year and now he was attacked by dysentery, which legend has since said was brought on by feasting too enthusiastically on peaches and cider. Without his relics or the effects of his chapel the sickness was an even more severe business than it would have otherwise been, since divine intervention, which was an important part of medical treatment at the time, was now much harder to request. His condition grew worse over the course of the next few days until John finally despaired of his life. At this point, unexpectedly, he turned his mind to atonement for his sins and granted land for a monastery to be founded in Hertfordshire in memory of Matilda de Briouze and her eldest son, whom he had starved to death. On 15 October he wrote miserably to the new Pope, Honorius III, begging for absolution and hoping

* In the thirteenth century the coastline of the Wash lay some way south of its present littoral. Thus a number of towns which were once on the coast of the Wash (such as King's Lynn) are now inland.

that God 'will look on us with the eye of his mercy, and deem us worthy to be placed in the number of the elect'.[264] Three days later he was on his deathbed; he died in Newark during a violent storm on the night of 18/19 October. William Marshal was at his side and described to his biographer a penitent king who apologized for his misdeeds before 'death, that great harrier, that wicked, harsh creature, took him under her control and never let him go.'[265]

John had ruled for seventeen and a half years, and his time on earth had ended in misery and failure. The king died with thunder booming in his ears and scant hope that his kingdom or his dynasty would survive his passing. His two sons by Isabella of Angoulême were perilously young: Henry was nine and Richard seven. (Their three girls, Joan, Isabella and Eleanor, were younger still.) In 1209 John had demanded that his barons swear allegiance to the then two-year-old Henry as his successor, and since 1212 the boy had been under the academic tutelage of John's staunch ally Peter des Roches, bishop of Winchester. But this hardly seemed a strong prospect on which to peg the future of the Plantagenet royal family or rebuild the shredded political stability of the realm.

John was not buried at Beaulieu Abbey, which he had founded at the beginning of his reign, for it was under enemy control. Instead, his entrails were removed from his corpse and taken for preservation by the abbot of Croxton, while his body was carried by a cortege of mercenaries to Worcester Cathedral. There he was buried next to the tomb of St Wulfstan, the tenth-century bishop known for his miracles, prolific church-building and campaigns against the slave trade.[266]

John's legs and torso were covered in a crimson-embroidered robe, his left hand held a sword in a leather scabbard and his crownless head was strapped into a monk's cowl.[267] Less than two years had passed since he had sat in much the same spot at Christmas 1214, enjoying a personal performance of '*Christus vincit*'. How things had changed. When the chronicler Matthew Paris reflected on the fate of John's soul, twenty years after his death, he famously remarked that 'England reeks with John's filthy deeds; the foulness of Hell is defiled by John.'[268] Surely, though, even John could not have plunged Hell into a very much worse state than the earthly realm he left behind.

Afterword

King John's eldest son was crowned Henry III on 28 October 1216 at Gloucester Abbey, with a small corps of long-suffering loyalists, William Marshal foremost among them. A new papal legate, Guala Bicchieri, was also at his side. Louis's forces still controlled London and the south-east and it was far from clear that the nine-year-old Henry would ever be accepted by his countrymen as king, let alone recover the formidable power that had been enjoyed by his father, uncle and grandfather. Aside from the immediate military necessity of waging a war against the rebels and the French invaders, it was now vital that the men around the young king offer their enemies some grounds for reconciliation – some gesture that would allow them to believe that with King John dead and buried, the greatest obstacle to peace had been removed.

As John had lain dying he had begged those around him to see that Marshal be given command of the kingdom in the name of his son. This was not controversial: although he was around seventy years old, Marshal was one of the most respected figures in England and one of only a small handful of men who had remained loyal to his king until the end. He accepted the post of regent with some reluctance, but once in post began drawing back to the royal cause those who had abandoned it as lost. He received invaluable support from Guala, who excommunicated all those who followed Louis. No bishop would crown a king who was exiled from the spiritual community of the Church. This bought time and gave slender hope to the loyalist cause. And Marshal's deft handling of the regency's difficult politics slowly began to bring John's enemies back to his son's cause.

Letters went out to barons offering recompense and restitution to any who would come over to the new king's side. More importantly, it was not long before the treaty John had begrudgingly agreed with his barons was dusted off and offered up as an emollient, to bring back into the fold those who might be wavering. Magna Carta was reissued for the first time on 12 November 1216, under the seals of William Marshal and Guala Bicchieri. This was an extraordinarily bold move. After all, the late Innocent III had condemned the charter as 'null and void of all validity forever' – hardly words that left a lot of room for interpretation. John had died fighting a war against everything the charter stood for. But Innocent and John were dead, and new circumstances dictated new thinking. It is to Marshal and Guala's credit that they were flexible enough to see that with some small but significant amendments (which included removing the troublesome 'security' clause) the charter did not have to be a stick to beat the Plantagenet crown. It could stand as the foundation of a new monarchy.

The effects of this new Magna Carta were encouraging but not immediate. We can see from its list of witnesses – most of the English bishops and now three earls besides Marshal – that it had convinced a few men to turn. Plenty, however, fought on. The war dragged on into 1217, heaping further misery on both sides: Marshal's biographer reported having seen a hundred Frenchmen lying slain on the ground between Winchester and Romsey, with hungry dogs ripping the flesh from their bones.[269] Yet eventually the resolve and resources of the French began to weaken. Louis left England to attend to business across the Channel for eight weeks in the early spring, and although he came back, his absence saw a trickle of further defections from the rebel camp. Fighting for an uncrowned French prince against a crowned English king whose government was committed to reform started to look less and less reasonable. The chronicler Roger of Wendover believed that for many of the rebels, eventually the only difficulty in switching sides was the shame of being thought a turncoat.[270]

Yet for all the flagging enthusiasm of the opposition and the growing confidence of the men around Henry, several months would pass before a decisive moment was reached in the war. This came at the battle of Lincoln, on 20 May 1217, when a powerful and impressively armed force led by William Marshal descended on the castle, routing the rebels who were camped there and capturing a large number of their leaders. It was a crushing defeat for Louis, from which his cause would never recover.

In August 1217, Hubert de Burgh destroyed a French fleet off the Kentish coast at the battle of Sandwich, and almost immediately a downcast Louis sought terms on which he could depart from England without losing too much face. Peace was made in the treaty of Lambeth on 20 September, and Louis departed the country with a massive bribe of ten thousand marks (a quarter of England's royal annual revenue) to salve his wounded pride. Once he was gone, the business of restoring some normality to government after two years of exhausting civil war began. The charter wrung from a reluctant King John at Runnymede was once again reissued.

This time it was accompanied by a new grant: the Charter of the Forest. This reversed the Plantagenet policy begun under Henry II of expanding the territories classed as forest land and subject to the burdensome system of forest law. The charter reduced the size of the royal forest and severely restricted the purview of forest justice and officials. The extent of forest land was to be as it stood on the day of Henry II's coronation in 1154. Free men were to be allowed to let their pigs forage in the forest; they were able to build mills, dig ponds and gather firewood without being prosecuted. 'Any archbishop, bishop, earl or baron whatever who passes through our forest shall be allowed to take one or two beasts under the supervision of the forester,' ran one clause, and another promised that 'no one shall henceforth lose life or limb' for poaching venison, although men found taking royal deer without permission could still be fined heavily, thrown in jail for a year and a day and exiled from England.[271] It was from 1217 that Magna Carta earned its famous name – in order to differentiate it from the Charter of the Forest.

The 1216 and 1217 reissues of Magna Carta contained some important variations from the text of the original. Strongly worded statements on foreign ministers, which had featured in 1215, were quietly dropped, since many of the men who surrounded Henry III in his minority – such as Peter des Roches – were themselves of alien birth. The clauses regulating purveyance were redrawn, and there were substantial tweaks made to provision for widows' rights and procedures for recovering debts, both to the crown and to Jewish moneylenders. A clause was introduced in 1217 ordering the destruction of castles that had been erected during the recent war. New restrictions limited the frequency with which sheriffs could hold their courts and the commitment to investigate historical abuses dating back to Henry II and Richard I's reigns disappeared.

It is telling that both the 1216 and 1217 reissues of Magna Carta were presented without the 'security clause'. The question of how to restrain an out-of-control king would remain alive for the duration of the middle ages and beyond, but in 1216 and 1217 it was shelved. Partly this was because its openly bellicose methods had justified civil war instead of promoting peace. More important, however, was the fact that in just two years Magna Carta had shifted in purpose. Although reissued on both occasions from the jaws of civil war, it was now no longer a peace treaty imposed by the king's enemies. Now it was an offering by the king's friends, designed to demonstrate voluntarily the commitment of the new regime to govern by principles on which the whole realm could agree. Magna Carta had mutated from a begrudgingly accepted text of compromise into an assurance of good faith. As it was copied out by clerks and distributed to the shires of England to be read aloud in the sheriffs' courts, the charter had taken on a new purpose.

William Marshal died in May 1219, and on his deathbed he warned the young Henry not to 'follow in the footsteps of some wicked ancestor'.[272] Stephen Langton, who returned to England in 1218 with his sentence of suspension lifted by the new Pope, worked until his death in July 1228 to ensure that the charter remained alive. For the rest of Henry's reign – indeed, for the rest of the thirteenth century – Magna Carta would be reconfirmed and reissued at moments of political instability or crisis.

In 1225 Henry III turned eighteen and another, revamped version of the charter was published, given by the king – according to the preamble – 'of our own spontaneous goodwill' ('*spontanea et bona voluntate nostra*'). [273] This was slightly disingenuous. As clause 37 of the 1225 edition of Magna Carta made clear, the charters were in fact reissued as one side of a political bargain. The king promised to observe and uphold the customs of the realm, and in return 'all of our realm have given us a fifteenth part of all their movables'. In other words, the king swapped a concession of liberties for tax revenue.

This would become an enduring practice. Over the course of the thirteenth and fourteenth centuries English government would become anchored by the principle that the king could exercise his right to tax his subjects only if he agreed to remedy grievances and reform his realm. In the 1225 edition of Magna Carta, that idea was made explicit for the first time. (The 1225 charter was also notable for its bestowal, in the preamble, of its liberties upon 'all of our realm'; specific clauses were still, however, restricted to 'free men'.)

Further reissues followed. In January 1237 both charters were again confirmed in binding and perpetual form, protected by a third 'small charter', whose witnesses included a few old men who had been at Runnymede in 1215. Once again a tax was granted. By this time something of a myth had started to grow. The charter was widely circulated with each revision and reissue. Magna Carta was referred to frequently in legal cases. Barons began to offer charters of liberties to their own tenants, which were clearly modelled on its form and content.

The charter was still specifically protected by the Church. English parish churches were the venues for readings of Magna Carta in the vernacular. Excommunication was pronounced as the penalty for disobedience in both 1225 and 1237; on 13 May 1253 a confirmation of both Magna Carta and the Charter of the Forest took place in Westminster Abbey, in which the archbishop of Canterbury and thirteen bishops passed that familiar sentence on those who ignored Magna Carta's provisions. (The saints called upon to observe the penalty included Edward the Confessor and Thomas Becket, both of whom had played their own small roles in the history of opposition to John and his Plantagenet relatives.) When the sentence was passed, the bishops all threw down the lit candles they had been holding and said together: 'Thus are extinguished and reek in Hell all those who attack this sentence.' King Henry promised to guard Magna Carta in all its terms, which he declared was his duty as a 'man, a Christian, a knight and an anointed king'.

In the century that followed John's promulgation of the charter at Runnymede, the collapse into civil war and the king's death, Magna Carta was probably copied out, in its various editions, over a thousand times. There remain in existence more than a hundred medieval copies, ranging from those official exemplifications of Magna Carta 1215, held in London, Salisbury and Lincoln, to privately made copies kept in abbeys and archives. One of the latter is the elegantly scripted copy among the records of Cerne Abbey in Dorset – a hybrid of the 1217 and 1225 editions, with the Charter of the Forest bolted directly on as though it were part of the same treaty.[274] These were not merely documents of antiquarian interest. The importance of the charter was clearly and regularly stated. Even where its clauses grew irrelevant and obsolete, much importance was still attached to the idea of Magna Carta as a bargaining chip, particularly in relation to taxation.

In 1242, at one of the earliest recorded parliaments in English history, Henry III requested financial aid from the realm to pay for a military expedition to France. He was refused, on the grounds that previous grants of taxation had not resulted in good governance, 'because the king had never, after the granting of the thirtieth [i.e. his requested tax], abided by his charter of liberties, nay had since then oppressed [his subjects] more than usual'.[275] When Henry and his eldest son Edward found themselves embroiled in a long war against Simon de Montfort, earl of Leicester, during the 1250s and 1260s, Magna Carta was again at the heart of the political wrangling. When de Montfort was at the peak of his powers during the first half of 1265 he not only forced Henry and Edward to swear an oath to obey his own constitution, which de Montfort had established the previous year, he also required the king to reconfirm Magna Carta and the Charter of the Forest. In a sense this took the charter back to its original state – the weapon of a radical rebellious faction in English politics seeking to extract promises from a king by intimidation. But de Montfort's insistence on reconfirming the charters in 1265 was also an illustration of just how symbolically potent the mere name of Magna Carta had become for anyone seeking to put their mark on English government. De Montfort sought legitimacy. He found it by wearing the badge of Magna Carta.[276]

Henry III confirmed or reissued Magna Carta on average about once every five years during his reign – and increasingly the charter was promulgated in French and English as well as the Latin in which it had first been written. It was known in Normandy, and became a model for charters of liberties negotiated there. By Henry's death in 1272 Magna Carta had become a political commonplace, whose significance, if not its precise detail, was etched deep into the minds of Englishmen of almost every literate rank. But the final, and in some ways definitive, version of the charter was produced not under Henry III but during the reign of Edward I (1272–1307).

The reign of this tall, imposing, warmongering king was – although broadly more successful than that of his father and grandfather – still troubled by moments of crisis. The worst came in 1297, when the crippling costs of Edward's wars of conquest in Wales and Scotland and resistance to French continental advances in Gascony were rejected by a coalition of barons and bishops, who revolted en masse against his heavy-handed rule and relentless financial demands. The compromise that was thrashed out included the *Confirmatio cartarum* (Confirmation of the Charters) of 10 October 1297, by which Magna Carta and the Charter of the Forest were reissued once more, accompanied by other concessions and guarantees of good government. Not all of these would be kept by the king or his descendants – in fact, the history of Magna Carta is largely the history of kings failing to stick to its terms. All the same, by the end of the thirteenth century a peace treaty that had lasted just a few weeks eight decades earlier had become, in many ways, the foundation stone of the whole system of English law and government.

Edward confirmed and reissued Magna Carta and the Charter of the Forest for one final time in 1300.* Subsequent medieval kings confirmed the charters' terms many times over, but Magna Carta was never again to be copied out and distributed in the same formal fashion as had first occurred in June 1215. Nevertheless, it was appealed to dozens of times in parliamentary petitions and private legislation. It also gave a model for the baronial opposition movements that sprang up during the reigns of Edward II (1307–27) and

---

* One of these 1300 editions came to light in February 2015 in the archives of the British seaside town of Sandwich, where it had been tucked away in a Victorian scrapbook. It is quite badly damaged but has still been estimated to be worth around £9.5 million ($15 million).

Richard II (1377–99), both of which attempted to restrain the king by ordinances and contracts and to force him to rule by co-operation with his leading subjects. Inevitably, time stripped Magna Carta of legal relevance. But its influence – and its legend – survived.

Appendices

The Text of Magna Carta, 1215
The Charter of the Forest, 1217

The Text of Magna Carta

1215

John, by the grace of God King of England, Lord of Ireland, Duke of Normandy and Aquitaine, Count of Anjou, to his archbishops, bishops, abbots, earls, barons, justices, foresters, sheriffs, reeves, officers and all his bailiffs and faithful subjects, greetings. Know that, for the sake of God and for the salvation of our soul and the souls of all our ancestors and heirs, to the honour of God and the exaltation of the holy Church, and for the reform of our realm, by the advice of our venerable fathers Stephen, Archbishop of Canterbury, Primate of All England and Cardinal of the Holy Roman Church; Henry, Archbishop of Dublin; William, Bishop of London; Peter, Bishop of Winchester; Jocelin, Bishop of Bath and Glastonbury; Hugh, Bishop of Lincoln; Walter, Bishop of Worcester; William, Bishop of Coventry; and Benedict, Bishop of Rochester; Master Pandulf, subdeacon and confidant of the lord pope; Brother Aymeric, Master of the Knights Templar in England; and the noble men William Marshal, Earl of Pembroke; William, Earl of Salisbury; William, Earl Warenne; William, Earl of Arundel; Alan of Galloway, Constable of Scotland; Warin FitzGerald; Peter FitzHerbert; Hubert de Burgh, Seneschal of Poitou;

Hugh de Neville; Matthew FitzHerbert; Thomas Basset; Alan Basset; Philip d'Aubigny; Robert de Roppel; John Marshal; John FitzHugh and other ofour faithful subjects:

1. Firstly, we have granted to God and confirmed by this, our present charter, for us and our heirs in perpetuity, that the English Church shall be free, and shall have its rights in full and its liberties intact; and we wish this to be thus observed, which is clear from the fact that, before the discord with our barons began, we granted and confirmed by our charter free elections, which are considered to be of the utmost importance and necessity to the English Church, and we obtained confirmation of this from our lord Pope Innocent III; which we shall observe and which we wish our heirs to observe in good faith in perpetuity. We have also granted to all the free men of our realm, for ourselves and our heirs in perpetuity, all the liberties written below, for them and their heirs to have and to hold of us and our heirs.

2. If any of our earls or barons, or others holding in chief* of us by knight service, dies, and at his death his heir is of full age and owes relief, he shall have his inheritance by paying the ancient relief: that is, for the heir or heirs of an earl, £100 for the whole earl's barony; for the heir or heirs of a baron, £100 for the whole barony; for the heir or heirs of a knight, 100 marks at most for the whole knight's fee; and anyone who owes less gives less, according to the ancient custom of fees.

---

* 'Holding in chief' – i.e. as tenant-in-chief, holding land directly from the Crown.

3. If, on the other hand, the heir of any such person has been underage and has been in wardship, when he comes of age he is to have his inheritance without paying relief and without a fine.

4. The guardian of the land of such an heir who is underage, shall not take from the heir's land any more than reasonable revenues, reasonable customs and reasonable services, and this shall be done without the destruction or waste of men or goods; and if we have committed the wardship of any such land to a sheriff or anyone else who answers to us for its revenues, and he destroys or wastes the lands, we will take amends from him, and the land shall be committed to two law-abiding and discreet men of the fee,* who will answer to us or the person we have assigned them, and if we give or sell the wardship of any such land to anyone, and he destroys or wastes it, he shall lose the wardship, and it shall be handed over to two law-abiding and discreet men of the fee who shall answer to us as previously said.

5. Moreover, so long as the guardian has wardship of the land, he shall maintain out of the revenues of the land the buildings, parks, fishponds, pools, mills, and other things pertaining to the land; and when the heir comes of age he shall restore to him all his land stocked with ploughs and growing crops, such as the agricultural season requires and the revenues of the land can reasonably sustain.

* 'Men of the fee' – men connected to the land in question.

6. Heirs shall be married without disparagement, provided that before a marriage is contracted, the heir's closest relatives are informed.

7. After the death of her husband a widow shall have her marriage portion and inheritance straightaway and without difficulty, nor shall she pay anything for her dower, her marriage portion or her inheritance which she and her husband held on the day of his death. She may remain in her marital home for forty days after his death, during which period her dower will be assigned to her.

8. No widow shall be forced to marry for as long as she wishes to live without a husband, provided that she gives security that she will not marry without our consent, if she holds of us, or without the consent of her lord of whom she holds, if she holds of someone else.

9. Neither we nor our bailiffs will seize any land or any rent for any debt, so long as the debtor's chattels are sufficient to pay the debt; nor are the pledges of the debtor to be distrained so long as the principal debtor has enough to pay the debt. And if the principal debtor defaults on the debt, not having the means to pay it, the pledges are to answer for it. And if they wish, they may have the debtor's lands and rents until they have had satisfaction for the debt they have settled for him, unless the principal debtor demonstrates that he is quit with regard to the pledges.

10. If anyone has taken any sort of loan from the Jews, great or small, and dies before the debt is settled, the debt shall not carry interest for as long as the heir is underage, whoever he holds from; and if that debt should fall into our hands, we will take nothing but the principal sum recorded in the charter.

11. And if anyone should die owing a debt to the Jews, his wife shall have her dower and pay nothing of that debt; and if he leaves surviving children who are underage, their needs are to be provided for according to the holding of the deceased, and the debt shall be paid from what remains, saving the service owed to the lords. Debts owed to others besides the Jews are to be dealt with in the same way.

12. No scutage or other aid is to be levied in our realm, except by the common counsel of our realm, unless it is to pay for the ransoming of our person, the knighting of our first-born son or the first marriage of our first-born daughter; and for these only a reasonable aid is to be taken. Aids taken from the City of London will be treated in the same way.

13. And the City of London shall have all its ancient liberties and free customs both on land and on water. Furthermore we wish and grant that all other cities, boroughs, towns and ports shall have all their liberties and free customs.

14. And for us to have common counsel of the realm for the levying of an aid (other than in the three cases previously

mentioned) or for the levying of a scutage, we will have archbishops, bishops, abbots, earls and greater barons summoned individually by our letters; and furthermore we will have a general summons, made by our sheriffs and bailiffs, of all of those who hold from us in chief for a fixed day, at least forty days away, and at a fixed place; and in all our letters we will explain the cause of the summons. And when the summons has thus been made, the business shall proceed on the agreed day according to the counsel of those present, even if not all of those summoned have come.

15. In future we will not grant to anyone that he may take an aid from his free men, except to pay a ransom on his person, or on the knighting of his first-born son, or on the first marriage of his first-born daughter; and for these there is only to be a reasonable aid.

16. No one is to be distrained to do more service for a knight's fee, or for any other free tenement, than is owed for it.

17. Common pleas are not to follow our court, but are to be held in some fixed place.

18. Recognizances of novel disseisin, mort d'ancestor and darrein presentment*are not to be held except in their proper county court, and in this way: we, or if we are out of the realm

* 'Novel disseizin, mort d'ancestor and darrein presentment' – common legal procedures initiated by writs of Chancery, all connected with ownership of property.

our Chief Justiciar,* shall send two justices to each county four times a year, who, with four knights of each county chosen by the county court, shall hold the said assizes in the county court, on the day and in the meeting place of the county court.

19. And if on the day of the county court the said assizes cannot be held, as many knights and free tenants [as are required] out of those who were present in the county court on that day will remain for the sufficient making of judgments, according to whether the business is great or small.

20. A free man may not be amerced [i.e. fined] for a small offence, except according to the nature of the offence; and for a great offence he shall be amerced according to the magnitude of the offence, saving his livelihood; and a merchant in the same way, saving his merchandise; and a villein shall be amerced in the same way, saving his growing crops, if they fall into our mercy. And none of the said amercements may be made, except upon the oaths of honest men of the neighbourhood.

21. Earls and barons are not to be amerced except by their peers, and only in accordance with the nature of the offence.

22. No clergyman is to be amerced on his lay tenement, except in accordance with the nature of his offence, in the way of others mentioned previously, and not in accordance with the size of his ecclesiastical benefice.

* '(Chief) Justiciar' – the principal royal servant in legal and political matters, effectively a chief minister, sometimes regent.

23. Neither town nor man shall be forced to build bridges over rivers, except those who are obliged to do so by custom and right.

24. No sheriff, constable, coroner or other of our bailiffs shall hold the pleas of our crown.

25. All counties, hundreds, wapentakes and ridings* shall be at their ancient farms, without any increment, except for our demesne manors.

26. If anyone holding a lay fee of us dies, and our sheriff or bailiff shows our letters patent of a summons for a debt which the deceased owed us, it is to be lawful for our sheriff or bailiff to attach and record the chattels of the deceased found on the lay fee, to the value of the debt, in the view of law-abiding men, so that nothing is to be removed from there, until the clear debt is paid to us, and the residue is to be relinquished by the executors to carry out the will of the deceased; and, if nothing is owed to us by him, all the chattels shall go to the deceased, saving reasonable portions for his wife and children.

27. If any free man dies intestate, his chattels are to be distributed by his closest kinsmen and friends, under the supervision of the Church, saving to everyone the debts that the dead man owed them.

* 'Hundreds, wapentakes and ridings' – administrative subdivisions of counties or shires, with their origins in Anglo-Saxon times; 'farms' – fixed sums of money due annually in taxation from an area of land.

28. No constable, or any of our bailiffs, shall take anyone's corn or any other chattels, unless he immediately pays for them in cash, or else he can agree with the seller to postpone payment.

29. No constable may compel any knight to give money instead of performing castle guard, if he is willing to perform that guard in person, or, if he is for some good reason unable to do it himself, through another reliable man. And if we have led or sent him in the army, he shall be relieved of guard duty, in accordance with the amount of time he spent in our military service.

30. No sheriff or bailiff of ours, or anyone else, may take any free man's horses or carts for transporting things, except with the free man's agreement.

31. Neither we nor our bailiffs may take anyone's timber to a castle or to any other business of ours, except with the agreement of the timber's owner.

32. We will not hold the lands of convicted felons for more than a year and a day, and then the lands will be returned to the lord of the fee.

33. In future, all fish-weirs will be completely removed from the Thames and the Medway and throughout the whole of England, except on the sea-coast.

34. The writ called Praecipe will not, in future, be issued to anyone for any holding in respect of which a free man could lose his court.

35. There shall be one measure of wine in the whole of our realm, and one measure of ale, and one measure of corn, namely, the quarter of London, and one width of dyed, russet and haberget cloths, namely two ells within the borders. Let it be the same for weights as it is for measures.

36. Nothing shall in future be given or taken for the writ of inquisition of life and limb, but it shall be freely given and not refused.

37. If anyone holds of us by fee-farm, socage or burgage,* and holds land of someone else by military service, we will not, by reason of the fee-farm, socage or burgage, have wardship of his heir or of his lands belonging to another man's fee. Nor will we have custody of that fee-farm, socage or burgage, except if the fee-farm, socage or burgage owes military service. We will not have custody of anyone's heir or anyone's lands which he holds of someone else by military service, by virtue of some petty serjeantry by which he holds of us by the service of rendering us knives, or arrows, or suchlike.

38. No bailiff is in future to put anyone to law by his accusation alone, without trustworthy witnesses being brought forward.

39. No free man is to be arrested, or imprisoned, or disseized, or outlawed, or exiled, or in any other way ruined, nor will

---

* 'Fee-farm, socage or burgage' – different forms of feudal tenure (where payments or military services are owed to the king in return for possession of land).

we go or send against him, except by the legal judgment of his peers or by the law of the land.

40. To no one will we sell, to no one will we deny or delay, right or justice.

41. All merchants are to be safe and secure in leaving and coming to England, and in staying and travelling in England, both by land and by water, to buy and sell without any evil tolls, but only by the ancient and rightful customs, save in time of war if they come from an enemy country. And if such are found in our land at the beginning of war, they will be detained without damage to their persons or goods, until it is clear to us or our Chief Justiciar how the merchants of our land are treated in the enemy country; and if ours are safe there, the others shall be safe in our land.

42. In future it is lawful for anyone, saving his allegiance to us, and except for a short period during time of war, to leave our realm and return, safe and secure by land and water, for the sake of the general good of the realm; except for those imprisoned or outlawed according to the law of the land, and people from the enemy country, and merchants – who shall be treated as previously described.

43. If anyone dies who held of any escheat, such as the honours of Wallingford, Nottingham, Boulogne, Lancaster, or of other escheats* which are in our hand and our baronies, his heir will

* 'Escheat' – land that reverted to its lord if the tenant were to die without an heir.

not pay any relief or do us any other service than he would have done to the baron if the barony was in the baron's hand; and we will hold it in the same manner as the baron held it.

44. From now on men who reside outside the forest will not come before our justices of the forest on a general summons, unless they are impleaded, or they are pledges for any person or persons who are attached for forest business.

45. We will not appoint justices, constables, sheriffs or bailiffs, other than those who know the law of the realm and intend to keep it well.

46. All barons who have founded abbeys, for which they have charters of the kings of England, or ancient tenure, shall have custody of the abbeys when they are vacant, as they should have.

47. All forests which have been afforested in our time shall be immediately disafforested, and let the same be done for riverbanks which have been fenced off during our time.

48. All evil customs, of forests and warrens, and of foresters and warreners, sheriffs and their officers, riverbanks and their keepers are immediately to be investigated in each and every county by twelve sworn knights of the same county, who are to be chosen by upright men of their county, and within forty days of the inquiry [the evil customs] are to be entirely abolished, provided that we, or our justiciar if we are not in England, know about it first.

49. We will immediately restore all hostages and charters that have been given to us by Englishmen as security for peace and faithful service.

50. We will completely remove from their offices the relations of Gerard d'Athée, so that from now on they shall have no office in England: Engelard de Cigogné, Peter and Guy and Andrew de Chanceaux, Guy de Cigogné, Geoffrey de Martini and his brothers, Philip Mark and his brothers, and his nephew Geoffrey, and all their followers.*

51. And immediately after the restoration of peace we will remove from the realm all foreign knights, crossbowmen, serjeants and mercenaries, who have come with horses and arms to the detriment of the kingdom.

52. If anyone has been disseized or dispossessed by us of lands, castles, liberties or of his rights, without lawful judgment of his peers, it shall immediately be restored to him. And if dispute should arise over this, then let it be settled by judgment of the twenty-five barons, as mentioned below in the security clause. For all those things of which anyone was disseized or dispossessed during the reign of King Henry our father or King Richard our brother, which we hold in our hand or which others hold, which we ought to warrant, we will have respite

* This group represented the only people to be condemned specifically by name in Magna Carta: the foreign mercenary captain Gerard d'Athée and his relatives had been rewarded for their service to John with high office in England and favour at court.

during the crusaders' term, excepting those cases when a plea was begun or an inquest made on our order before we took the cross; but when we have returned from our pilgrimage, or if by chance we do not go on our pilgrimage, we will immediately do full justice.

53. We shall have the same respite, and in the same manner, in doing justice on disafforesting or retaining those forests that Henry our father or Richard our brother afforested, and concerning wardships of lands which are part of another fee, wardships which we have held by reason of a fee which someone held of us by knight service, and of abbeys which were founded on a fee other than ours, in which the lord of the fee has claimed his right. And when we return, or if we do not go on our pilgrimage, we will immediately do full justice to those complaining about these things.

54. No man shall be arrested or imprisoned because of the appeal of a woman for the death of anyone other than her husband.

55. All fines which were made with us unjustly and contrary to the law of the land and all amercements made unjustly and contrary to the law of the land shall be completely remitted, or shall be settled by the twenty-five barons mentioned below in the security clause, or by the judgment of the majority of them, together with the aforementioned Stephen, archbishop of Canterbury, if he can be present, and others such as he may wish to bring with him for this purpose. And if it is not possible for him to attend, let the business proceed without

him, provided that if any one or more of the twenty-five barons are in such a suit, they shall be removed from this particular judgment, and shall be replaced in this case only by others chosen and sworn in by the twenty-five.

56. If we have disseized or deprived Welshmen of lands or liberties or other things without lawful judgment of their peers, in England or in Wales, they are to be returned to them immediately. And if a dispute arises about this, then it is to be settled in the March by judgment of their peers, for English tenements according to the law of England, for Welsh tenements according to the law of Wales, for tenements of the March according to the laws of the March. And the Welsh will do the same to us and ours.

57. However, with regard to all of the possessions of which any Welshman has been disseized or dispossessed without the lawful judgment of his peers, by King Henry our father, or King Richard our brother, and which we have in our hand, or which others hold which we ought to warrant, we will have respite for the common crusaders' term, except in cases where a plea was started or an inquest held by our instruction before we took the cross; however, when we return, or if by chance we do not go on crusade, then we will immediately do justice according to the laws of Wales and the parts previously mentioned.

58. We will immediately restore the son of Llywelyn and all the hostages from Wales, and charters that were delivered to us as security for peace.

59. We will deal with Alexander, king of the Scots, regarding the return of his sisters and hostages and his liberties and rights in accordance with the way we deal with our other barons of England, unless it should be otherwise under the charters which we have from his father, William, former king of Scots. And this will be by judgment of his peers in our court.

60. All the previously mentioned customs and liberties which we have granted in our kingdom as far as we are concerned with regard to our own men, shall be observed by all men of our realm, both clergy and laity, as far as they are concerned with regard to their own men.

61. Since we have granted all these things for God and for the correction of our kingdom, and for the better settlement of the discord that has arisen between us and our barons, wishing these things to be enjoyed with full and firm stability in perpetuity, we make and grant them the following security: namely, that the barons are to choose twenty-five barons of the realm, whoever they wish, who with all their strength should observe, uphold and cause to be observed the peace and liberties which we have granted to them and confirmed to them in this present charter, so that if we or our justiciar, or our bailiffs, or any other of our officers shall in any way offend against anyone, or transgress against any of the articles of peace or security, and the offence has been shown to four of the said twenty-five barons, those four are to go to us, or our justiciar if we are out of the kingdom, setting forth the offence and demand that it be set right without delay. And if within

the space of forty days of being shown the offence, we do not set right or if we are out of the realm, our justiciar does not set it right, the said four barons are to refer the case to the rest of the twenty-five barons, and those twenty-five barons, with the community of the whole realm shall distrain and distress us in all ways possible, by taking castles, lands, possessions and in any other ways they can, until it has been put right in accordance with their judgment, saving our person and the persons of our queen and children. And once redress has been made let them obey us as they did before. And whoever of the land wishes may swear that he will obey the orders of the said twenty-five barons and with them distress us as much as he can, and we publicly and freely give permission to swear to whoever wishes to do so, and we will never prohibit anyone from swearing. Furthermore we will compel all those of the land who do not wish to swear with the twenty-five barons to distrain and distress us with them to swear as has been said. And if any of the twenty-five barons should die, or leave the land, or is in any other way prevented from doing his duties as previously mentioned, the remainder of the aforementioned twenty-five barons are to elect another in his place, by their own discretion, who will be sworn in the same manner as the rest. Furthermore, in everything that has been entrusted to the twenty-five barons to undertake, if it should happen that the twenty-five are present and disagree among themselves on anything, or if any of them, having been summoned, will not or cannot attend, whatever the majority of those present shall provide or command shall be considered as fixed and binding, as if all the twenty-five had agreed to it. And the aforementioned twenty-five swear that they will faithfully observe all the aforesaid and cause it to be observed to their fullest ability. And we will ask nothing of anyone, either ourselves or through anyone else, through which any of these grants and liberties shall be revoked or diminished. And if any such thing shall be obtained, let it be null and void and we will never make use of it, through ourselves or through anyone else.

62. And we have fully remitted and pardoned all ill-will, indignation and rancour that has arisen between us and our men, clergy and laity, during the time of discord. Moreover, we have fully remitted to all men, clergy and laity, all the trangressions committed as the result of that discord between Easter in the sixteenth year of our reign until the establishment of peace, and as far as we are concerned, they are completely forgiven. And in addition we have had letters patent made by Lord Stephen, archbishop of Canterbury, Lord Henry, archbishop of Dublin, and the aforesaid bishops, and Master Pandulf testifying to this security and the aforesaid grants.

63. Wherefore we wish and firmly command that the English Church shall be free and that men in our kingdom have and hold all the aforesaid liberties, rights and grants, well and in peace, freely and quietly, fully and completely, for themselves and their heirs of us and our heirs, in all things and in all places, in perpetuity as has been said. This has been sworn to both on our behalf and on behalf of the barons, that all the previously mentioned things shall be observed in good faith and without

evil intent. Witnessed by the above-mentioned and many others. Given by our hand in the meadow called Runnymede, between Windsor and Staines, on the fifteenth day of June, in the seventeenth year of our reign.

The Charter of the Forest
1217

HENRY, by the grace of God, king of England, lord of Ireland, duke of Normandy, Aquitaine, and count of Anjou, to the archbishops, bishops, abbots, priors, earls, barons, justiciaries, foresters, sheriffs, governors, officers, and all his bailiffs and faithful subjects, Greeting.

Know that we, for the honour for God and for the salvation of our own soul and the souls of our ancestors and successors, for the exaltation of Holy Church and the reform of our realm, have granted and by this present charter have confirmed for us and our heirs for ever, by the counsel of our venerable father, the lord Gualo, cardinal priest of St Martin and legate of the apostolic see, of the lord Walter archbishop of York, William bishop of London and the other bishops of England and of William Marshal earl of Pembroke, guardian of us and of our kingdom, and of others our faithful earls and barons of England, these underwritten liberties to be held in our kingdom of England for ever.

1. In the first place, all the forests made by our grandfather king Henry, shall be viewed by good and lawful men, and if

he made any other than his own proper woods into forests to the damage of him whose wood it was, it shall forthwith be disafforested. And if he made his own proper woods forest, it shall remain forest, saving the common right of pasturage, and of other things in the same forest, to those who were formerly accustomed to have them.

2. Men who live outside the forest, from henceforth shall not come before our justiciaries of the forest, upon a common summons, unless they are impleaded there or are sureties for any other persons who were attached for something concerning the forest.

3. Also all woods which were afforested by King Richard our uncle, or by King John our father, until our own first Coronation, shall forthwith be disafforested, unless they shall be our demesne woods.

4. Archbishops, bishops, abbots, priors, earls, barons, knights and freeholders who have woods within forests shall have them the same as they held them at the time of the first coronation of our grandfather king Henry,* so that they shall be discharged forever of all purprestures, wastes, and assarts made in their woods after that time until the beginning of the second year of our coronation.† And those who in future

---

* Sunday 19 December 1154

† Purpresture was trespass and the erection of illegal dwellings. Waste was worthless land that had been cleared but lay uncultivated. Assart was land cleared for cultivation.

shall without our licence make wastes, purprestures or assarts within them, shall answer for such wastes, purprestures or assarts.

5. Our regarders shall go through the forests to make a view as it was used to be made at the time of the first coronation of our grandfather, king Henry, and not otherwise.

6. The inquisition or view for declawing dogs living within the forest,* for the future shall be when the view ought to be made, namely, the third year in three years; and then it shall be done by the view and testimony of lawful men, and not otherwise. And he whose dogs shall be found then still clawed, shall give three shillings for mercy, and for the future no one's ox shall be taken for failure to declaw. Such declawing also shall be done by the assize commonly used; which is, that three claws shall be cut off outside the ball of the fore-foot. Nor shall dogs be declawed from henceforth, excepting in places where it hath been customary to expeditate them from the time of the first coronation of king Henry our grandfather.

7. No forester nor beadle shall for the future make any scotale,† nor collect sheaves of corn or oats, or any grain, or lambs, or swine, nor shall make any gathering but by the

---

* Declawing or expedition meant cutting off the claws of a dog, to inhibit it from chasing deer.

† Scotale was the keeping of an ale-house within a forest by an officer of the forest, who might abuse his position to get trade.

view and oath of twelve regarders; and when they shall make
their view: as many foresters shall be appointed to keep
the forests, as they shall think reasonably sufficient for the
purpose.

8. No swainmote for the future shall be held in our kingdom,*
excepting thrice a year; namely, in the beginning of fifteen
days before the feast of Saint Michael when the agistators
meet for the agisting of our (royal) demesne woods; and
about the feast of Saint Martin, when our agistators ought
to receive our pannage-dues: and in those two swainmotes
the foresters, verderers, and agistators shall meet, and
no others by distraint; and the third swainmote shall be
held in the beginning of the fifteen days before the Feast
of Saint John the Baptist concerning the fawning of our
does; and at that swainmote the tenants shall meet the
foresters and verderers, and no others shall be distrained
to be there. Moreover every forty days through the whole
year, the foresters and verderers shall meet for seeing to
attachments of the forests, as well of vert as of venison,†
by the presentment of the foresters themselves and before
those who are attached. And the aforesaid swainmotes shall
not be holden, except in those counties where they were
accustomed to be held.

---

* Swainmote was a court held before the foresters as judges, by the
steward of the court, with swains, i.e. freeholders within the forest,
making up the jury.
† Vert was green forest vegetation, which formed cover or providing
food for deer.

9. Every free man shall agist his own wood in the forest as he wishes and have his pannage.* We grant also that every free-man may drive his swine through our demesne wood freely and without impediment to agist them in his own woods or anywhere else as he wishes. And if the swine of any free-man shall remain one night in our forest, he shall not on that account lose anything of his for it.

10. No man henceforth shall lose life or limb for taking our venison, but if he shall be seized and convicted of taking venison he shall be fined heavily if he has the means to pay; but if he has not the means, he shall lie in our prison for a year and a day; and if after a year and a day he can find sureties, he shall leave prison; but if not, he shall abjure the kingdom of England.

11. Whatever archbishop, bishop, earl or baron shall be passing through our forest, it shall be lawful for them to take one or two deer under the view of the forester, if he shall be present; but if not, he shall cause a horn to be blown, lest it should seem like theft.

12. Every free-man for the future, may, without being prosecuted, erect a mill in his own wood or upon his own land which he has in the forest; or make a warren, or pond, or marl-pit, or ditch, or turn it into arable land, so that it be not to the detriment of any of the neighbours.

---

* Agistment pasture is livestock for a fee. Pannage was the right to allow pigs to forage in woodland, for which a fee might be charged.

13. Every free-man shall have the eyries of hawks, sparrowhawks, falcons, eagles and herons in his own woods, and he shall likewise have the honey found in his woods.

14. No forester from henceforth, who is not a forester in fee-farm, giving to us rent for his bailiwick, shall take any cheminage,* within his bailiwick; but a forester in fee, paying to us rent for his bailiwick, shall take cheminage; that is to say, for every cart two-pence for the one half year, and two-pence for the other half year; and for a horse that carries burdens, one half-penny for the one half year, and one half-penny for the other half year: and not that excepting of those who come out of their bailiwick by licence of their bailiff as dealers, to buy underwood, timber, bark, or charcoal; to carry it to sell in other places where they will: and of no other carts nor burdens shall any cheminage be taken; and cheminage shall not be taken excepting in those places where anciently it used to be and ought to be taken. Also those who carry wood, bark, or coal, upon their backs to sell, although they get their livelihood by it, shall not for the future pay cheminage. Also cheminage shall not be taken by our foresters, for any besides our demesne woods.

15. All persons outlawed for forest offences from the time of king Henry our grandfather up to our first coronation, shall be released from their outlawry without legal proceedings; and they shall find sureties that for the future they will not trespass unto us in our forests.

* Cheminage was a toll levied on transport in the forest.

16. No castellan or other person shall hold forest pleas whether concerning vert or venison but every forester-in-fee shall attach forest pleas as well concerning both vert and venison and shall present them to the verderers of the provinces; and when they have been enrolled and put under the seals of the verderers they shall be presented to our chief forester, when he comes into those parts to hold forest pleas and before him they shall be determined.

And these liberties concerning the forests we have granted to all men, saving to the archbishops, bishops, abbots, priors, earls, barons, knights, and others, ecclesiastical as well as secular; Templars and Hospitallers, their liberties and free customs, in forests and outside, in warrens and other places, which they had previously. All these aforesaid customs and liberties which we have granted to be observed in our kingdom for as much as it belongs to us; all our whole kingdom shall observe, clergy as well as laity, for as much as belongs to them. Because we have at present no seal, we have caused the present charter to be sealed with the seals of our venerable father the lord Gualo, cardinal-priest of St Martin, legate of the apostolic see, and of William Marshal earl of Pembroke, guardian of us and of our kingdom. Witness the before-named and many others. Given by the hands of the aforesaid lord, the legate, and of William Marshal at St Paul's, London, on the sixth day of November in the second year of our reign.

Acknowledgements

Thanks must go to my agent, Georgina Capel, for her brilliance and support. Anthony Cheetham first suggested this book and I owe him my thanks for (another) very good idea. For Head of Zeus Richard Milbank and Eleanor Rees both worked to craft and polish the final manuscript, while Georgina Blackwell helped me greatly in assembling the images. Joy de Menil, my editor in the US, worked on another version of this text and her improving hand has therefore been at work beneath many of its chapters. I was greatly assisted by the staff at the National Archives in London and Washington DC, the British Library and the London Library. A number of brilliant scholars have also offered me their time, thoughts and comments during the time I have been working on this book. Particular thanks to Julian Harrison and Dr Claire Breay at the British Library, Dr Nick Barratt at the National Archives, Professor Elizabeth Eva Leach at the University of Oxford, Dr Eleanor Giraud at Lincoln College, Oxford, Professor Miri Rubin and Dr Thomas Asbridge at Queen Mary University of London, Professor David Carpenter at King's College London, Professor Louise Wilkinson at Canterbury Christ Church University, Dr Kate Wiles and Dr Helen Castor. Marta Musso and Chiara Zanforlini helped with aspects of the research.

Lastly, the biggest thanks of all are to my girls, Jo, Violet and Ivy Jones. With love, as always.

Bibliography

PRIMARY

Amt, E., and Church, S. D. (ed. and trans.), *Dialogus de Scaccario and Constitutio Domus Regis*, new edn, Oxford, 2007

Appleby, J. T. (ed.), *The Chronicle of Richard of Devizes of the Time of King Richard the First*, London, 1963

Berry, V. G. (ed. and trans.), *Odo of Deuil, De profectione Ludovici VII in Orientem*, New York, 1948

Bird, J., Peters, E., and Powell, J. M., *Crusade and Christendom: Annotated Documents In Translation from Innocent III to the Fall of Acre 1187–1291*, Philadelphia, 2013

Brewer, J. S., Dimock, J. F., and Warner, G. F. (eds), *Giraldus Cambrensis, Opera*, London, 1879–80

Carlin, M., and Crouch, D., *Lost Letters of Medieval Life*, Philadelphia, 2013

Chaplais, P. (ed.), *Diplomatic Documents Preserved in the Public Record Office*, London, 1964

Cheney, C. R., and Semple, W. H. (eds), *Selected Letters of Pope Innocent III Concerning England (1198–1216)*, London, 1953

Chew, H. M., and Weinbaum, M. (eds), *The London Eyre of 1244*, London, 1970

Craw, W., *An Edition of the Histoire des ducs de Normandie et rois d'Angleterre contained in the French MS.56 of the John Rylands Library*, University of Glasgow PhD thesis, 1999

Darlington, R. (ed.), *The Vita Wulfstani of William of Malmesbury: to which are added the extant abridgements of this work and the miracles and translation of St Wulfstan*, London, 1928

Douglas, D. C. et al. (eds), *English Historical Documents II 1042–1189*, 2nd edn, London, 1981

Douglas, D. C. et al. (eds), *English Historical Documents III 1189–1327*, London, 1975

Downer, L. J. (ed. and trans.), *Leges Henrici Primi*, Oxford, 1972

Dubin, N. E., *The Fabliaux*, New York/London, 2013

Fairweather, J. (ed. and trans.), *Liber Eliensis: A History of the Isle of Ely*, Woodbridge, 2005

Fallows, N. (trans.), *The Book of The Order of Chivalry by Ramon Llull*, Woodbridge/Rochester, 2013

Flavius Vegetius Renatus, *De Re Militari (Concerning Military Affairs)*, Driffield, 2012

Flower, C. T. et al. (eds), *Curia Regis Rolls of the Reigns of Richard I and John*, 20 vols, London, 1922–

Garmonsway, G. M. (ed. and trans.), *The Anglo-Saxon Chronicle*, 2nd edn, London, 1972

Gerald of Wales, *The Journey through Wales*, Harmondsworth, 1976

Giles, J. A. (ed. and trans.), *Roger of Wendover's Flowers of History*, 2 vols, London, 1849

Giles, J. A. (ed. and trans.), *Matthew Paris's English History*, 3 vols, London, 1852–4

Giles, J. A. (ed. and trans.), *William of Malmesbury's Chronicle of the Kings of England*, London, 1847

Green, M. H. (ed.), *The Trotula: A Medieval Compendium of Women's Medicine*, Philadelphia, 2001

Goldschmidt, E. (ed.), *Burchardus de Bellevaux: Apologia de Barbis*, Cambridge, 1935

Hardy, T. D., *A Description of the Patent Rolls in the Tower of London*, London, 1835

Hardy, T. D. (ed.), *Rotuli chartarum in Turri londinensi asservati*, vol. I, 1199–1216, London, 1837

Hardy, T. D. (ed.), *Rotuli litterarum clausarum in Turri londinensi asservati*, 2 vols, London, 1833–4

Hardy, T. D. (ed.), *Rotuli litterarum patentium in Turri londinensi asservati*, London, 1835

Holden, A. J., Gregory, S., and Crouch, D. (ed. and trans.), *History of William Marshal*, 3 vols, Oxford, 2002–6

Holt, A. and Muldoon, J., *Competing Voices from the Crusades*, Oxford/Westport, 2008

James, M. R. (ed. and trans.), Brooke, C. N. L. and Mynors, R. A. B. (revised), *Walter Map: De nugis curialium: Courtiers' Trifles*, Oxford, 1983

Luard, H. R. (ed.), *Matthew Paris: Flores historiarum*, London, 1890

Luard, H. R. (ed.), *Annales monastici*, 5 vols, London, 1864–9

Luard, H. R. (ed.), *Matthaei Parisiensis, monachi Sancti Albani: Chronica majora*, 7 vols, London, 1872–3

Michel, F. (ed.), *Histoire des ducs de Normandie et des rois d'Angleterre*, Paris, 1840

Ohlgren, T. H. (ed.), *Medieval Outlaw Tales: Twelve Tales in Modern English*, rev. edn, West Lafayette, 2005

Riley, H. T. (ed.), *The Annals of Roger de Hoveden: Comprising the History of England, and of Other Countries of Europe from AD 732 to AD 1201*, 2 vols, London, 1853

Riley, H. T. (ed.), *Chronicles of the Mayors and Sheriffs of London: 1188–1274*, London, 1863

Robertson, J. C. (ed.), *Materials for the History of Thomas Becket*, Rolls Series, 1875–85

Rothwell, H., *English Historical Documents III 1189–1327*, new edn, London/New York, 1996

Rymer, T. (ed.), *Foedera, conventiones, literae, et cujuscunque generis acta publica vol I.i.*, The Hague, 1745

Stevenson, J. (ed.), *Chronica de Mailros*, Edinburgh, 1835

Stevenson, J. (ed.), *Radulphi de Coggeshall Chronicon Anglicanum*, London, 1875

Stevenson, J. (ed. and trans.), *The Church Historians of England (Pre-Reformation Series)*, 5 vols, London, 1853

Stevenson, J. (ed. and trans.), *Gerald of Wales: On the Instruction of Princes*, London, 1858

Stubbs, W. (ed.), *The Historical Works of Gervase of Canterbury*, 2 vols, London, 1872–3

Stubbs, W. (ed.), *Memoriale fratris Walteri de Coventria*, 2 vols, London, 1872

Thomson, R. M. (ed.), *The Chronicle of The Election of Hugh Abbot of Bury St Edmunds and Later Bishop of Ely*, Oxford, 1974

Thorpe, L. (ed. and trans.), *Geoffrey of Monmouth: The History of the Kings of Britain*, London, 1966

Traill, D. A. (ed. and trans.), *Walter of Châtillon: The Shorter Poems: Christmas hymns, love lyrics, and moral-satirical verse*, Oxford, 2013

Tyson, M. (ed.), 'The Annals of Southwark and Merton Priory' in *Surrey Archaeological Collections 36*, Guildford, 1925

Upton-Ward, J., *The Rule of the Templars*, Woodbridge, 1992

Walsh, P., and Kennedy, M. (ed. and trans.), *William of Newburgh: The History of English Affairs*, 2 vols, Warminster, 1998–2007

SECONDARY

Allen Brown, R., *Allen Brown's English Castles*, new edn, Woodbridge, 2004

Baker, T., *Medieval London*, London, 1970

Barron, C. M., *London in the Later Middle Ages: Government and People, 1200–1500*, Oxford, 2004

Bartlett, R., *England under the Norman and Angevin Kings 1075–1225*, Oxford, 2000

Bartlett, R., *Trial by Fire and Water*, Oxford, 1986

Benham, W., *Old St Paul's Cathedral*, London, 1902

Birch, D. A., *Pilgrimage to Rome in the Middle Ages*, Woodbridge, 2000

Bradbury, J., *The Medieval Siege*, Woodbridge, 1992

Bradbury, J., *Philip Augustus: King of France 1180–1223*, London, 1998

Breay, C., and Harrison, J., *Magna Carta: Law, Liberty, Legacy*, London, 2015

Burke, J., *Life in the Castle in Medieval England*, London, 1978

Canning, J., and Oexle, O. G. (eds), *Political Thought and the Realities of Power in the Middle Ages*, Göttingen, 1998

Carlin, M., *Medieval Southwark*, London, 1996

Carpenter, D. A., *Magna Carta*, London, 2015

Carpenter, D. A., *The Reign of Henry III*, London/New York, 1996

Castles of England and Wales, 6 vols, London, 1929–70

Chaplais, P., *English Diplomatic Practice in the Middle Ages*, London, 2003

Church, S. D., *King John: England, Magna Carta and the Making of a Tyrant*, London, 2015

Church, S. D. (ed.), *King John: New Interpretations*, Woodbridge, 1999

Clarke, P. D., *The Interdict in the Thirteenth Century: A Question of Collective Guilt*, Oxford, 2007

Colvin, H. M. (ed.), *The History of the King's Works*, vols I and II, London, 1963

Crouch, D., *The English Aristocracy 1070–1272: A Social Transformation*, New Haven/London, 2011

Dodson, A., *The Royal Tombs of Great Britain: An Illustrated History*, London, 2004

Duby, G., *The Legend of Bouvines: War, Religion and Culture in the Middle Ages*, Cambridge, 1990

Dyer, C., *Everyday Life in Medieval England*, new edn, London/New York, 2000

Feasey, H. J., *Ancient English Holy Week Ceremonial*, London, 1897

Finucane, R. C., *Soldiers of the Faith: Crusaders and Moslems at War*, London, 1983

Fried, J., and Lewis, P. (trans.), *The Middle Ages*, Cambridge/London, 2015

Goldberg, P. J. P., and Riddy, F. (eds), *Youth in the Middle Ages*, York, 2004

Gravett, C., *Norman Stone Castles (2) Europe 950–1204*, Oxford, 2004

Green, V., *An Account of the Discovery of the Body of King John in the Cathedral Church of Worcester, July 17, 1797, From Authentic Communications, With Illustrations and Remarks*, London/Worcester, 1797

Griffith-Jones, R., and Park, D. (eds), *The Temple Church in London: History, Art and Architecture*, Woodbridge, 2010

Haig, M., *The Templars: History and Myth*, London, 2008

Harper-Bill, C., and Vincent, N. (eds), *Henry II: New Interpretations*, Woodbridge, 2007

Harrison, D., *The Bridges of Medieval England: Transport and Society, 400–1800*, Oxford, 2004

Harvey, J. H., *The Medieval Architect*, Wayland, 1972

Hiley, D., *Western Plainchant: A Handbook*, Oxford, 1993

Hindle, B. P., *Medieval Roads and Tracks*, Princes Risborough, 1998

Holt, J. C., *Magna Carta*, 2nd edn, Cambridge, 1992

Holt, J. C., *The Northerners: A Study in the Reign of King John*, Oxford, 1961

Housley, N., *Fighting for the Cross*, New Haven/London, 2008

Hughes, R., *Rome*, London, 2011

Hunt, R. W., and Gibson, M., *The Schools and the Cloister: The Life and Writings of Alexander Nequam (1157–1217)*, Oxford, 1984

Hutton, R., *The Stations of the Sun: A History of the Ritual Year in Britain*, Oxford, 1996

Jobson, A. (ed), *English Government in the Thirteenth Century*, Martlesham, 2004

Jones, D., *Magna Carta: The Making and Legacy of the Great Charter*, London, 2014

Jones, P. M., *Medieval Medicine in Illuminated Manuscripts*, London, 1998

Jope, E. M. (ed.), *Studies in Building History: Essays in Recognition of the Work of B. H. St J. O'Neil*, London, 1961

Kantorowicz, E. H., *Laudes regiae: A Study in Liturgical Acclamations and Mediaeval Ruler Worship*, Berkeley, 1958

Keen, M., *Medieval Warfare: A History*, Oxford, 1999

Keene, D., *Survey of Medieval Winchester*, 2 vols, Oxford, 1985

Klemettilä, H., *Animals and Hunters in the Late Middle Ages*, New York/ Abingdon, 2015

Labarge, M. W., *A Baronial Household of the Thirteenth Century*, Brighton, 1965

Lobel, M. D., *Historic Towns Atlas: The City of London from Prehistoric Times to c.1520*, III, Oxford, 1989

Loengard, J. S. (ed.), *Magna Carta and the England of King John*, Woodbridge, 2010

MacCulloch, D., *A History of Christianity*, London, 2009

Malden, H. E. (ed.), *Magna Carta Commemoration Essays*, London, 1917

McGrail, S., *Boats of the World: From the Stone Age to Medieval Times*, Oxford, 2004

McLynn, F., *Lionheart and Lackland: King Richard, King John and the Wars of Conquest*, London, 2007

McSheffrey, S., *Marriage, Sex and Civic Culture in Late Medieval London*, Philadelphia, 2006

Moore, J. C., *Pope Innocent III: To Root Up and Plant*, Leiden, 2003

Norwich, J. J., *The Popes: A History*, London, 2011

Orme, N., *Medieval Children*, New Haven/London, 2001

Orme, N., *Medieval Schools*, New Haven/London, 2006

Piponnier, F., and Mane, P., *Dress in the Middle Ages*, trans. C. Beamish, New Haven/London, 1997

Poole, A. L., *From Domesday Book to Magna Carta 1087–1216*, Oxford/New York, 1951

Postles, D., *Naming the People of England, c.1100–1350*, Newcastle, 2006

Power, E., and Postan, M. M. (ed.), *Medieval Women*, Cambridge, 1975

Purton, P., *A History of the Late Medieval Siege*, Woodbridge, 2010

Ridyard, S. J., *The Medieval Crusade*, Woodbridge 2004

Robinson, J., *Masterpieces of Medieval Art*, London, 2008

Rogers, C. J. (ed.), *The Oxford Encyclopedia of Medieval Warfare and Military Technology*, 3 vols, Oxford, 2010

Rubin, M., *Corpus Christi: The Eucharist in Late Medieval Culture*, Cambridge, 1991

Sandoz, E., *The Roots of Liberty: Magna Carta, Ancient Constitution and the Anglo-American Tradition of Rule of Law*, Columbia, 1993

Saul, N. (ed.), *The Oxford Illustrated History of Medieval England*, Oxford, 1997

Schofield, J., *London 1100–1600: The Archaeology of a Capital City*, Sheffield, 2011

Schofield, P. R. (ed.), *Seals and Their Context in the Middle Ages*, Oxford, 2015

Serjeantson, D., and Rees, H., *Food, Craft and Status in Medieval Winchester*, Winchester, 2009

Starkey, D., *Magna Carta: The True Story behind the Charter*, London, 2015

Strickland, M (ed.), *Anglo-Norman Warfare: Studies in Late Anglo-Saxon and Anglo-Norman Military Organization and Warfare*, Woodbridge, 1992

Treharne, E., *Gluttons for Punishment: the Drunk and Disorderly in Early English Homilies*, Brixworth, 2007

Vincent, N., *Peter des Roches: An Alien in English Politics 1205–1238*, Cambridge, 1996

Vincent, N. (ed.), *Magna Carta: The Foundation of Freedom 1215–2015*, London, 2014

Wallis, F., *Medieval Medicine: A Reader*, Toronto, 2010

Warren, W. L., *Henry II*, new edn, New Haven/London, 2000

Warren, W. L., *King John*, new edn, New Haven/London, 1997

Weiser, F. X., *Handbook of Christian Feasts and Customs*, New York, 1958

Yates, R., *History and Antiquities of the Abbey of St Edmund's Bury*, London, 1843

ARTICLES

Baldwin J. W., 'Master Stephen Langton, Future Archbishop of Canterbury: The Paris Schools and Magna Carta', *English Historical Review* 123, 2008

Barratt, N., 'The English Revenues of Richard I', *English Historical Review* 116, 2001

Barratt, N., 'The Revenue of King John', *English Historical Review* 111, 1996

Bradley, R. S., Hughes, M. K., and Diaz, H. F., 'Climate in Medieval Time', *Science*, 2003

Broadberry, S., Campbell, B. M. S., and van Leeuwen, B., 'English Medieval Population: Reconciling Time Series and Cross Sectional Evidence', qub.ac.uk, 2010

Carpenter, D. A., 'Archbishop Langton and Magna Carta: His Contribution, His Doubts and His Hypocrisy', *English Historical Review* 126, 2011

Church, S. D., 'King John's Last Testament and the Last Days of His Reign', *English Historical Review* 125, 2010

BIBLIOGRAPHY

Crockford, J., 'Peripatetic and Sedentary Kingship: The Itineraries of John and Henry III', *Thirteenth Century History* 13, 2011

Gillingham, J., 'From Civilitas to Civility: Codes of Manners in Medieval and Early Modern England', *Transactions of the Royal Historical Society*, 2002

Hansen, P. V., 'Reconstructing a Medieval Trebuchet', *Military History Illustrated Past and Present* 27, 1990

Keefe, T. K., 'King Henry II and the Earls: The Pipe Roll Evidence', *Albion* 13, 1981

Kerr, M. H., Forsyth, R. D., and Plyley, M. J., 'Cold Water and Hot Iron: Trial by Ordeal in England', *Journal of Interdisciplinary History* 22, 1992

Levin, C., 'A Good Prince: King John and Early Tudor Propaganda', *Sixteenth Century Journal* 11, 1980

Masschaele, J., 'Transport Costs in Medieval England', *Economic History Review* 46, 1993

Moore, T., 'The Loss of Normandy and the Invention of Terre Normannorum, 1204', *English Historical Review* 125, 2010

Pennington, K, 'The Rite for Taking the Cross in the Twelfth Century', *Traditio* 30, 1974

Rousseau, C. M., 'Neither Bewitched nor Beguiled: Philip Augustus's Alleged Impotence and Innocent III's Response', *Speculum* 89, 2014

Steiner, E., 'Naming and Allegory in Late Medieval England', *Journal of English and German Philology* 106, 2007

Thomas, H. M., 'Shame, Masculinity and the Death of Thomas Becket', *Speculum* 87, 2012

Notes

1   Holden, A. J., Gregory, S. and Crouch, D. (ed. and trans.), *History of William Marshal* (Oxford, 2002–6), II, 253

2   Ibid. 254–5

3   Magna Carta 1215, clause 61

4   Printed in Douglas, D. C. et al. (eds), *English Historical Documents III 1189–1327* (London/New York, 1975), 324–6

5   Magna Carta 1215, clause 63

6   Payment was raised from the royal treasure by the king's personal order on 19 January 1215. Hardy, T. D. (ed.), *Rotuli litterarum clausarum in Turri londinensi asservati* (London, 1833), I, 183. Twenty-five shillings was the customary payment or presbyterium owed to anyone who sang this song for a king. Kantorowicz, E. H., *Laudes regiae: a study in liturgical acclamations and mediaeval ruler worship* (Berkeley, 1958), 173

7   The *laudes* of Worcester is printed with musical notation in Kantorowicz, *Laudes regiae*, 217–19

8   Hardy, T. D., *A Description of the Patent Rolls in the Tower of London* (London, 1835), 'Itinerary of King John'

9   Gerald of Wales, *The Journey through Wales* (Harmondsworth, 1976), 234–43

10 According to Gerald of Wales, Henry II wrote this in a letter to Manuel Comnenus, Emperor of Constantinople. Gerald of Wales, *The Journey through Wales*, 234

11 Ibid., 199–200, 87–8

12 Traill, D. A. (ed. and trans.), *Walter of Châtillon: the Shorter Poems: Christmas hymns, love lyrics, and moral-satirical verse* (Oxford, 2013), 84–5

13 Hardy, *Rotuli litterarum clausarum*, I, 139

14 Ambler, S., 'Christmas at the Court of King John' at The Magna Carta Project blog (magnacartaresearch.blogspot.co.uk)

15 These recipes date from fourteenth- and fifteenth-century cooks'

manuscripts – one of many useful modern editions of medieval recipes, complete with twenty-first-century adaptations for home cooking, is Black, M., *The Medieval Cookbook* (London, 1992)

16 Hardy (ed.), *Rotuli litterarum clausarum*, quoted in Vincent, N. C., 'King John's Diary and Itinerary', The Magna Carta Project, magnacarta.cmp.uea.ac.uk

17 A month later Hugh de Neville claimed back from the Exchequer the money for the ninety beasts he brought to Worcester for the Christmas feasting. Hardy (ed.), *Rotuli litterarum clausarum*, I, 184

18 See for example, royal orders on 29 January 1215 ordering the distribution of barrels and casks of red and white wine across the realm, from Wallingford in the Thames valley to Wakefield in Yorkshire. Hardy (ed.), *Rotuli litterarum clausarum*, I, 185

19 See, for example, archaeological findings in Keene, D., *Survey of Medieval Winchester* (Oxford, 1985) I, 53

20 'The city of Worcester: Introduction and borough', *A History of the County of Worcester* IV (London, 1924), 376–90 and fn 50

21 Darlington, R., *The Vita Wulfstani of William of Malmesbury: to which are added the extant abridgements of this work and the miracles and translation of St Wulfstan* (London, 1928), 35–43 *passim*

22 Riley H. T. (ed.), *The Annals of Roger de Hoveden: Comprising the History of England, and of Other Countries of Europe from AD 732 to AD 1201* (London, 1853), I, 256

23 Broadberry, S., Campbell, B. M. S., and van Leeuwen, B., 'English Medieval Population: Reconciling Time Series and Cross Sectional Evidence', qub.ac.uk (2010), 22. See also a survey of older work in Bartlett, R., *England under the Norman and Angevin Kings 1075–1225* (Oxford, 2000), 290–6

24 Quoted in Poole, A. L., *From Domesday Book to Magna Carta 1087–1216* (Oxford/New York, 1951), 36

25 Stubbs, W. (ed.), *Memoriale fratris Walteri de Coventria* (London, 1872), II, 142

26 Stubbs, W. (ed.), *The Historical Works of Gervase of Canterbury* (London, 1872–3), II, 92

27 Giles, J. A. (ed. and trans.), *Roger of Wendover's Flowers of History* (London, 1849), II, 304

28 Goldschmidt, E., *Burchardus de Bellevaux: Apologia de barbis* (Cambridge, 1935)

29   On medieval roads see Hindle, B. P., *Medieval Roads and Tracks*
      (Oxford, 2008). On the legacy of Roman roads, however, see
      Harrison, D., *The Bridges of Medieval England* (Oxford, 2004), 48–52

30   James, M. R. (ed. and trans.), Brooke, C. N. L. and Mynors, R. A. B.
      (rev.), *Walter Map: De nugis curialium: Courtiers' Trifles* (Oxford, 1983),
      370–1

31   Green, V., *An Account of the Discovery of the Body of King John in
      the Cathedral Church of Worcester, July 17th 1797, From Authentic
      Communications, With Illustrations and Remarks* (London/Worcester,
      1797), 4. The average height of male skeletons excavated during
      the middle ages is 5' 7¼" – Schofield, J., *London 1100–1600: The
      Archaeology of a Capital City* (Sheffield, 2011), 199

32   Hardy, *Description of the Patent Rolls*, 60

33   Appleby, J. T. (ed. and trans.), *The Chronicle of Richard of Devizes of
      the Time of King Richard I* (London, 1963) 32, 20

34   Holden et al. (eds), *History of William Marshal*, I, 384–5, 449

35   Thomson, R. M. (ed.), *The Chronicle of the Election of Hugh Abbot of
      Bury St Edmunds and Later Bishop of Ely* (Oxford, 1974), 171

36   BL MS Cotton Claudius DII, f.116 – the image dates from the
      fourteenth century

37   Hardy (ed.), *Rotuli litterarum clausarum*, I, 184

38   John's baggage train was infamously lost in the Wellstream, near
      the Wash in East Anglia, shortly before his death in 1216. For a
      convenient collation of chronicler accounts of the accident (and
      thus descriptions of John's baggage train itself) see Warren, W. L.,
      King John (new edn, New Haven, 1997), 278

39   Masschaelle, J., 'Transport Costs in Medieval England' in *Economic
      History Review* 46 (1993), 270

40   Discussed by Masschaelle, J., 'The English Economy' in Loengard,
      J. S. (ed.), *Magna Carta and the England of King John* (Woodbridge,
      2010) 162–3 and confirmed in Hardy (ed.), *Rotuli litterarum
      clausarum*, I, 183, when John orders a cart 'with good iron tires' for
      the use of the queen.

41   James, Brooke and Mynors, *Walter Map*, 477 and 103

42   Nicholas Vincent suggests Guiting, correcting T. A. Hardy's
      earlier itinerary, which read 'Geiting' as 'Geddington' in
      Northamptonshire. Vincent, 'King John's Diary & Itinerary'

43   Hardy (ed.), *Rotuli litterarum clausarum*, I, 182. The king of Norway
      at this time was Inge Bårdsson, also known as Inge II.

44   Upton-Ward, J., *The Rule of the Templars* (Woodbridge, 1992), 25, 30, 32, 36

45   Griffith-Jones, R. and Park, D., *The Temple Church in London: History, Architecture and Art* (Woodbridge, 2010), 4

46   Ibid., 10

47   Hardy, T. D. (ed.), *Rotuli chartarum in Turri londinensi asservati* (London, 1837), I, 203–4

48   William the Breton's account of Bouvines may be found conveniently translated into English at http://deremilitari. org/2014/03/the-battle-of-bouvines-1214/, along with many other contemporary and near-contemporary accounts. See also Bradbury, J., *Philip Augustus: King of France 1180–1223* (London, 1998) and Duby, G., *The Legend of Bouvines: War, Religion and Culture in the Middle Ages* (Cambridge, 1990) for detailed accounts of the battle based on original sources.

49   See *Relatio Marchianesis de Pugna Bouvinis* at http://deremilitari. org/2014/03/the-battle-of-bouvines-1214

50   Holden et al. (eds), *History of William Marshal*, II, 242–3. This was theoretically hearsay, since Marshal was not present at Bouvines. All the same, it is a pithy and accurate assessment.

51   Ibid.

52   Ibid., 41

53   For a considered argument about John's reputation during his own lifetime, see Gillingham, J., 'Historians without Hindsight' in Church, S. D. (ed.), *King John: New Interpretations* (Woodbridge 1999), 3–26

54   See, for example, Hardy (ed.), *Rotuli litterarum clausarum*, I, 186 in the long list of instructions sent on 1 February 1215 to Henry, archbishop of Dublin.

55   The letter, copied into the document known as the Black Book of the Exchequer (National Archives, E 164/12) is printed in Latin and English in Loengard, *Magna Carta*, 168–79

56   Giles (ed.), *Roger of Wendover's Flowers of History*, II, 303–4

57   Douglas, D. C. et al. (eds), *English Historical Documents II* (2nd edn, London, 1981) 432–4

58   On the Bury St Edmunds meeting, Vincent, 'King John's Diary and Itinerary', http://magnacarta.cmp.uea.ac.uk/read/ itinerary/Drama_and_jokes_at_Bury_St_Edmunds expresses strong doubts about 'the entirely unsubstantiated account

of a baronial meeting at Bury' as related by Wendover. But Carpenter, D. A., *Magna Carta* (London, 2015), 292 makes a strong case for it happening on 19 October.

59   Stubbs (ed.), *Memoriale fratris Walteri de Coventria*, II, 218

60   Hardy, T. D. (ed.), *Rotuli litterarum patentium in Turri londinensi asservati* (London, 1835), 126, but note the important correction in Vincent, N. C., 'The Conference at the New Temple, January 1215', The Magna Carta Project http://magnacarta.cmp.uea.ac.uk/read/feature_of_the_month/Jan_2015

61   See Colvin, H. M. (ed.), *The History of the King's Works* (London, 1963), I, 80

62   Ambler, 'Christmas at the Court of King John'

63   Michel, F. (ed), *Histoire des ducs de Normandie et des rois d'Angleterre* (Paris, 1840), 105

64   Serjeantson, D. and Rees, H., *Food, Craft and Status in Medieval Winchester* (Winchester, 2009), 167

65   Hardy, *Description of the Patent Rolls*, 67

66   Douglas et al. (eds), *English Historical Documents III*, 823

67   Bartlett, *England under the Norman and Angevin Kings*, 579–80

68   Treharne, E., *Gluttons for Punishment: the Drunk and Disorderly in Early English Homilies* (Brixworth, 2007), 19; Appleby, *Chronicle of Richard of Devizes*, 75

69   Giles, J. A. (ed. and trans.), *William of Malmesbury's Chronicle of the Kings of England* (London 1847)

70   Fairweather, J. (ed. and trans.), *Liber Eliensis: A History of the Isle of Ely* (Woodbridge, 2005)

71   Douglas et al. (eds), *English Historical Documents III*, 828

72   Matthew Paris's glorious map British Library MS Royal 14 c vii f2v–2r is digitized and may be viewed online at bl.uk. For a discussion of this and alternative routes to Rome, see Birch, D. A., *Pilgrimage to Rome in the Middle Ages* (Woodbridge, 2000), 42–55

73   Chaplais, P., *English Diplomatic Practice in the Middle Ages* (London, 2003), 28, translated by Vincent, N. C. in 'The Conference at the New Temple, January 1215', The Magna Carta Project

74   Dante Alighieri, *Paradiso*, canto XXXI, 35–6

75   I have drawn here on the translation in Stevenson, J., (ed. and trans.), *Gerald of Wales: On the Instruction of Princes* (London, 1858), 106

76   Dubin, N. E. (trans.), *The Fabliaux* (New York/London, 2013), 937–41, 929–31

77   Bartlett, *England under the Norman and Angevin Kings*, 435

78   Douglas et al. (eds), *English Historical Documents III*, 751–2

79   Church, *King John*, 163–4 quoting Pipe Roll 14 John 44–5

80   Cheney, C. R. and Semple, W. H. (eds), *Selected Letters of Pope Innocent III Concerning England (1198–1216)* (London, 1953), 149–51

81   K. Harvey, 'The Freedom of Election Charter', The Magna Carta Project http://magnacarta.cmp.uea.ac.uk/read/feature_of_the_month/Aug_2014

82   Chaplais, *English Diplomatic Practice*, 28–9

83   Ibid.

84   Stevenson, *Gerald of Wales: On the Instruction of Princes*, 63

85   According to the Arab historian Beha ed-Din and the anonymous Christian author of *De expugatione terrae sanctae per Saladinium*. Both are printed and translated in Holt, A. and Muldoon, J., *Competing Voices from the Crusades* (Oxford/Westport, 2008), 114–18

86   See Andrea, A. J., 'Innocent III, the Fourth Crusade and the Coming Apocalypse' in Ridyard, S. J., *The Medieval Crusade* (Woodbridge, 2004), 105

87   Stubbs (ed.), *Memoriale fratris Walteri de Coventria*, II, 219

88   Berry, V. G. (ed. and trans.), *Odo of Deuil, De profectione Ludovici VII in Orientem* (New York, 1948), 14–19

89   Finucane, R. C., *Soldiers of the Faith: Crusaders and Moslems at War* (London, 1983), 42

90   Housley, N., *Fighting for the Cross* (New Haven/London, 2008), 53

91   Printed in Pennington, K., 'The Rite for Taking the Cross in the Twelfth Century' in *Traditio* 30 (1974); translated in Bird, J., Peters, E. and Powell, J. M., *Crusade and Christendom: Annotated Documents in Translation from Innocent III to the Fall of Acre 1187–1291* (Philadelphia, 2013)

92   Hardy (ed.), *Rotuli litterarum clausarum*, I, 188–92

93   Ibid., 184–5, 189, 191

94   Ibid., 191

95   James, Brooke and Mynors, *Walter Map*, 12–13

96   A good starting point on this topic is Fried, J., *The Middle Ages* (Cambridge/London, 2015), 328–73

97   Alfanus quoted in Green, M. H. (ed.), *The Trotula: A Medieval Compendium of Women's Medicine* (Philadelphia, 2001), 9

98   Jones, P. M., *Medieval Medicine in Illuminated Manuscripts* (London, 1998), 62

99   BL Sloane MS 1977 f.2 – see also Wallis, F., *Medieval Medicine: A Reader* (Toronto, 2010), 181–5

100   Green, *Trotula*, 123

101   Ibid., 168–9

102   Feasey, H. J., *Ancient English Holy Week Ceremonial* (London, 1897), *passim*; Hutton, R., *Stations of the Sun: A History of the Ritual Year in Britain* (Oxford, 1997), 182–97

103   Feasey, *Ancient English Holy Week Ceremonial*, 114–15

104   Hardy (ed.), *Rotuli litterarum clausarum*, I, 196

105   Ibid., 195

106   Ibid.

107   Cheney and Semple (eds), *Selected Letters of Pope Innocent III*, 194–5

108   Ibid., 196

109   Carpenter, *Magna Carta*, 298

110   Fallows, N. (trans.), *The Book of the Order of Chivalry: Ramon Llull* (Woodbridge and Rochester, 2013), 44–55

111   In modern translation, see Thorpe, L. (ed. and trans.), *Geoffrey of Monmouth: The History of the Kings of Britain* (London, 1966)

112   Labarge, M. W., *A Baronial Household of the Thirteenth Century* (Brighton, 1965), 78–9, 111, 175

113   A lovely example of an aquamanile may be found at the British Museum, collection number P&E 1853,0315.1, photographed and described in Robinson, J., *Masterpieces of Medieval Art* (London, 2008), 240–1

114   Stubbs (ed.), *Memoriale fratris Walteri de Coventria*, II, 219

115   Michel (ed.), *Histoire des ducs de Normandie et des rois d'Angleterre*, 145. On the naming of the Northerners more generally see Holt, J. C., *The Northerners* (Oxford, 1961), 8–16

116   Michel (ed.), *Histoire des ducs de Normandie et des rois d'Angleterre*, 115

117   Bartlett, *England under the Norman and Angevin Kings*, 213

118   Michel (ed.), *Histoire des ducs de Normandie et des rois d'Angleterre*, 119

119   Giles (ed.), *Roger of Wendover's Flowers of History*, II, 305

120   Holden et al. (eds), *History of William Marshal*

121   Ibid., II, 63, 65, 121

122   Ibid., I, 285

123   Ibid., I, 83–95

124   Giles (ed.), *Roger of Wendover's Flowers of History*, II, 306

125   The Unknown Charter is held at the Archives Nationales in Paris where it is classified J.655. It is printed in Latin and discussed in

Holt, J. C., *Magna Carta* (2nd edn, Cambridge, 1992), 418–28, where its provenance is dated to between January and June 1215. An English translation of John's supposed concessions is in Rothwell, H. (ed.), *English Historical Documents III 1189–1327* (London/New York, 1996), 310–11. David Carpenter suggests that the Unknown Charter was written some time between the New Temple meeting in January and the fall of London on 17 May and leans towards an earlier date within this window. Carpenter, *Magna Carta*, 314

126   Douglas et al. (eds), *English Historical Documents II*, 432–4

127   Giles (ed.), *Roger of Wendover's Flowers of History*, II, 306

128   John's offers of reconciliation were described in a letter to the Pope the following month, printed in Rymer, T. (ed.), *Foedera, conventiones, litterae et cujuscumque generis acta publica etc*, vol. I.i (The Hague, 1745), 66–7

129   Cheney and Semple (eds), *Selected Letters of Pope Innocent III*, 214–15

130   Tyson, M., 'The Annals of Southwark and Merton' in *Surrey Archaeological Collections* 36 (1925), 49

131   Both are printed in Latin in Holt, *Magna Carta*, 492–3

132   Hardy (ed.), *Rotuli litterarum clausarum*, I, 204

133   Flower, C. T. et al. (eds), *Curia Regis Rolls of the Reigns of Richard I and John*, VII (1935), 247

134   Kerr, M. H., Forsyth, R. D., and Plyley, M. J., 'Cold Water and Hot Iron: Trial by Ordeal in England' in *Journal of Interdisciplinary History* 22, 582–3

135   Ibid. Body fat makes a significant difference in human buoyancy, since fat floats much more easily than muscle and bone.

136   Hardy, *Description of the Patent Rolls*, 101–2

137   Ohlgren, T. H. (ed.), *Medieval Outlaw Tales: Twelve Tales in Modern English* (rev. edn, West Lafayette, 2005), 147

138   Ibid., 197, 212

139   Stubbs (ed.), *Memoriale fratris Walteri de Coventria*, II, 219

140   Giles (ed.), *Roger of Wendover's Flowers of History*, II, 307

141   On Northampton Castle see Colvin (ed.), *History of the King's Works*, II, 750–3 and Page, W. (ed.), 'The borough of Northampton: Description', *A History of the County of Northampton: Volume 3* (1930), 30–40

142   Vincent, 'King John's Diary and Itinerary: 15–24 February', The Magna Carta Project, magnacarta.cmp.uea.ac.uk, citing Vincent,

N. C., 'The Seals of King Henry II and His Court', in Schofield, P. R. (ed.), *Seals and Their Context in the Middle Ages*, (Oxford, 2015), 7–33, especially 17 figure 2.11, 19

143 Hardy, *Rotuli litterarum patentium*, 129

144 Geoffrey de Martigny would be named in clause 50 of Magna Carta as one of the kinsmen of Gerard d'Athée who was to be removed from England. The others included Engelard and Guy de Cigogné, Peter, Guy and Andrew de Chanceaux, de Martigny's brothers, Philip Mark and his brothers and a nephew called Geoffrey.

145 Giles (ed.), *Roger of Wendover's Flowers of History*, II, 307. William de Beauchamp was one of the rebels who was excommunicated by Pope Innocent III for defying John.

146 Ibid., 307.

147 Holden et al. (eds), *History of William Marshal*, II, 255

148 Wendover erroneously gives the date as Sunday 24 May.

149 Giles (ed.), *Roger of Wendover's Flowers of History*, II, 307. See also Stubbs (ed.), *Memoriale fratris Walteri de Coventria*, II, 220

150 Dyer, C., 'The Economy and Society' in Saul, N. (ed.), *The Oxford Illustrated History of Medieval England* (Oxford, 1997), 155

151 Holden et al. (eds), *History of William Marshal*, I, 482–3

152 Fitzstephen's description of London is printed in slightly truncated form in *English Historical Documents II*, and in its full Latin transcription in Robertson, J. C., *Materials for the History of Thomas Becket* (Rolls Series, 1875–85), III, 2–13

153 Baker, T., *Medieval London* (London, 1970), 163–7

154 Ohlgren (ed.), *Medieval Outlaws*, 144

155 Thorpe (ed.), *Geoffrey of Monmouth: The History of the Kings of Britain*, 262

156 Hardy, *Description of the Patent Rolls*, 67–8

157 Schofield, J., *London 1100–1600: The Archaeology of a Capital City* (Sheffield, 2011), 159–62

158 Ibid., 109

159 Lobel, M. D., *Historic Towns Atlas: The City of London from Prehistoric Times to c.1520*, III, 31

160 Appleby (ed.), *Chronicle of Richard of Devizes*, 64-7

161 Riley, H. T. (ed.), *Chronicles of the Mayors and Sheriffs of London: 1188–1274* (London, 1863), 179–87

162 ibid., 1–8

163 The assize is translated in Rothwell (ed.), *English Historical Documents III*, 849–54

164 Bartlett, *England under the Norman and Angevin Kings*, 345

165 Chew, H. M., and Weinbaum, M. (eds), *The London Eyre of 1244* (London, 1970), items 40, 180

166 Ibid., items 121, 48, 85, 57, 71

167 Stubbs (ed.), *Memoriale fratris Walteri de Coventria*, II, 220

168 For a concise survey of London's relationship with the Norman and Plantagenet kings, see Bartlett, *England under the Norman and Angevin Kings*, 342–4

169 Giles (ed.), *Roger of Wendover's Flowers of History*, II, 307–8

170 James, Brooke and Mynors, *Walter Map*, 476–7

171 Ibid., 496–7

172 *A Linguistic Atlas of Late Medieval English* (online edition), http://www.lel.ed.ac.uk/ihd/elalme/intros/atlas_gen_intro.html, 1.1.2

173 Bartlett, *England under the Norman and Angevin Kings*, 500

174 Flower et al. (eds), *Curia Regis Rolls* VII. For a convenient list of names of those who appear in the court records, see 464–9.

175 Ibid., 296

176 Steiner, E., 'Naming and Allegory in Late Medieval England', *Journal of English and German Philology* 106.2 (2007), 248. See also more generally Postles, D., *Naming the People of England c.1100–1350* (Newcastle, 2006), *passim*

177 Mills, A. D., *A Dictionary of British Place Names* (Oxford, 2011). Thanks to Dr Kate Wiles for this reference and for her invaluable advice on the origins of Runnymede's name.

178 Luard, H. R. (ed.), *Matthew Paris: Flores historiarum* (London, 1890), II, 153. I am very grateful to Professor David Carpenter for this reference.

179 Maddicott, J. R., 'Edward the Confessor's Return to England in 1041' *in English Historical Review*, 119 (2004), 661–3

180 Stevenson, J. (ed.), *Radulphi de Coggeshall Chronicon Anglicanum* (London, 1875), 172

181 Hardy (ed.), *Rotuli litterarum clausarum*, I, 193

182 Colvin (ed.), *History of the King's Works*, II, 864–5

183 Luard, H. R. (ed.), *Matthaei Parisiensis, monachi Sancti Albani: Chronica majora* (London, 1872–3), II, 611

184 Hardy (ed.), *Rotuli litterarum patentium*, 138, 142

185 Hardy (ed.), *Rotuli litterarum clausarum*, I, 213–14

186 Ibid., 213

187 Ibid., 214

188 Printed in Latin in Holt, *Magna Carta*, 429–40 and in English in Rothwell (ed.), *English Historical Documents III*, 311–16

189 Carpenter, D. A., 'The Dating and Making of Magna Carta' in Carpenter, D. A., *The Reign of Henry III* (London/New York, 1996), 16; Carpenter, *Magna Carta*, 342

190 Hardy (ed.), *Rotuli litterarum patentium*, 142–3

191 Thomson (ed.), *Chronicle of the Election of Hugh, Abbot of Bury St Edmunds*, 170–1

192 Ibid.

193 Carpenter, *Magna Carta*, 361

194 Revelation 4:1–11

195 Amt, E., and Church, S. D. (ed. and trans.), *Dialogus de Scaccario: the Dialogue of the Exchequer by Richard fitzNigel* (Oxford, 2011), 86–7

196 Fryde, N. M., 'The Roots of Magna Carta: Opposition to the Plantagenets' in Canning, J., and Oexle, O. G. (eds), *Political Thought and the Realities of Power in the Middle Ages* (Göttingen, 1998), 59–60

197 Carpenter, *Magna Carta*, 366–7

198 Printed in Holt, *Magna Carta*, 490–1

199 Stubbs (ed.), *Memoriale fratris Walteri de Coventria*, II, 222

200 Ibid., 221

201 Hardy (ed.), *Rotuli litterarum clausarum*, I, 215

202 Hardy (ed.), *Rotuli litterarum patentium*, 144

203 Giles (ed.), *Roger of Wendover's Flowers of History*, II, 338

204 Carpenter, *Magna Carta*, 388–9

205 Printed in Holt, *Magna Carta*, 498

206 Michel (ed.), *Histoire des ducs de Normandie et des rois d'Angleterre*, 151

207 Luard (ed.), *Matthaei Parisiensis*, II, 611

208 Luard, H. R. (ed.), *Annales monastici* (London, 1864–9), III, 43

209 Cheney and Semple (eds), *Selected Letters of Pope Innocent III*, 212–16

210 Chaucer, G., *The Canterbury Tales*, The Wife of Bath's Tale, lines 65, 182–4, 402–3

211 I Timothy 2:9–12

212 Appleby (ed.), *Chronicle of Richard of Devizes*, 10

213 This translation is owed to Orme, N., *Medieval Schools*, (New Haven/London, 2006), 104

214 Chew, H. M., and Weinbaum, M., 'Crown Pleas: 25 Henry III–27

Henry III (nos 152–80)', in *The London Eyre of 1244*, online edition
www.british-history.ac.uk/london-record-soc/vol6/pp59-72

215 A view most notably held by Ariès, P., *Centuries of Childhood*
(London, 1962), and contested vigorously and convincingly in
Orme, N., *Medieval Children* (New Haven/London, 2001), which
the present account follows.

216 Luard (ed.), *Annales monastici*, III, 44

217 For this and the account that follows see Giles (ed.), *Roger of
Wendover's Flowers of History*, II, 336; Stubbs (ed.), *Memoriale fratris
Walteri de Coventria*, II, 226

218 Giles (ed.), *Roger of Wendover's Flowers of History*, II, 337

219 Downer, L. J. (ed. and trans.), *Leges Henrici Primi* (Oxford, 1972), 109,
117

220 Colvin (ed.), *History of the King's Works*, I, 59–60

221 For an overview of castles and castle-building in this age see
Colvin (ed.), *History of the King's Works*, I, 64–81, which follows
Brown, R. A., 'Royal Castle-Building in England, 1154–1216' in
English Historical Review 70 (1955), 353–98. See also Allen Brown, R.,
Allen Brown's English Castles (new edn, Woodbridge, 2004), chapter
3, 34–63

222 Allen Brown, R., 'Rochester Castle' in *Castles of England and Wales,
Supplement I*, 8–10

223 Giles (ed.), *Roger of Wendover's Flowers of History*, II, 335

224 Ibid.

225 Ibid.

226 Ibid., 336

227 Bradbury, J., *The Medieval Siege* (Woodbridge, 1992), 10–11

228 Stubbs (ed.), *Memoriale fratris Walteri de Coventria*, II, 226

229 Giles (ed.), *Roger of Wendover's Flowers of History*, II, 337–8

230 Ibid., 338

231 Ibid., 339

232 Klemettilä, H., *Animals and Hunters in the Late Middle Ages* (New
York/Abingdon, 2015), 24

233 Serjeantson and Rees, *Food, Craft and Status in Medieval Winchester*,
148–51

234 For Fitzstephen see above, chapter 5. The most accessible edition
of the description of London is in Douglas et al. (eds), *English
Historical Documents II*, 1024–30

235 Bodleian Library, MS Bodley 764

236 Stubbs (ed.), *Memoriale fratris Walteri de Coventria*, II, 217

237 An English translation of the canons of the Fourth Lateran Council may be found in Rothwell (ed.), *English Historical Documents III*, 643–76

238 James, Brooke and Mynors, *Walter Map*, 118–21

239 This translation from Peter of Cornwall's *Liber revelationum* may be found in Bartlett, *England under the Norman and Angevin Kings*, 478

240 On this subject in general see Rubin, M., *Corpus Christi: The Eucharist in Late Medieval Culture* (Cambridge, 1991)

241 Giles (ed.), *Roger of Wendover's Flowers of History*, II, 344

242 Cheney and Semple (eds), *Selected Letters of Pope Innocent III*, 220

243 Giles (ed.), *Roger Wendover's Flowers of History*, II, 348

244 Ibid.

245 Holden et al. (eds), *History of William Marshal*, II, 255–6

246 Stubbs (ed.), *Memoriale fratris Walteri de Coventria*, II, 227

247 Hosler, J. D., 'Mercenaries' in Rogers, C. J., *The Oxford Encyclopedia of Medieval Warfare and Military Technology* (Oxford, 2010), III, 1–3

248 James, Brooke and Mynors, *Walter Map*, 118

249 Holden et al. (eds), *History of William Marshal*, II, 256–7

250 See for example Hardy (ed.), *Rotuli litterarum clausarum*, I, 238

251 Giles (ed.), *Roger of Wendover's Flowers of History II*, 349

252 Dyer, C., *Everyday Life in Medieval England* (new edn, London/New York, 2000), 134

253 Bartlett, *England under the Norman and Angevin Kings*, 184

254 Flower et al. (eds), *Curia Regis Rolls* VII, 467–8

255 BL Add MS 8167, transcribed and translated in Carlin, M., and Crouch, D. (ed. and trans.), *Lost Letters of Medieval Life: English Society 1200–1250* (Philadelphia, 2013), 274–7

256 Bartlett, *England under the Norman and Angevin Kings*, 252

257 Translation from Bennett, M., 'Wace and Warfare' in Strickland, M. (ed.), *Anglo-Norman warfare: studies in late Anglo-Saxon and Anglo-Norman military organization and warfare* (Woodbridge, 1992), 233

258 This Biblical wisdom was noted by the royal treasurer Richard FitzNigel in the introduction to his Dialogue of the Exchequer. Amt and Church (eds), *Dialogus de Scaccario*s, 3

259 Stevenson (ed.), *Radulphi de Coggeshall*, 177

260 Luard (ed), *Matthaei Parisiensis*, II, 642

261 Holden et al. (eds), *History of William Marshal*, II, 256–7

262 Ibid., 256–9

263 On John's losses in the Wash, including these translations of Coggeshall and Wendover, see Warren, *King John*, Appendix C, 278–85

264 Translation from Carpenter, *Magna Carta*, 405

265 Holden et al. (eds), *History of William Marshal*, II, 260–1

266 Darlington, *Vita Wulfstani*, 35–43 *passim*

267 Green, *Account of the Discovery of the Body of King John*, 4–5. Carpenter, *Magna Carta*, 406 identifies this as perhaps being the cap of unction worn by the king at his coronation.

268 Luard (ed.), *Matthaei Parisiensis*, II, 669

269 Holden et al. (eds), *History of William Marshal*, II, 256–7

270 Giles (ed.), *Roger of Wendover's Flowers of History*, II, 205

271 The text of the Charter of the Forest is translated and printed in Douglas et al. (eds), *English Historical Documents III*, 337–40

272 Holden et al. (eds), *History of William Marshal*, II, 406–7

273 The 1225 edition of Magna Carta is translated and printed in Douglas et al. (eds), *English Historical Documents III*, 341–9

274 Carpenter, D. A., 'The Cerne Abbey Magna Carta', The Magna Carta Project http://magnacartaresearch.org/read/feature_of_the_month/Apr_2014

275 The account of this episode by Matthew Paris may be found in Luard (ed.), *Matthaei Parisiensis*, IV, 185–7

276 Ambler, S. T., 'Henry III's Confirmation of Magna Carta in March 1265', The Magna Carta Project, http://magnacarta.cmp.uea.ac.uk/read/feature_of_the_month/Mar_2014

List of Illustrations

Index